Senses' Tender

William K. Buckley

# Senses' Tender

## Recovering the Novel
## for the Reader

PETER LANG
New York • Bern • Frankfurt am Main • Paris

**Library of Congress Cataloging-in-Publication Data**

Buckley, William K.
    Senses' tender : recovering the novel for the reader /
William K. Buckley.
      p.  cm.
    Bibliography: p.
    Includes index.
    1. English fiction—20th century—History and
criticism—Theory. etc.  2. Reader-response criticism.
3. De Forest, John William, 1826-1906. Miss Ravenel's
conversion from secession to loyalty.  4. Céline, Louis-
Ferdinand, 1894-1961—Criticism and interpretation.
I. Title.
PR826.B78     1989     823'.91'09—dc19     89-2759
ISBN 0-8204-0724-0                      CIP


**CIP-Titelaufnahme der Deutschen Bibliothek**

**Buckley, William K.:**
Senses' tender : recovering the novel for the
reader / William K. Buckley. — New York; Bern;
Frankfurt am Main; Paris: Lang, 1989.
    ISBN 0-8204-0724-0

© Peter Lang Publishing, Inc., New York 1989

Printed by Weihert-Druck GmbH, Darmstadt, West Germany

For my students

## Acknowledgments

I am grateful to the President's Council on the Humanities at Indiana University for the funds which helped me complete this book.

For his kind reading of the text and helpful suggestions, I thank Wayne Burns; and my appreciation is offered to Joe Butler and Jim Flynn for the many conversations we have had over the years. For her careful and patient typing, I thank Margaret Wheeler, and for their support I thank the Academic Affairs Office of Indiana University, Northwest.

Sections of this book first appeared in literary journals. An early version of the first two chapters appeared as "Contextualist Criticism in the Classroom" in *Recovering Literature*, 8, 1 (Spring, 1980), 5-23. The section on realism in Chapter 1 is a revision of the essay "Realism Still Knocking on Academe's Door," from *Studies in the Novel*, 18, 3 (Fall, 1986), 314-19. Chapter 3 is a revised version of an essay that appeared under the same title in *Liberal and Fine Arts Review*, 5, 1 (January, 1985), 43-54. "Dissident Notes on *Ulysses*," Chapter 4, is the revision of an essay that first appeared in *North Dakota Quarterly*, 51, 4 (Fall, 1983), 80-86. Chapter 5 is a revision of an essay from *Recovering Literature*, 5, 3 (Winter, 1976), 53-75. Chapter 6 is a revised version of an essay on Céline from *Studies in the Novel*, 18, 1 (Spring, 1986), 51-65. I thank the editors for permission to reprint this material.

# Table of Contents

Preface                                                                            1

## Part I
## Tentative Discussions

Chapter 1: Introduction                                                            9

Chapter 2: Contextualist Criticism                                                25

## Part II
## Tentative Applications

Chapter 3: *Lady Chatterley's Lover*: D.H. Lawrence's Answer to the "Nightmare
of History" in James Joyce and Virginia Woolf                                     43

Chapter 4: Dissident Notes on *Ulysses*.                                          53

## Part III
## Further Applications

Chapter 5: *Miss Ravenel's Conversion*: The Discreet Suspension of
Melodrama for the Sake of "The Panzaic."                                          67

Chapter 6: Louis-Ferdinand Céline's Novels: The Indiscreet Glance at the
Real from *Journey to the End of the Night to Rigadoon*.                          81

## Part IV
## Conclusion

Chapter 7: The Unpredictable Classroom                                            95

Appendix: *The Panzaic Principle*, Wayne Burns                                   105

Bibliography: Contextualist Criticism.                                           147

Index                                                                           155

Loerke:    " . . . a work of art . . . has nothing to do with anything
           but itself, it has no relation with the everyday world of
           this and other, there is no connection between them,
           absolutely none, they are two different and distinct
           planes of existence, and to translate one into the other is
           worse than foolish, it is a darkening of all counsel, a
           making confusion everywhere. Do you see, you must
           not confuse the relative world of action with the
           absolute world of art."

Ursula:    "As far as your world of art and your world of reality,"
           she replied, "you have to separate the two, because you
           can't bear to know what you are. You can't bear to
           realize what a stock, stiff, hide-bound brutality you *are*
           really, so you say it's the world of art. The world of art
           is only the truth about the real world, that's all -- but
           you are too far gone to see it."

                                         D.H. Lawrence, Chapter XXIX,
                                         *Women in Love*

# PREFACE

Now, in reality, the world have paid too great a compliment to critics, and have imagined them men of much greater profundity than they really are. From this complaisance the critics have been emboldened to assume a dictatorial power, and have so far succeeded that they are now become the masters, and have the assurance to give laws to those authors from whose predecessors they originally received them.

Henry Fielding, *Tom Jones*, Book V.

## 1. Fixing the Limits of My Critical Approach

Over the centuries literary criticism has taken a beating now and then by many famous authors. Fielding's wry comments on critics are peppered all throughout *Tom Jones*, and they aptly summarize complaints about what this book is going to do. Fielding sees critical activity as sometimes silly, sometimes snobbish, and always dull. D.H. Lawrence, E.M. Forster, and Louis-Ferdinand Céline have made equally pithy statements about criticism in our century.[1] It is, then, at no small risk when I say that the purpose of this book is to come to grips with how the novel works its way on us as readers. Silly, snobbish, and dull I hope it not to be. After all, criticism is an old habit. Plato's remark that poets were a danger to the state and Aristotle's definition of tragedy began it all, I suppose. Famous literary men have practiced it too: Shakespeare's brief comment in *Hamlet* that skewers genres, Dryden's long essay on drama, Pope's famous poem on criticism, Johnson's critique of Shakespeare, Shelley's defense of poetry, Zola's manifesto on the novel, Tolstoy's views on art, Henry James' theories on what the novel should do, Twain's slap at Cooper, Lawrence's essays on the novel, Sartre's comments on writing, and many more.[2] My plans in this volume are decidedly more modest. For this book is intended to be a brief introductory text for students to use in courses on the novel, a book more interested in helping students and teachers *experience* a novel rather than defensively interpret it. Interpretation obviously occurs in a class, since students and teachers bring with them a kaleidoscope of perspectives and opinions.[3] However, my perspective does not uphold the notion that criticism should dominate the novel in a classroom; instead, it proposes to help a classroom break up into individual experiences with a book before defensive interpretation. For the demand from academia now is not so much for talk about our lives as human beings in a real world, but for how our talk is structured; and this, useful as it may be as interpretation, kills off the atmospheric "poetry" in a class more than anything I know. This "poetry," this electric awareness that is sometimes heavy or light, and which comes from an in-class perception that a novel can suddenly and actually say something about our lives, is what my perspective seeks to protect from "theory." It is the *integrity of the unpredictable illumination* which my tentative remarks hope to support. I am not against theory; I'm not saying that the author's intention is eternally clear and therefore theory is foolish.[4] There are theories in this book. Nor am I saying that novels mold us into narcissistic and passive observers.[5] I am positing with John Dewey in his *Art As Experience* (1934) that as we read we must accept the possibility of going through "in our own vital processes" what the artist went through, before we theorize. The critical perspective in this book supports this idea, and refuses to start with a way of looking at literature that spiritualizes the novel out of existence.[6] "The intensely, stifling human quality of the novel is not to be avoided," says Forster in *Aspects of the Novel* (1927); "the novel is sogged with humanity; there is no escaping the uplift or the downpour, nor can they be kept out of criticism. We may hate humanity, but if it is exorcised or even purified the novel wilts; little is left but a bunch of words."[7]

2

Let me start by suggesting that when we criticize literature, we pay honor to art forms that have satisfied our hunger for a peculiar truth about out world: that there is, in reality, an enticing *danger* living at the heart of it, a danger that is heavy, moist, and breathing, like that great wall of African vegetation in Conrad's *Heart of Darkness*, that "rioting invasion of soundless life," that "rolling wave of plants, piled up, crested, ready to topple over the creek, to sweep every little man of us out of his little experience."[8] I see criticism not as talk between academic critics who seem eager to defuse this danger in art (since they smell the vegetation so keenly); rather, I see criticism to be a path for both student and teacher to walk on, right through those breathing walls of reality and up to the novel, in order to confront the danger. And danger is there, since, as Joyce Cary points out in *Art and Reality* (1958), the "reality which smashes every ideologue and his system is human nature."[9] Perhaps criticism is a way of testing the maps we find in a novel, to see if we can use them to find our way into what D.H. Lawrence called the "grisly dark" of new knowledge. I'm saying that the danger of new feelings and ideas is inherently in the novel, for I believe the novelist has a sixth sense for feeling it. Now I don't believe that my feelings about how novels contain dangerous ideas is new; but I do believe that my position is of value, based as it is on feelings apart from my conventional moral and civic training, and on the way I've seen literature take hold of a student. Sometimes, in the classroom, the student experiences with a great novel what Charles Sanders Peirce has called an *abduction*. These two ideas -- that novels hold out dangerous feelings and ideas and that they abduct us -- fixes, more or less, the limits of my approach. What is this danger? Where in the novel does it live? And how does it work its way on us as readers? These questions will be answered in Chapters 1 and 2.

Danger to one's ideas has been a topic for treatment in literature for quite some time. Chaucer's characters experience it in *The Canterbury Tales*, Don Quixote found out about it riding with Sancho Panza, as did Prince Hal drinking with Falstaff in *Henry IV, Part I*. Gulliver discovers such danger among the Yahoos in *Gulliver's Travels*, as does Jude feel it with Arabella in *Jude the Obscure*, and Clifford, in seeing the change in Connie as her relationship grew with a gamekeeper in *Lady Chatterley's Lover*. Wayne Burns has specifically defined this danger in his *The Panzaic Principle* (1965), using D.H. Lawrence's essays on the novel, José Ortega Y Gasset's *Meditations on Quixote* (1914), and Stephen C. Pepper's *The Basis of Criticism in the Arts* (1945). I base my critical views on Lawrence, Burns, Pepper, and John Dewey; and their hypotheses concerning the function of literature fixes, again, the limits of my approach. Lawrence, Burns, Pepper, and Dewey believe, as I do, that literature does, indeed, refer to the world. Current critical theories, with their emphasis upon the nature of *reference* in language, or even in their philosophical "joy" in seeking out gaps and holes in verbal meaning, do not hold out very much for me as a teacher since the students in my classroom would find them incomprehensible obstacles to their eager search for meaning in their lives.[10] The contextualist approach, which emphasizes the degree to which the reader *will* get the novel mixed up with his personal life, is therefore antithetical to our popular and cherished criticisms. Our current critics spend most of their time "moving around books," as Forster says in *Aspects of the Novel*, "instead of through them" (p. 13). "The reader," he says, "must sit down alone and struggle with the writer, and this the pseudo-scholar will not do. He would rather relate a book to the history of its time, to events in the life of its author, to the events it describes, above all to some tendency" (p. 14). Contextualism sees the critic as a reader struggling *alone* with the novel, as someone who reads the novel without relying so much on classifications or tendencies. For a novel to the contextualist is something more than an object of appreciation or an expression of an ideology. "The final test," Burns says, "is the quality and amount of illumination that a novel gives the reader through the connections it makes. How it obliges him to make the connections is not finally crucial, since the 'how,' in so far as it depends on unity, structure, and pattern, is only a means to the illuminative end . . . ." Novels are "still 'slices of life,' no matter how refined or elaborate the techniques of slicing, and they still demand that the reader connect up the life that they present with his own."[11] The deeper and more honest this connection turns out to be in the classroom, the more likely it is that a teacher will *not* spend inordinate amounts of time drawing endless distinctions between life and literature.

In claiming that connections between the "life" in the novel and the life of its readers are real, contextualist criticism refuses conservative partnership with the moral approach (Ian Watt's *The Rise of the Novel* [1957] and Wayne Booth's *The Rhetoric of Fiction* [1961]), the formistic approach (Cleanth Brook's "The Formalistic Critic" [1951]), the traditional (T.S. Eliot's essays), and the structuralist-deconstructionist approach (Barthes, Lacan, Derrida). And although contextualist criticism does stress reader-reaction, it remains subversive to current "reader-response" theories; for it does not emphasize reading "communities," or claim that a novel exists entirely as a reader's subjective re-creation of it.[12] It may be true, as Wolfgang Iser maintains, that "as we read we react to what we ourselves have produced, and it is this mode of reaction that, in fact, enables us to experience the text as an actual event."[13] But contextualism goes a bit further than this, as does Burns in *The Panzaic Principle*, and emphasizes that the connections readers make "give the lie to their own and critics' abstractions about the novel."[14] The major function of the teacher of fiction is not "to help students identify their own collectivities, their group or class interests"[15] [although there is nothing to prevent us from calling this valuable too], but rather to help students see how the real connections they make with the novel may *subvert their own individual or class interests and the ideals of literary criticism.* To get discussion going in this direction the following question from David Bleich's *Readings and Feelings* (1975) is useful: "What is it you think you are reacting to?"[16] Answers will be individual responses to the material, which will, hopefully, allow the class to see just how the novel can sometimes "give the lie" to the abstractions we want the novel to be. (How a novel gives the lie to its author's intentions is the subject of Chapter 4, "Dissident Notes on *Ulysses*").

2. Spotlighting Questions Which Contextualist Criticism Tries To Answer.

"Even where we can establish the existence of certain features" in a work of art, state Radford and Minogue in *The Nature of Criticism* (1981), "this . . . doesn't in all cases establish how we should respond to them, so that what critical analysis can establish is still further limited."[17] Contextualism agrees, but reminds us that when the contextualist does "criticize" he does not emphasize how we *should* respond to anything. Nor do I mean to suggest with Gerald Graff that we need what he calls "better contextualizing" (i.e., "to teach not the texts themselves" since "all courses are courses in theory," but to "situate ourselves in reference to those texts" *Professing Literature* [Chicago: University of Chicago Press, 1987, pp. 256; 262]). Instead, the contextualist looks at how the student *does* respond, and goes from there; and since the kinds of questions he asks in order to illuminate the connection between a reader and a novel are not based on scientific methodologies, he does not worry about being "limited." Some of the questions that contextualist criticism asks are as follows:

a. *Has the novelist intensified his material in order to achieve for the reader a vivid experience?* When the contextualist judges degrees of vividness, he judges the degree of illumination about life achieved by the writer, the depth and spread of it. He will note the degree of cognitive and emotional tension in a reader as the reader discusses the material, and he will look to see how the novelist increases intensity by the use of *conflict*, struggles which break up habit, conventions, traditions, and ideologies. Contextualist criticism analyzes the details of such struggles in order to understand the depth and spread of intensity, and takes the aesthetic value of conflict very seriously.

b. *Is the aesthetic distance between the reader and the novel kept close or distant?* Traditional concepts of aesthetic distance have stressed that readers must maintain cool objectivity in the face of art if pleasure or value is to be gained. In his chapter on contextualist criticism from *The Basis of Criticism in the Arts* (1945), Stephen C. Pepper maintains that in proportion as these conflicts "of instinctual impulse and social interest" do touch us "the aesthetic value of the experience is increased."[18] The concept of cool aesthetic distance is challenged by contextualist criticism because the feelings of readers and those feelings explored in the novel may be coincidental; and in their attempt to keep their distance from the novel readers will keep *secrets* concerning the collision between their lives and the novel's new ideas which challenge them to feel and think differently. Chapter 3 discusses aesthetic distance.

      c. *Does the novel stay close to the problems of living* ? While judging the relation of the work of art to its immediate social context, the contextualist critic will say that a novel is a great work of art if it stays close to revealing the social battle between human impulse and civic interest, between our basic facts of life and our blind *ideals* about them. How close a novel stays to the problems of living is the basis for contextualist value judgments.

      d. *Does the novel set up conflict between itself and the reader's preconceived ideas* ? Contextualist criticism relies on D.H. Lawrence's essays on the novel, and on Wayne Burns' *The Panzaic Principle.* Both authors believe that when ideals are undermined by the novel, illumination takes place. How the novel undermines our ideals is the subject for discussion in determining the intensity of aesthetic experience.

Indiana University
Northwest

W.K.B.
Chicago, 1989

# Notes

[1] See: D.H. Lawrence's essay "John Galsworthy" (1928) in A. Beal, ed. *Selected Literary Criticism* (New York: The Viking Press, 1966), pp. 118-119; E.M. Forster's *Aspects of the Novel* (New York: Harcourt, Brace and World, Inc., 1927), pp. 7-14; and Louis-Ferdinand Céline's *Conversations with Professor Y*, trans. S. Luce (Hanover and London: University Press of New England, 1986).

[2] See: Plato's *The Republic*, Book X; Aristotle's *Poetics*, XIII-XIV; *Hamlet*, II, ii ll. 415-21; John Dryden, *An Essay of Dramatic Poesy* (1668); Alexander Pope, *An Essay on Criticism* (1711); Samuel Johnson, *Preface to Shakespeare* (1765); Shelley's *A Defense of Poetry* (1840); Emile Zola's *The Experimental Novel* (1893); Leo Tolstoy's *What is Art* ? (1898); James' "The Art of Fiction" (1884); Mark Twain's "Fenimore Cooper's Literary Offenses" (1895); D.H. Lawrence's "The Novel" in *Phoenix II*, and his "Why the Novel Matters" and "Morality and the Novel"; Jean-Paul Sartre's *What is Literature* (1949).

[3] For an introduction to contemporary literary criticism consult: Forster's *Aspects of the Novel* (1927); I.A. Richards' *Practical Criticism* (1929); L.M. Rosenblatt's *Literature As Exploration* (1938); J.C. Ransom's *The New Criticism* (1941); Welleck and Warren's *Theory of Literature* (1942); S.E. Hyman's *The Armed Vision* (1947); S.O. Lesser's *Fiction and the Unconscious* (1957); W.S. Scott's *Five Approaches of Literary Criticism* (1962); R. Scholes, *Structuralism in Literature* (1974); Terry Eagleton, *Literary Theory: An Introduction* (1983).

[4] As do Knapp and Michaels in "Against Theory" from W.J.T. Mitchell, ed., *Against Theory: Literary Studies and the New Pragmatism* (Chicago: Univeristy of Chicago Press, 1985), pp. 11-30, and in "Against Theory -- 2" *Critical Inquiry*, 14, 1 (Autumn, 1987), pp. 49-68. See also: Wimsatt and Beardsley's "The Intentional Fallacy" in *On Literary Intention* (Edinburgh, University Press, 1976), pp. 1-13, and M. Steig's "The Intentional Phallus: Determining Verbal Meaning in Literature" *Journal of Aesthetics and Art Criticism* (Fall, 1977), pp. 51-61.

[5] As does Lennard J. Davis in *Resisting Novels: Ideology and Fiction* (New York: Methuen, 1987), Chapter one.

[6] John Dewey, *Art as Experience* (New York: Capricorn Books, 1934) "We lay hold of the full import of a work of art only as we go through in our own vital processes the processes the artist went through in producing the work. It is the critic's privilege to share in the promotion of this active process. His condemnation is that he so often arrests it" (325); "Theory can start with and from acknowledged works of art only when works of art are set in a niche apart instead of being celebrations, recognized as such, of the things of ordinary experience . . . . the trouble with existing theories is that they start from a ready-made compartmentalization, or a conception of art that spiritualizes it out of connection with the objects of concrete experience" (11).

[7] E.M. Forster, *Aspects of the Novel*, p. 24. Hereafter references are included in the text.

[8] Joseph Conrad, *Heart of Darkness* (New York: W.W. Norton and Company, 1971), p. 30.

[9] Joyce Cary, *Art and Reality* (Anchor Books, 1958), p. 172.

[10] See: Jacques Derrida, "Structure, Sign, and Play in the Discource of the Human Sciences," *The Languages of Criticism and the Sciences of Man* (Baltimore: Johns Hopkins, 1970). For a critique of this approach, consult G. Hartman's *Criticism in the Wilderness* (New Haven, Conn.: Yale University Press, 1980).

[11] Wayne Burns, "On Reading Novels: An Outline for a Contextualist Primer," *Recovering Literature*, 10 (1982), pp. 33-41. See also: Wayne Burns, *Journey Through The Dark Woods* (Seattle: The Howe Street Press, 1982).

6

12 See: Stanley Fish, *Is There a Text in This Class?* (Harvard University Press, 1980) and David Bleich, *Readings and Feelings* (NCTE, 1975). For a comprehensive introduction to "reader-response" theory consult J.P. Tompkins, ed., *Reader-Response Criticism* (Baltimore: John Hopkins University Press, 1980).

13 Wolfgang Iser, *The Act of Reading: A Theory of Aesthetic Perception* (The Johns Hopkins University Press, 1978), pp. 128-29.

14 Burns, "On Reading Novels," p. 37.

15 Robert Scholes, *Textual Power: Literary Theory and the Teaching of English* (New Haven, Conn.: Yale University Press, 1985), p. 23.

16 Bleich, *Readings and Feelings,* p. 10.

17 Colin Radford and Sally Minogue, *The Nature of Criticism* (Sussex: The Harvester Press, 1981), p. 61.

18 Stephen C. Pepper, *The Basis of Criticism in the Arts* (Cambridge, Mass: Harvard University Press, 1945), p. 67.

PART I

TENTATIVE DISCUSSIONS

# CHAPTER 1

## INTRODUCTION

1. Certainties in Contextualist Criticism

Contextualism is not an excessively analytical theory; it does not dissect a novel in order to determine which part demands a feeling of delight -- this is *mechanistic* criticism, whose best known proponent is Santayana in his *Sense of Beauty* (1896). Nor is contextualism interested in discovering how the novel is organized, or how it does or does not fully integrate our feelings according to some harmonious ideal about what novels should do -- this is *organicist* criticism, whose best known practitioners are Coleridge, Henry James, and Percy Lubbock. (Hegel, Stephen Pepper said, took the aesthetic value of "harmony" and "rolled it ponderously over the whole field of cultural history").[1] Nor does contextualism concern itself with finding critical values in the artistic imitation of the *norm* or the *universal*, or in how the novel conforms to our social milieu -- this is *formistic* criticism, and its spokesmen are Aristotle, T.S. Eliot, and Wellek and Warren. (Formism seeks out in a novel what Pepper calls "perceptions satisfying in themselves to the normal man."[2] We may, perhaps, even include Marxian social realism here, since Engels has said that realism is the "truthful reproduction of typical characters under typical circumstances").[3] Briefly stated, *contextualism* is interested in discussing the deeply felt experiences we may have as we unexpectedly connect up with passages in novels, and its major proponents are D.H. Lawrence, E.M. Forster, Stephen C. Pepper, and Wayne Burns.

To understand how contextualism is different from other criticisms, we must first look at the point of origin for contextualism, what Pepper calls the "historic event."

> By historic event, however, the contextualist does not mean primarily a past event, one that is, so to speak, dead and has to be exhumed. He means the event alive in its present . . . The real historic event, the event in its actuality, is when it is going on *now*, the dynamic dramatic active event . . . it is an act in and with its setting, an act in its context.[4]

The contextualist critic regards the "act in its context" as a certainty, and he likes to describe it. He sees a reader's experience in discussing a novel to be an interesting "act in its context."

In *Aspects of the Novel*, E.M. Forster listed what he called main facts in human life: birth, food, sleep, love, and death. I want to keep these facts as examples of certainties in the historic event because contextualism often appeals to them, and uses their degree of presentation in fiction for measures of beauty. The standard of beauty for the contextualist critic is what Pepper calls *intensity and depth of experience* (*BCA*, p. 57), and it is my hypothesis in this study that if a reader experiences *conflict* when reading a novel, if he is confronted with any of the above facts of life in such a way as to upset his preconceived ideas about them, then his experience with that novel will be most intense, deep, and beautiful. Beauty to the contextualist could be the intensity experienced at the ugliness of death, or the intensity from social peace or chaos. It could be the danger our senses pose to our intellectualizations about human behavior, or to our respect for law, custom, religious training, educational expectations, or Kantian judgments of taste. Beauty could be the danger sexuality poses to our idealized conceptions of love, honesty, and charity, as it does so vividly in Thomas Hardy's *Jude the Obscure* (1896). This concept of the *historic event*, the concept of the novel as an *act* in context, and this idea that as readers we can experience *conflict* as we read or discuss novels, gives to contextualism a powerful critical view. I do not deny the validity of other criticism; I do claim, however, that contextualist criticism relies upon facts in real and literary experience to explain both reader comments and the meaning of the novel. I further claim, with Wayne Burns, that our most intense and deep experiences in reading come when our ideals are attacked by novels.

## 2. A Definition of Terms

Closely associated with my use of *historic event* and *reader conflict* are other terms useful for making contextualist judgments: *aesthetic distance, emotion, feeling, realism,* the *novel* , and *reading experience.*

### Aesthetic Distance.

Traditional concepts of aesthetic distance stress that readers maintain cool objectivity in the face of art in order to get aesthetic pleasure or value. You should, in other words, appreciate Duke Orsino's speech on love in *Twelfth Night* but not compare his remarks to what you hear in life and give up on "love" altogether. Very few people, Stephen Pepper says, have noticed the reverse of this idea:

> . . . that in proportion as these conflicts do touch you (to the point of not precipitating action) the aesthetic value of the experience is increased.
> Most of what we have taken to be our greatest art is outright tragedy or contains tragic portions. To a hedonist this is a mystery. Why in the temple of pleasure do we set up a god of sorrow? A contextualist explains that when the center of aesthetic interest is placed on vivid realization of experience, then the attraction of the artist to tragic subject matter is seen as inevitable. Conflicts of instinctive impulse and social interest stir our awareness of experience to the deepest, and the further they can be carried in a work of art towards their full tragic import the more vivid our realization. Tragedy in art then becomes no paradox.
> (*BCA* , p. 67)

I want to call attention to Pepper's phrase: "conflict of instinctive impulse and social interest stirs our awareness to the deepest." These kinds of conflicts might cause a reader to lose his objectivity about a novel, to (and here I extend Pepper's view) bolt into action. Surely teachers experience the following in their classrooms now and then: a young woman approaches her professor of modern literature after class and reports that after reading James Joyce's *Portrait of the Artist as a Young Man* all her emotions and ideas about her religious faith have been destroyed, or a young graduate student complains that his marriage is now a shambles after reading passages of D.H. Lawrence's *Women in Love* to his new bride. Contextualist criticism recognizes these results as part of the aesthetic experience, and wants to explore how and why they happen. Fashionable criticism has reinforced the idea of cool aesthetic distance by building solid walls of unknown variables between words and experience. Today there is such a plethora of semiotic theories that claim language cannot refer to anything that one is stumped at where to begin reading about such views. Why do such theories mystify language, make it a new religion, an angry god? Such critical fundamentalism smacks too much of its political equivalent. "Perhaps we are *here*," Rilke says in his "The Ninth Elegy," "in order to say... house, bridge, fountain, gate, pitcher, fruit-tree, window

. . . / to say them *more* intensely than the Things themselves ever dreamed of existing . . . / *Here* is the time for the *sayable*, here is its homeland./ Speak and bear witness. More than ever/ the Things that we might experience are vanishing, for/what crowds them out and replaces them is an imageless act./ . . . . these Things,/ which live by perishing . . . look to us for deliverance: us, the most transient of all." If we live in the age of fashionable high-tech intellectualism [as Russell Jacoby describes it in *The Last Intellectuals: American Culture in the Age of Academe* (1987)], then now is, indeed, "the time for the *sayable.*" Despite what is fashionable, this study maintains that there is, after all, a connection between a word and the thing it refers to, and between a text and a reader -- classroom experiences substantiate this.[5] Aesthetic distance is not cool but hot, and fraught with danger; and literary criticism, whether it likes it or not, must refer to the heavy presence of reality in literature. For the monsters we call *reality*, the objects of Kurtz's "horror" in *Heart of Darkness,* are all those "sexual, revolutionary, deterministic, or psychic energies that novelists and intellectuals confront even as they try to avert them."[6] Our real world is always quietly at work undermining the philosopher's model of it. Teachers who tell their students that language cannot correspond to reality assume "that the way meanings *originate* determines their ability or lack of ability to refer to external reality."[7] Our "modern anxiety," says Graff, "that sign and meaning, meaning and referent, do not correspond is often accompanied by another emotion -- a desire that they not correspond. It is often unclear in modern critical polemics whether we have no choice but to remain in our prison-houses of language or consciousness, or whether we might depart from these prison-houses but *ought not to want to*, lest we compromise the autonomy of human consciousness. Underlying our programmatic skepticism there is frequently a programmatic moralism that assumes man is somehow demeaned if he imitates nature or takes his cues from sources outside his own mind."[8]

What those two students experienced when they had finished reading Joyce and Lawrence was a sudden, unstructured, receptivity. The authors took them by surprise. Opposed to the act of criticism, their reading acts increased the intensity of their life experiences. It is these kinds of students, who, because they are willing to compromise the "autonomy" of their minds, find that their aesthetic experiences are really human ones. If I start with my definition of aesthetic distance as *our objectivity under attack*, and with my definition of aesthetic experience as *human, passional experience*, then my exploratory definitions of "feeling" and "emotion" emerge.

## Feelings and Emotions

Right away we can see that if contextualist criticism views tragic art as conflict between instinctive impulse and social restraint, then a description of our *feelings* as we experience conflict is in order. Take those two students I mentioned. The young woman said that her original religious *emotions* were destroyed; yet, she also admitted that she *felt* Joyce was right about a lot of things. The young man complained that his marriage was a wreck; yet, he too admitted that he *felt* Lawrence described a number of painful truths. Used for a long time in literary criticism, these words "feeling" and "emotion" have not been fully distinguished, except in a few cases where preliminary distinctions have been drawn.[9]

Feelings, it seems to me, have their life in immediate sensual apprehension; emotions, on the other hand, are half way to becoming intellectualized feelings. Feelings can provoke thought -- instinctively -- but emotion, ego-bound and protective of ideas, remains suspiciously and continually mouthed by culture. Somehow feelings are deeper experiences in rebellion from the stereotypical emotional responses to our environment. They are subversive to emotions like "admiration," "edification," "fairness," "charity," and "brotherly love." Somehow emotions can "understand" and thrive in such ideas. Inside us as clichés, emotions like "love," "religious faith," "patriotism," and "fairness," for example, are used by speechmakers to get us to do something, or to give us political convictions of one kind or another. The end of such art, as Donald Davie says, is "emotional inflammation." Thus, in *rhetorical* literature:

> The signals are cues not to action but emotion; and since
> the audience, if it is at all sophisticated, recognizes these

as the terms of the contract, there is an unpleasant flavour of
masturbation about the whole transaction. "Oh," says the
compliant reader, "he wants me to feel indignant, does he?
Very well, I think I can manage that." And he duly
manipulates himself into the state required of him. Getting
the cues and responding to them is what such a reader
understands as experiencing literature; and he finds it
enjoyable, since he is getting something for nothing. He
experiences emotion without having to suffer its occasion or
act upon its prompting.[10]

I agree with Davie here, yet perhaps we have got to start with this kind of "emotion" before we get
*through* it to our feelings -- to how we actually respond to a novel apart from the rhetorical
instructions given by the author, teacher, or critic. Teachers are always eager to protect the stable
atmosphere of a classroom, to protect their students from the pain and challenge of literature by
telling them where to look for *emotional* cues: the result is a peculiar release of tension in the
reader that lessens the chance for independent feelings to erupt and bring new thought. Critics are
eager to promote their perspective, to control student response in the belief that "criticism" will
provide a truth. Authors who are jittery about unstructured reactions to what they see as their
authorial intention often given stage directions in novels. In fact, not to be triggered in some
"emotional" way, not to be inflamed or intimidated by esoteric theories is actually, as Davie claims,
"an affront" to modern readers who have been

schooled in a rhetorical theory of literature so as to think
that the writer's prime duty is to him, the reader, rather than
to his own experience, his own subject . . . does
Shakespeare cue in the playgoer how to feel about the
spectacles he represents in *A Midsummer Night's Dream*, in
*As You Like It*, in *Much Ado About Nothing* ? . . . . Dr.
Johnson, who preferred Shakespeare's comedies to his
tragedies, did not feel affronted: but it seems that we do.[11]

Real instinctual feelings in an author, which often reflect our own, and which do not require
"emotional cues" from a teacher or critic, can lead to vivid reader-experiences. That's why
Stephen Pepper suggests for the contextualist aesthetic field the *voluntary but vivid intuitions of the
qualities in a situation* (*BCA*, p. 56). If, however,

one wants to get at the particular force of contextualistic
criticism, he does better not to think about the pleasure
(leave that to the mechanist) but about the experience. The
contextualist is a gourmand for experience. The stress is on
the experience, the unique quality of the experience, and it
is this that is quantified to give the contextualistic aesthetic
standard. *The more vivid the experience and the more
extensive and rich its quality, the greater its aesthetic value* .
(*BCA*, p. 57)

Now let me look at those two students again. Both the young woman's experience with *Portrait*
and the young man's experience with *Women in Love* brought them new feelings from disturbing
ideas -- they freely admitted that. Their experiences were unexpected, surprising to their usual
intellectualized emotions about religious faith and marriage. But if their feelings were felt by them
to be parallel with the character's feelings, and I believe that they were, then I claim the more vivid
their reading experiences must have been.[12]

True, in *The Basis of Criticism in the Arts* Pepper uses the word "emotion" and not "feeling" in his definition of contextualist aesthetic experience; however, in the following quote he gives such interesting and added dimensions to the word "emotion" that his remarks will help my tentative distinctions between emotion and feeling.

> You remember William James identified emotion with the fusion (that was his own word) of organic and kinesthetic sensations. There is no very good reason why he should not have included the external sensations also when these are present. Actually, in any emotional reaction there is no clear separation of visual, auditory, or tactile sensations from the internal and dynamic ones. The sound of thunder is with difficulty distinguished from its fearfulness . . . .This basic insight of the James-Lange theory of emotion appears to hold in spite of all the criticisms of it. Only, *what James should have stressed was not the kind of sensations that make an emotional quality, but the manner of their appearance, their fusion.* In short, vividly fused experience is, for aesthetic purposes at least, a very convenient definition of emotional experience. (*BCA*, p. 64; emphasis added)

*Fusion*, a meshing of kinesthetic feeling with intellectualized emotion, is, I maintain, a fact in the reading act, and contextualist criticism appeals to this fact for its definition of aesthetic experience. Fusion may set up in the reader a conflict between instincts and cultural expectations. For "emotion is," John Dewey has said, "psychologically, the adjustment or tension of habit and ideal, and the organic changes in the body are the literal working out, in concrete terms, of the struggle of adjustment . . . .emotion in its entirety is a mode of behavior which is purposive, *or has intellectual content.*"[13] This *initial* tension between habit and ideal reflects the tension between raw feeling and emotions. A scene from George Orwell's *Down and Out in Paris and London* (1933) will illustrate:

> One night, in the small hours, there was a murder just beneath my window. I was woken by a fearful uproar, and, going to the window, saw a man lying flat on the stones below; I could see the murderers, three of them flitting away at the end of the street. Some of us went down and found that the man was quite dead, his skull cracked with a piece of lead piping. I remember the colour of his blood, curiously purple, like wine; it was still on the cobbles when I came home that evening, and they said the school-children had come from miles round to see it. But the thing that strikes me in looking back is that I was in bed and asleep within three minutes of the murder. So were most of the people in the street; we just made sure that the man was done for, and went straight back to bed. We were working people, and where was the sense of wasting sleep over a murder?[14]

Between habit and ideal in this passage is the tension between the pull of sleep and what the character *should* have done. Our *emotions* with this passage may cause us to ask what we would have done, but our *feelings* align themselves with the pull of sleep.

14

Raw feelings, those expressed in real life or even in reaction to a novel, are, therefore, less idealistic -- if not downright anti-idealistic. Emotions, on the other hand, recollected feelings at the mercy of cultural pressure, are probably idealistic, because they help us do what we think we should be doing.

*Realism.*

I have been belaboring the obvious in my claim that novels provoke feelings. Yet this obvious point seems "old fashioned" and "naive" today, since so much of our literary criticism denies that literature is realistic. Academic arguments might declare that Orwell's book on Paris and London doesn't show what it means to be down and out -- that it may not is acceptable. But when these arguments claim that literature as a general rule cannot reflect reality, then obvious reaffirmations of known facts have to be made. For no matter how efficiently we pad our university walls with esoterica or muffle our office doors with theory, the subversive knock of reality will be heard. Reacting to the work of Zola and others, Marcel Proust said that the nineteenth-century conception of the novel as a "cinematographic parade" was "absurd," since merely to describe things in order to carve out a clear view of the world cuts off communication between ourselves and the past. "The reality to be expressed," he said, "was to be found, not in the outward appearance of the subject, but in the extent to which this impression had penetrated to a depth where that appearance was of little importance."[15] Despite Proust's dismissal of the realistic novel at the end of *Remembrance of Things Past* (1913-1927), "realism" still intrigues the novelist. Robbe-Grillet's *ciné-romans* (and even more so his *Snapshots* [1962]) are intended rejections of nineteenth-century realistic techniques; yet upon closer reading we discover that these works embrace *the detail* more than ever. There is even a term to decribe the experimental techniques of Márquez and Cortázar: "magic realism." The term explains how Latin-American authors combine magic events in fantastic worlds with realistic qualities. Other modern authors could be described as realists too: Dreiser, Ellison, Solzhenitsyn, and Vonnegut, to name only a few. Yet realism knocks with persistence on the office doors of literary critics as well. Studies in literary realism flood our libraries: Georg Lukács's *German Realists of the Nineteenth Century* (1951), Ian Watt's *The Rise of the Novel* (1957), René Wellek's "The Concept of Realism in Literary Scholarship" in *Concepts of Criticism* (1963), and George J. Becker's *Documents of Modern Literary Realism* (1963) are some of the more important historical and theoretical explorations. What must be pointed out now, however, is that both writers and critics hear wildly different things in that knock. They no longer hear Zola, who maintained that the "experimental novelist is therefore the one who accepts proven facts, who points out in man and in society the mechanism of the phenomena over which science is mistress, and who does not interpose his personal sentiments, except in the phenomena whose determinism is not yet settled, and who tries to test, as much as he can, this personal sentiment, this idea *apriori,* by observation and experiment."[16] Virginia Woolf satirized such a position in her short story "An Unwritten Novel," and Bertolt Brecht has sidestepped Zola with politics. "Realism means," Brecht says in *Aesthetics and Politics* (1980), "discovering the causal complexes of society/unmasking the prevailing view of things as the view of those who are in power/writing from the standpoint of the class which offers the broadest solutions for the pressing difficulties in which human society is caught up."[17] William Dean Howells simply stated: "Realism is nothing more and nothing less than the truthful treatment of material, and Jane Austen was the first and the last of the English novelists to treat material with entire truthfulness."[18] George J. Becker's *Master European Realists of the Nineteenth Century* (1982) takes a more historical approach by reiterating the characteristics of the realistic movement, fitting the technical contributions of Flaubert, Zola, the Goncourts, Tolstoy, Dostoevsky, and Chekhov to "the movement," and concluding with traditional critical language about realism: Galdós comes about as close to being the "*compleat realist* in the novel that Chekhov is in the short story and the drama."[19] Galdós's novels, for Becker, look at the proverbial huge "slices" of Madrid life. Elizabeth Ermarth's *Realism and Consensus in the English Novel* (1983) says that in realistic fiction there is a fixed and arbitrary nature to the spectator, that this arbitrary spectator, in creating a homogeneous viewpoint, draws more attention to his own methods of perception than to the things perceived. Looking at the novels of Defoe, Richardson, Austen, Dickens, and Eliot, Ermarth says the narrator is a "nobody," neither an individual nor someone who is corporeal, but rather a "collective result," a "specifier of consensus," dependent upon distance and memory.[20]

My intention is not to review the complete history of realism here, but to state, simply, that I do not believe the realistic narrator is a "nobody." I believe he is alive, idiosyncratic, and susceptible to the pain of the world because he is the creation of an author who believes that his novel can indeed describe the world he lives in. I still believe in authorial intention, in the rage of Dickens for example, in the passion of D.H. Lawrence, in the psychological analysis of Mann, in the pronouncements of Dostoevsky in *Notes from the Underground* or Ellison in *Invisible Man.* I believe with Alex Comfort that the realistic novelist is a writer with a "medical, level eye," who does not sentimentalize human behavior.[21] I believe that great realists described the causes of hunger, sexual feeling, and death, and that they felt the power of language could help the reader ferret out meaning in his life. I still believe, in other words, that if I read Orwell's *Down and Out in Paris and London* (1933), I would find out what it meant to be down and out in those cities in 1933. If this means that I am, according to Derrida, "sad, *negative*, nostalgic, guilty," and even a bit like Rousseau, and maybe, in the final analysis, naive, well then so be it.[22] For I am still convinced that a great novel can illumine quotidian history. Novels give significance to the complaints of reality, and realism, a way of literary perception as old as the Greeks, gives credence to the critical notion that *context creates form,* that the world shoves its way into the imagination of the novelist, who, if asked as he walked down a dirt road to repudiate the existence of the idea of a stone, would, in that context, and with Dr. Johnson, kick a rock.

A useful and traditional definition of realism-naturalism by M.H. Abrams is as follows:

> A thoroughgoing realism involves not only a selection of subject matter but, more importantly, a special literary manner as well: the subject is represented, or "rendered," in such a way as to give the reader the illusion of actual experience . . . it is a mode of fiction that was developed by a school of writers in accordance with a special philosophical thesis. This thesis, a product of post-Darwinian biology in the mid-nineteenth century, held that man belongs entirely in the order of nature and does not have a soul or any other connection with a religious or spiritual world beyond nature; that man is therefore merely a higher-order animal whose character and fortunes are determined by two kinds of natural forces, heredity and environment. He inherits his personal traits and his compulsive instincts, especially hunger and sex, and he is helplessly subject to the social and economic forces in the family, the class, and the milieu into which he is born.[23]

Even more useful is Harry Levin's definition:

> We lose little by confining our attention to that terrain of experience which philosophical sophistication would label "naive realism." Its classical gesture occurred when Dr. Johnson kicked the stone. Characteristically it manifests itself by repudiating some manifestation of idealism.[24]

Contextualist criticism takes note of Abrams' definition, but finds real interest in what Levin calls "naive realism" because it was the repudiation of idealism in Joyce's *Portrait* and Lawrence's *Women in Love* that challenged the conventional emotions about marriage and religion in those

16

two students of mine.  Using  Abrams' definition, the contextualist will describe the "illusion of actual experience" in the novel, and he will agree with Levin that realism manifests itself by repudiating some form of idealism.  To take this manifestation of repudiated idealism in a young reader seriously, is to appeal to that fragile, delicate, vocal response from a student who, after putting down a novel, tells us that he is burning at the stake, signaling to us through the flames, as Antonin Artaud says in *The Theatre and Its Double* (1958).[25]

Since I emphasize the objectivity of pain in getting new knowledge, my definition of realism may appear to have the reader passive.  Yet unstructured passivity is really the mind opening and asking questions about reality, after the shock of new knowledge has subsided.  Victims in shock are passive; when they awake, they ask questions.  I see the reader of literature as Rainer Maria Rilke saw the panther:

His sight from ever gazing through the bars
has grown so blunt that it sees nothing more.
It seems to him that thousands of bars are
before him, and behind them nothing merely.

The easy motion of his supple stride,
which turns about the very smallest circle,
is like a dance of strength about a center
in which a mighty will stands stupefied.

Only sometimes when the pupil's film
soundlessly opens   . . . then one image fills
and glides through  the quiet tension of the limbs
into the heart and ceases and is still.[26]

Ian Watt, whose views Pepper would call *organicist*, claims that "the novel's realism does not reside in the kind of life it presents, but in the way it presents it."[27]  Near the end of his *The Rise of the Novel* (1957), Watt announces that the "ultimate cohesive force of the book [*Tom Jones*] resides not in the characters and their relationships, but in an intellectual and literary structure which has a considerable degree of autonomy."[28]  Surely Fielding did not write *Tom Jones* to impress us with his "structure," or to have us laugh at its "organization." All throughout *Tom Jones*, Fielding critiques this demand for structure [Book V, Chp. 1], and reaffirms his love for the reader.  What we do find in this novel, as in all great novels, are, indeed, "characters and their relationships;" and it is because such relationships are often parallel to our own lives that the book works in any classroom.  Fielding likes the idea of having unsuspecting and "passive" readers, minds able to let go for the sake of surprise.  It is modern literary theory that does not see reality in the novel, not Fielding, or a reader.  It is modern literary theory that rejects surprise.  Today, using the terminology of a ghostly metaphysics, this rejection has gone deep.  Fictional *relationship* -- that crucial, obvious, and painful fact of life so necessary to a novelist and his readers -- has been spiritualized.  In this strange world, in this "rarefied region of the undecidable," literature is "emptied of all linguistic force except the force of its own duplicitous self-consciousness."[29]  Such critical idealism has its roots in Roland Barthes' "An Introduction to the Structural Analysis of Narrative" (1966), where it is claimed that

Narrative does not make people see, it does not imitate;
the passion that may consume us upon reading a novel is
not that of a "vision" (in fact, strictly speaking, we "see"
nothing).  It is the passion to discover meaning, it is a
striving towards a higher order of relation, which also
carries its emotions, its hopes, its threat, its triumphs.
What goes on in a narrative is, from the referential (real)
point of view, strictly *nothing*.  What does "happen" is

language per se, the adventure of language, whose advent
never ceases to be celebrated.[30]

Searches for "higher order" meanings or languages "per se" have been more than
adequately described by the Marxists as samples of *real* estrangement; in fact, this search for the
elusive nature of language makes socialist realism look not only quaint but attractive. Under
capitalism, Georg Lukács says in "The Ideal of the Harmonious Man in Bourgeois Aesthetics"
(1970), the "bleaker and emptier life becomes . . . the more intense is the yearning after beauty."[31]
He states directly that dominant formistic and organicist criticisms have become hothouse
cultivations of "exaggerated subjectivity," and "foggy mysticism."[32] The "avant-garde critics," he
says, "fail to go beyond the distortion of the abstract anti-historicism of the academics."[33] For all
of its insight into abstract theories of criticism, however, socialist realism is not the kind of realism
contextualist criticism can accommodate either. In the final analysis it is propaganda [i.e., the
individual "will enjoy greater freedom to choose a place for himself" in a socialist society Lukács
says in *Realism in Our Time* (1971).][34]

More acceptable to contextualist criticism is the kind of realism that affirms *a solid
confrontation between the novelist and his world and between the reader and the novel*, the kind of
realism that sees the novelist as someone trying to fuse his sense of life into a "novel," the kind
which sees a reader as someone struggling with words on a page. Even more acceptable, and, in
fact, what contextualist criticism affirms, is the kind of realism that shows how art can be
subversive. "Art does not provide knowledge of reality by reflecting it photographically or 'from a
particular perspective,'" argues Adorno in "Reconciliation under Duress," "but by revealing
whatever is veiled by the empirical form assumed by reality" (*Aesthetics and Politics* [London:
Verso, 1980], p. 162). Literature is anchored to our world "where we still twist and turn on that
hard bed, too belabored and aching from the stones of fact to be able to escape into dreams."[35]

*Novels*

In the last fifty years or so, novelists and critics have been announcing that the novel has
committed suicide with the tools of academic interests and gimmick writers, lost its interest in
reality, or endured inevitable historical death.[36] The modern novel, these critics claim, has dried up
because novelists have pushed their craft into a state of entropy where a lot of paraphrasing,
borrowing, copying, or modeling goes on.[37] The novel has become for these critics static,
directionless -- dead; and in turn, some novelists have become smug in their perceptions about the
"death" of their art. D.H. Lawrence explained how all this came about when he wrote his essays
on the novel in the 1920's. He said in "Why the Novel Matters" ( *circa* 1925) that at its best, the
novel can help a person be alive, be a "whole man alive," and that when you read a novel, you can
develop an "instinct for life, if you will, instead of a theory of right and wrong, good and bad."[38]
In "Morality and the Novel" (1925) he claimed the real business of art was to "reveal the relation
between man and his circumambient universe, at the living moment" (*SLC*, p. 108). The novel, to
Lawrence, is the "highest example of subtle inter-relatedness that man has discovered. Everything
is true in its own time, place, circumstance, and untrue outside of its own place, time,
circumstance. If you try to nail anything down, in the novel, either it kills the novel, or the novel
gets up and walks away with the nail " (*SLC*, p. 110). And in an essay that has been frequently
overlooked -- "Surgery for the Novel -- Or a Bomb" (1923) -- Lawrence says that the serious
writer can get "senile-precocious," absorbedly self-conscious, and self-satisfied with that old tune
about the death of twentieth-century culture (*SLC*, p. 115). All these remarks share a common
critique: modern readers, writers, and critics have given up on feelings of aliveness because they
have swallowed the idea that death reigns supreme in the twentieth-century. I rely on D.H.
Lawrence's definition of the novel because he gives the novel a way out of its entropy. If the
novel has a future, he says, its got to have the courage to

> tackle new propositions without using abstractions; it's got to present us with new, really new feelings, a whole line of new emotion, which will get us out of the emotional rut. Instead of snivelling about what is and has been, or inventing new sensations in the old line, it's got to break a way through, like a hole in the wall. And the public will scream and say it is sacrilege: because, of course, when you've been jammed for a long time in a tight corner, and you get really used to its stuffiness and its tightness, till you find it suffocatingly cosy; then, of course, you're horrified when you see a new glaring hole in what was your cosy wall (*SLC,* pp. 117-118).

Since contextualist criticism affirms what Lawrence calls "really new feelings," that public scream at the new hole in the culture wall, it relies on Lawrence's definition of the novel:

> The novel is the highest form of human expression so far attained. Why? Because it is so incapable of the absolute . . . . There may be didactic bits, but they aren't the novel. And the author may have didactic "purpose" up his sleeve . . . . But even a didactic purpose . . . cannot put to death the novel.
>
>     . . . It is such a bore that nearly all great novelists have a didactic purpose, otherwise a philosophy, directly opposite to their passional inspiration. In their passional inspiration, they are all phallic worshipers. From Balzac to Hardy, it is so. Nay, from Apuleius to E.M. Forster.
>     Now in a novel there's always a tom-cat, a black tom-cat that pounces on the white dove of the Word, if the dove doesn't watch it; and there is a banana-skin to trip on; and you know there is a water-closet on the premises. All these things help to keep the balance.[39]

"Black tom-cats" of reality that pounce on our philosophy, "banana-skins" that remind us of the vulnerability of our bodies, and the water-closet that tells us of the functions which undermine the "poetry" of life: these are the images Lawrence uses to show us the conflict between the real and the ideal, what Wayne Burns has called the "Panzaic principle" -- that voice of reality in Sancho Panza undermining Don Quixote's dreams.

To help bring itself back from "the dead," Lawrence advised that a novel be 1. " *Quick,*" that is, alive, or consisting of "an odd, sort of fluid, changing, grotesque or beautiful relatedness" to life (*Phoenix II,* p. 420). In other words, "the man in the novel must be 'quick' . . . . he must have a quick relatedness to all the other things in the novel"; 2. "*Interrelated,* in all its parts, vitally, organically. For the relatedness and interrelatedness of all things flows and changes and trembles like a stream, and like a fish in the stream the characters in the novel swim and drift and float and turn belly-up when they're dead" (p. 422); and 3. "*Honourable.*" "Tolstoi, being a great creative artist, was true to his characters. But being a man with a philosophy, he wasn't true to his *own character.* Character is a curious thing. It is the flame of a man, which burns brighter or dimmer, bluer or yellower or redder, rising or sinking or flaring according to the draughts of circumstance and the changing air of life, changing itself continually, yet remaining one single, separate flame, flickering in a strange world: unless it be blown out at last by too much adversity" (*Phoenix II,* p. 423).

> And the honour, which the novel demands of you, is
> only that you shall be true to the flame that leaps in you . . .
> Whichever flame flames in your manhood, that is you, for
> the time being. It is your manhood, don't make water on it,
> says the novel. (*Phoenix II*, pp. 425-26)

Contextualist criticism sees the perception of *quickness, interrelatedness*, and *honor* in a novel as part of our aesthetic experience, and finds that these qualities often allow us to see the conflict between reality and idealism.

*Reading Experience*

"Pristine" is how the American pragmatist William James described the original texture of our experiences in life, before we have had a chance to analyze and label them. When we have such pristine experiences, we find ourselves participating in them to such a great extent that when they are over we realize that we have learned something. Pristine experiences occur with novels, too, as we read, and before criticism has had a chance to analyze and label our reactions. When we do put the book down and begin to discover what we have experienced, we look at how our reactions stand in relation to the *textual facts* of the novel.

If, then, a student has a pristine experience as he is reading, how does knowledge happen? James says that knowing is a particular kind of relation, that the relations which connect our experiences (exemplified by the graph above) must be experienced, and that this whole process is very real. [40] This unique interplay between readers and novels is the reading experience, and it is something contextualist criticism will not deny. As a teacher I will not hold, on the one hand, that the author's intentions *must* shape all student response to the novel; nor will I claim, on the other hand, that a student re-writes the novel as he or she reads it. I will claim, however, that if readers sustain and nourish an intellectual openness, then, as Elizabeth Freund puts it, whatever is "counter, original, spare," or "strange" in a great novel will be experienced by such readers. [41]

Popular literary criticisms, with their representational theories of perception, claim that immediate data of perception are subjective impressions to which external objects gravitate. These kinds of theories, William James responds, violate the reader's "sense of life" [i.e., Lawrence's "flame"]. [42] As students interplay with the novel in their reading experiences, and as they discuss the text in class, their "sense of life" may evoke the *quickness* and *interrelatedness* of their own connections with the book. The power of these new feelings -- realities substantiated by references to the text -- will either provoke students to accept such new feelings, or cause them to fight to get free from them.

21

Notes

1 Stephen C. Pepper, *The Basis of Criticism in the Arts* (Cambridge, Mass.: Harvard University Press, 1945), p. 75. As did structuralism with its "unified field theory" (Geoffrey Hartman, "Structuralism: The Anglo-American Adventure," J. Ehrmann, ed. *Structuralism* (New York: Anchor Books, 1970), p. 139.

2 Ibid., p. 107. Hereafter abbreviated as *BCA* in text.

3 Friedrich Engels, "On Socialist Realism," *Literature and Art by Karl Marx and Friedrich Engels* (New York: International Publishers, 1947), p. 41.

4 Stephen C. Pepper, *World Hypotheses* (Berkeley: University of California Press, 1970), p. 232.

5 See: A.C. Purves and R. Beach, *Literature and the Reader* (NCTE, n.d.), and C.R. Cooper, ed., *Researching Response to Literature and the Teaching of Literature* (Norwood, NJ: Ablex Publishing Co., 1985).

6 George Levine, *The Realistic Imagination* (Chicago and London: University of Chicago Press, 1981), p. 25.

7 Gerald Graff, *Literature Against Itself* (Chicago: University of Chicago Press, 1979), p. 20.

8 *Ibid.*, p. 22.

9 A. Berndstron, *Art, Expression, and Beauty* (New York: Holt, Rinehart and Winston, 1969); D. Davie, *The Poet in the Imaginary Museum* (New York: Persea Books, Inc., 1977); John Dewey, *Art As Experience* (Capricorn Books, 1932); I.A. Richards, *Practical Criticism* (New York: Harcourt Brace and World, Inc., 1929); I.A. Richards, *Complementaries: Uncollected Essays* (Cambridge: Harvard University Press, 1976); J.W. Krutch, *Experience and Art* (New York: Collier Books, 1962); S.O. Lesser, *Fiction and the Unconscious* (New York: Vintage Books, 1957).

10 Donald Davie, *The Poet in the Imaginary Museum* (New York: Persea Books, Inc., 1977), p. 243.

11 Ibid., pp. 247-48.

12 As far as pleasure is concerned, I offer the following episode. After I had taught D.H. Lawrence's *The Plumed Serpent* to a college class of Mexican-Americans, a young woman walked into my office at the end of the course and said: "If that's what men are like in Mexico, then I want to go there right away." I never found out whether she had left for Mexico or not, although it was rumored that she had. Yet this remark substantiates, tentatively I believe, the contextualist definition of aesthetic distance, the contextualist description of aesthetic experience, and my tentative definition of feeling. I am not saying that Lawrence knew exactly what Mexican men were like, or that what his novel presented was real; in fact, if that young woman took his book to be an exact description of Mexican men then she might have been suffering from her own quixotic misunderstanding. I am saying that a possibility for new behavior presented itself to the young student, and she took it.

13 John Dewey, "The Theory of Emotion," *The Early Works of John Dewey,* ed. JoAnn Boydston (Carbondale: Southern Illinois University Press, 1971), pp. 170-71. (Emphasis added). To borrow a phrase from social psychologists, we can also say that emotions are "hedonically polarized feelings" (R.L. Morgan and D. Heise, "Structure of Emotions," *Social Psychology Quarterly*, 51, 1 (1988), p. 19.

14 George Orwell, *Down and Out in Paris and London* (New York and London: Harcourt, Brace, and Jovanovich, 1933), p. 91.

22

15 Marcel Proust, *Remembrance of Things Past, II* (New York: Random House, 1932), p. 1009.

16 J.H. Smith and E.W. Parks, eds. *The Great Critics* (New York: Norton, 1967), p. 911.

17 Bertolt Brecht, "Popularity and Realism," *Aesthetics and Politics* (London: Verso, 1980), p. 82.

18 Smith and Parks, *The Great Critics*, p. 904.

19 George J. Becker, *Master European Realists of the Nineteenth Century* (New York: Frederick Ungar, 1982), p. 239.

20 Elizabeth D. Ermarth, *Realism and Consensus in the English Novel* (Princeton, NJ: Princeton University Press, 1983), pp. 65-66.

21 See: Alex Comfort, *The Novel and Our Time* (London: Phoenix House, 1948), p. 74.

22 See: Jacques Derrida, "Structure, Sign, and Play in the Discourse of the Human Sciences," in *The Structuralist Controversy*, eds. R. Maclosey and E. Donato (Baltimore: John Hopkins University Press, 1972), p. 264.

23 M.H. Abrams, *A Glossary of Literary Terms* (New York: Holt, Rinehart and Winston, Inc., 1957), pp. 153-54.

24 Harry Levin, *Contexts of Criticism* (Cambridge: Harvard University Press, 1957), pp. 68-69.

25 Antonin Artaud, *The Theatre and Its Double* (New York: Grove Press, 1958), p. 13.

26 R.M. Rilke, *Selected Poems* (Berkeley: University of California Press, 1964), p. 65.

27 Ian Watt, *The Rise of the Novel* (Berkeley: University of California Press, 1957), p. 11.

28 Ibid., p. 277.

29 Frank Lentriccia, *After The New Criticism* (Chicago: University of Chicago Press, 1980), p. 254.

30 Roland Barthes, "Introduction à l'analyse structurale des récits," *Communications*, 8 (1966); trans by L. Duisit, pp. 26-27.

31 Georg Lukács, *Writer and Critic* (New York: Grosset and Dunlap, 1970), p. 89.

32 Ibid., p. 194.

33 Ibid., p. 201.

34 Georg Lukács, *Realism in Our Time* (New York: Harper and Row, 1964), p. 112.

35 George J. Becker, ed. *Documents of Modern Literary Realism* (Princeton, NJ: Princeton University Press, 1963), p. 38.

36 Of the many who have proclaimed this thesis, here are some of the more famous: Ortega y Gasset's *The Dehumanization of Art* (1948) and George Steiner's *Language and Silence* (1967).

37 Bernard Bergonzi explores the development of this famous argument in his *The Situation of The Novel* (London: Macmillan, 1970), Chapter I "The Novel No Longer." The paradox is that the novel, "which seems so open to life, and to give, as Lawrence saw, a total picture of man in all his variety and fullness, is intimately connected with a particular technology and form of commercial development, neither of which may be permanently protected from obsolescence. There is a further paradox in the fact that despite the commitment of novelists to the power and authority of the fictional form, critics have for a long time been predicting the end of the novel, in tones ranging from cool indifference to apocalyptic gloom. The apocalypticism may, indeed, be inherent in the form. The novel is concerned, above all, with carving shapes out of history, with imposing a beginning, a middle and an end on the flux of experience, and there might

be obscure connections between the need for a novelist to find an end for his novel, and the preoccupations of critics with seeing an end for all novels" (p. 13).

[38] A Beal, ed., D.H. Lawrence: *Selected Literary Criticism* (New York: Viking Press, 1966), p. 107. (Hereafter abbreviated as *SLC* in the text.)

[39] W. Roberts and H.T. Moore, eds. *Phoenix II* (New York: Viking Press, 1970), pp. 416-18. (Hereafter abbreviated as *Phoenix II* in the text).

[40] C.H. Seigfried explains it this way: "As soon as the flux of pure experience is given it turns 'ordinary,' and 'tends to fill itself with emphases, and these salient parts become identified and fixed and abstracted; so that experience now flows as if shot through with adjectives and nouns and prepositions and conjunctions.' Ordinary experience is composed of explicit relations just as much as of explicit objects" (*Chaos and Context* [Athens: Ohio University Press, 1978], p. 53).

[41] Elizabeth Freund, *The Return of the Reader* (London and New York: Methuen, 1987), p. 154.

[42] J.J. McDermot, ed., *The Writings of William James* (Chicago and London: University of Chicago Press, 1977): "Let [the reader] begin with a perceptual experience, the 'presentation,' so called, of a physcial object, his actual field of vision, the room he sits in, with the book he is reading as its centre; and let him for the present treat this complex object in the common-sense way as being 'really' what it seems to be, namely, a collection of physical things cut out from an environing world of other physical things with which these physical things have actual or potential relations. Now at the same time it is just *those self-same things* which his mind, as we say, perceives; and the whole philosophy of perception from Democritus's time downwards has been just one long wrangle over the paradox that what is evidently one reality should be in two places at once, both in outer space and in a person's mind. 'Representative' theories of perception avoid the logical paradox, but on the other hand they violate the reader's sense of life, which knows no intervening mental image but seems to see the room and the book immediately just as they physically exist" (p. 173). If we read Katherine Lever's *The Novel and the Reader*, a primer for students and critics, we can understand just how far behind we have left the idea that novels, and the people who read them, live in a context: "The fact is that the relation of novel and reader is not all there is to be known about a novel. It has an origin in the mind, life, and environment of the novelist and it has effects radiating into time and space" (New York: Appleton-Century-Crofts, Inc., 1960), p. 96. At the same time it is surprising to discover the similarities between, say, the theories of Stanley Fish and remarks on the reader by Percy Lubbock in his *The Craft of Fiction* (New York: Compass Books, 1957), p. 17 especially.

# CHAPTER 2

## Contextualist Criticism

### 1. Stephen Pepper and the Contextualist Field[1]

The essential ingredient in the field of our reading experience is the *felt quality* of our response to a novel. *Quality* is the felt character of the reading event, [2] and when we analyze it we find in it the following categories: *spread, change, and fusion. Spread* is the present quality of the event that may fan out into the future or back again into the past; it may often spread out in wild and numberless ways, some too large and wide for us to chart, and others too small for us to detect. Often, in frustration, after realizing that we cannot fully control the unexpected moments in life, we monotonously proclaim permanent ways of harnessing the free flow. We decide to deny the impatient spread of events, and we isolate ourselves from them. We start to rob meaning from reality out of revenge, to strip definitions from words, to decontextualize language itself. Some believe this activity symptomatic of individual adjustments to our world; others claim it is human to want to abolish spontaneous actions that would bring about historically difficult consequences. *Change* remains, however, and it is a constant occurrence in contextualist perception.[3] Familiar sights may look strange one day since the quality of the whole may have altered a detail, or textures may have been rearranged. If change is so radical, then how does the contextualist admit accountable fields of unified experience? He answers that the quality of an event has a high or low intensity of *fusion*. The contextualist looks at the details of an event, and decides how they contribute to the vividness of perception. Fusion happens not only in a mind but also in the event, because the "organization of any individual thing," George Mead has said, "carries with it the relation of this thing to processes that occurred before this organization set in."[4]

In Wilfred Gibson's war poem "In The Ambulance," we can observe networks of spread, change, and fusion.

> Two rows of cabbages
> Two of curly-greens,
> Two rows of early peas,
> Two of kidney-beans.
>
> That's what he keeps muttering,
> Making such a song,
> Keeping other chaps awake
> The whole night long.
>
> Both his legs are shot away,
> And his head is light,
> So he keeps on muttering
> All the blessed night:
>
> Two rows of cabbages,
> Two of curly-greens,
> Two of early peas,
>
> Two of kidney-beans.[5]

26

The *spread* of this poem is the forward reach of it to the future -- the soldier's most likely death in stanza three -- a future which aligns itself with a backward reach to the past: the soldier planting his two-row English victory garden at home before joining up. *Change* in the poem takes place in the second stanza. Tension increases and changes the context of the poem, taking us from those garden images in a man's delirium, those furrows for planting, to the parallel image of trench warfare. *Fusion*, the felt quality of the conflict in the poem, is the degree to which our thoughts and feelings merge these images.

At the same time we apprehend *quality*, we apprehend *texture*: the *context* and *strands* of an event, the parts and positions of it. "Both his legs are shot away" is a disturbing *strand* -- a contributing detail -- to the texture of this poem. The title "In the Ambulance" is the *context*. If we heighten, then, our contextual awareness to the *strands* and *context*, and to the *spread, change*, and *fusion* in this poem, and if all this awareness happens at once in our reading experience, we will feel an intense irony. I don't mean to say, with Cleanth Brooks, that irony is the "most general term that we have for contextual qualification" in determining what poetry might be. [6] I am saying that irony neither rests solely in the language nor in the intentions of an author, but comes to the text from a reader too. We know that there is a peculiar relationship at that point of ironic revelation between an author and his character, when the author withholds information from him. But sometimes between a *reader* and an author there is intentional irony, since an author may treat his reader "more as a victim than as a confederate"; that is, "the artist acts as an *eiron* in the traditional Socratic sense. The victimization of the reader (the idea of . . . being placed at a disadvantage because of a deficiency in knowledge . . .) is finally intended as a way of bringing the reader closer to the truth about himself."[7] To "make irony anything more than a subcategory of contextual qualification," McKee says, "is to risk losing sight of the element of victimization in irony, as the New Critics did."[8] Contextualist criticism is interested in this kind of irony because when we learn truths about ourselves, we experience, sometimes reluctantly, our most intense fusions with novels. The degree to which the reader gets his perception fused measures both the beauty of the text and the intensity of reader-illumination.

2. Contextualist Criticism: Definition and Brief Application

A concise and more functional definition of my approach may now be offered. Contextualist criticism is a method of inquiry that determines: 1) how the reading of a novel emerges as a vivid experience, and 2) how the reading reveals aspects of human behavior formerly blocked from understanding by habits of perception (automatic apprehension), conventional opinions (rules of verbal behavior recognized by people as substitutes for individualistic behavior), and ideological training (public education which gives a reader the content of socially acceptable thought). In explaining how a novel emerges as a vivid experience, contextualist criticism explores the *quality* and *texture* of a scene, and claims *conflict* as a source for intense experience. If vivid perceptions of quality, texture, or conflict fail to take place, the contextualist critic determines that the scene lacks beauty.

In *The Great War and Modern Memory* (1975), Paul Fussell notes that after reading World War I memoirs he finds one particular phenomenon that occurs with a great deal of repetition and similarity. Soldiers "locate, draw forth, and finally shape into significance events which otherwise would emerge without meaning into the general undifferentiated stream" by a "paradigm of ironic action." He calls this process the "mechanism of irony-assisted recall," and it depends upon what contextualist criticism calls the recognition of certain *strands* in a fused sight.[9] Fussell gives us the following example:

Sir Geoffrey Keynes . . . John Maynard's brother, was
a highly sophisticated scholar, surgeon, author, editor,
book collector, and bibliographer, with honorary doctorates
from Oxford, Cambridge, Edinburgh, Sheffield,
Birmingham, and Reading. In 1968 he recalled an incident
of January 26, 1916. A German shell landed near a British
artillery battery and killed five officers, including the major
commanding, who were standing in a group. "I attended as
best I could to each of them," he remembers . . . He then
wonders why he remembers so clearly this relatively minor
event: "Far greater tragedies were happening elsewhere all
the time. The long, drawn-out horrors of Passchendaele
were to take place not far away." It is, he concludes, the
small ironic detail of the major's dead dog that enables him
"to see these things as clearly today as if they had just
happened": "The pattern of war is shaped in the individual
mind by small individual experiences, and I can see these
things as clearly today as if they had just happened, down
to the body of the major's terrier bitch . . . lying near her
master."[10]

The kind of recall Keynes described above depends upon similar mechanisms readers use
in experiencing a novel. Readers look for details, qualities, and textures that will help them
understand why a scene remains fused in their memories. John Dewey remarks that a new poem
is "created by everyone who reads poetically -- not that *its* raw material is original for, after all, we
live in the same old world, but that every individual brings with him, when he exercises his
individuality, a way of seeing and feeling that in its interaction with the old material creates
something new, something previously not existing in experience." A work of art, Dewey claims,
is a work of art "only when it lives in some individualized experience."[11] Keynes brought with
him to this scene an individualistic, irony-assisted recall that remembered the body of the dog next
to the body of the soldier. This scene, in turn, releases many layers of meaning about war to us
because there is an interplay between pure experience and recalled memory that gives new
knowledge to readers who might visualize such an event. To understand the irony, we have to
look at that *strand* of the "body of the major's terrier bitch . . . lying near her master" and decide on
how this detail functions ironically, how it operates to fuse the whole scene in memory. If a
contextualist critic, in exercising what Dewey calls his individuality (seeing something new in old
material), takes this scene and says something new about war, or even about Keynes, he is
looking at the quality and the texture of this scene, and deciding whether, in this case, the last
sentence can accommodate critical judgments. When I isolated that scene from Orwell's *Down and
Out in Paris and London* in Chapter One, I said that it emphasized my point about the reality of
sleep. I concentrated on that last sentence, which for me fused the scene: "we were working
people, and where was the sense of wasting sleep over a murder?" That sentence seemed to vivify
the quality and texture of Orwell's whole event for me. In other words, both scenes from Orwell
and Keynes have a *spread* that is fraught with suspense -- they move, so to speak, toward a
conclusion. I would, as a critic exercising an individuality, underline certain words in the Orwell
scene in order to characterize the quality and texture of it. Why, for example, were *schoolchildren*
coming from *miles* to see the victim? Or, at the end of the paragraph, why did Orwell call losing
*sleep* over such an event to be foolish? I pointed to the clash between our instinctual needs and
our social obligations. Keynes has underscored the sight of a terrier bitch next to her master,
which, in turn, led Fussell to emphasize the function of irony in recall. My point is that not only
does contextualist criticism look for details in a text that would make a scene vivid, or emphasize
the clash between reality and idealism, or expose irony, but it also looks for sudden breaks in the
text which give new knowledge -- as if, at least in the above examples, the last sentence to a special
paragraph fuses the details of that paragraph into vivid reader-experience. Contextualist criticism is

interested in these points in narration or in dialogue where a "turn" to new knowledge occurs, where a "change" of tone is heard, or where a "break" in the text comes to announce a startling fact. These occurrences are not purely linguistical, but are more tonal, qualitative, and provocative to a reader. In a more general sense, these changes could be new events discussed by an author for the first time -- changing, as a result, the history of fiction. Weddings, for example, in eighteenth-century and nineteenth-century novels, come near the end of a chapter or near the end of the novel so that the author can avoid any discussion of sexual intercourse. With D.H. Lawrence's *Lady Chatterley's Lover*, however, a break from this tradition appears -- a break which illustrated a real change in feeling and attitude. To illustrate what I mean by changes which move away from expected tones, and by breaks from expected feelings (which usually evoke in a reader his *conventional* responses), let's look at how Ferdinand describes his friend's death in Louis-Ferdinand Céline's *Journey to the End of the Night* (1932).

> . . . . But there was nobody but me, really me, just me, by his side -- a quiet real Ferdinand who lacked what might make a man greater than his own trivial life, a love for the life of others. I hadn't any of that, or truly so little of it that it wasn't worth showing what I had. I wasn't death's equal. I was far too small for it. *I had no great conception of humanity. I would even, I believe, have more easily felt sorry for a dog dying than for Robinson, because a dog's not sly; whereas, whatever one may say, Léon was just a bit sly. I was sly too; we were all sly* . . . All the rest of it had fallen by the wayside and *even those facial expressions, which are still in some use by a death-bed,* I'd lost as well . . . My feelings were *like a house you only keep for the holidays.* They were barely habitable . . .
>
> It was as if now he were trying to assist us to live. As if he had sought out pleasant things for us to stay on for. He held onto each of us by a hand. *I kissed him. That is all there is that one can do in such cases, without going wrong.* We waited. He said nothing now. A little later, an hour perhaps, not more, the haemorrhage did come, in an abundant, an internal, an overpowering flood. It carried him off.
>
> His heart began to beat faster and faster and then very fast indeed. It was racing after the worn-out blood, thin and far away in his arteries, tingling at his finger tips. *The pallor spread up* from his neck and covered his whole face. The end came, choking. He went, as if he had taken a spring, and gripping onto both of us with both his arms.
>
> Then almost at once there he was back again before our eyes, his face strained, already beginning to take on his dead man's weight.
>
> We stood up and we disengaged ourselves from his hands. They stayed up in mid-air, his hands, quite stiff, and blue and discoloured in the light of the lamp.
>
> Now, in that room, it was *as if Robinson were a foreigner who'd come from a frightful land, whom no one would dare speak to .* (emphasis added)[12]

The "break" in our conventional ideas on sorrow occurs with: "I had no great conception of humanity. I would even, I believe, have more easily felt sorry for a dog dying than for Robinson, because a dog's not sly; whereas . . . Leon was just a bit sly. I was sly too; we were all sly." The "turn" to unexpected feeling over a scene like this occurs with: "My feelings were like a house you only keep for holidays. They were barely habitable." And at the end of this scene, you get a powerful change of tone that unifies the *strands* of the entire incident: "it was as if Robinson were a foreigner who'd come from a frightful land, whom no one would dare speak to." The quality of this passage is vivid, since the speed with which Robinson's death is described characterizes the *spread* of the movement of the episode -- even the spread of Robinson's last pallor joins to vivify the scene. There are *changes* of feelings from compassion to lack of pity to admissions of slyness. The degree of *fusion* is high -- especially if you note the details in the last two paragraphs. The texture is rich and complex, the *context* of Céline's attack on our conventional responses to death so subtly determined as it is by the *strands* of Ferdinand's feelings and Robinson's last body movements. The pallor spreading up from Robinson's neck, the strained face, the blue hands -- these are *factual*, aesthetic, and medical immediacies that determine how vivid the quality of our experience with this scene will be. Ferdinand's comments on slyness are the felt immediacies that challenge our notions of expected emotions during what would otherwise be called a "respectful" situation. Céline takes us underneath conventional responses to death because his tone refuses to let us cue our public emotions. The whole scene shows just how limited our conceptualizations can be in the face of the materiality of life, and it attacks our habits of perception and conventional talk about death. It even undermines our modern defense of irony, Fussell's "rhetorical" irony in Keynes' memoir. For part of Céline's exposure of our defense mechanisms rests on his belief that ideals cannot exist in the real world.[13]

### 3. Wayne Burns and *The Panzaic Principle*

In analyzing the power of Céline's passage above, the contextualist might ask the following questions:

1. How did Céline achieve this qualitative scene?
2. How great is its aesthetic distance?
3. Did the scene stir enough conflict in us to cause us to think about our conventionalized emotions about death?
4. What is the relation between Céline's novel and its social context?

Wayne Burns answers these kinds of questions. He draws out of the contextualist world view unexpected implications behind contextualism's insistence that the more intense our experience with a novel, the greater the novel's aesthetic value. Denying that art is solely the technique used to produce it,[14] Burns claims that only by means of an "epigonic awareness" (what Kafka called a "sharper light taken from our time") can the artist strengthen his "difference (the dimmer light emanating from himself"): thus achieving "the intensity necessary to illuminate the darkness that is modern civilization."[15] "I am a contextualist," Burns recently declared, "one who sees form as a means to an end, not an end in itself; and one who, on the positive side, believes that a good or a great novel must somehow illuminate the experiential world that its fictional world connects up with."

> How the novel achieves this illumination cannot of course be prescribed: from a contextualist point of view anything that works, that makes for illumination, is good, regardless of what it looks like or how it does what it does -- although it is my contention . . . that the Panzaic principle, by connecting the experiential with the fictional and bringing out the discrepancies between the real and the ideal in both worlds, has provided a good part of the illumination in just about every English novel of the nineteenth century.[16]

After reviewing the idealistic reaction *Don Quixote* has received from modern critics, Burns argues that, from their point of view (one which suggests that Don Quixote is a hero since readers attach a symbolic value to his quest), these critics are right to separate the Don from his partner Sancho, the servant who reminds us of our materiality. Critics usually recognize the power Sancho embodies to upset the ideals of Don Quixote, but more often they reject the broader implication of his power for our own culture. Paraphrasing Flaubert, Burns says: "For Sancho's belly has not only burst the seams of Venus' girdle, it has given the lie to Dulcinea and in fact all of Don Quixote's ideals -- much as Lady Chatterley's guts give the lie to Clifford and his ideals in *Lady Chatterley's Lover.*

> My dear, you speak as if you were ushering it all in!
> [i.e., 'the life of the body'] . . . Believe me, whatever God
> there is is slowly eliminating the guts and alimentary system
> from the human being, to evolve a higher, more spiritual
> being.
> Why should I believe you, Clifford, when I feel that
> whatever God there is has at last wakened up in my guts, as
> you call them, and is rippling so happily there, like Dawn?
> Why should I believe you, when I feel so very much the
> contrary.[17]

"In life the rightness of the guts (as against the mind) will depend on one's point of view," Burns points out. "In Lawrence's as in all other novels, however, the guts are always right; it is an axiom or principle of the novel that they are always right, that the senses of even a fool can give the lie to even the most profound abstractions of the noblest thinker. And it is this principle I have designated the Panzaic principle, after Sancho Panza."[18]

*The Panzaic Principle* is neither an ideology nor a new genre; and it does not claim that all of fiction must be subsumed under "Panzaic vision." Rather, it is an axiom that can be observed functioning in great novels where ideals are present, and where that clash between instinct and culture takes place. Wayne Booth is mistaken when he says in *A Rhetoric of Irony* [University of Chicago Press, (1974)] that "Wayne Burns asks me to see Sancho Panza as *the* moral center of *Don Quixote*" (p. 57). Burns does not ask us to see a "Panzaic" character as the moral center of any novel, since nothing in fiction is "Panzaic in itself . . . nothing can be Panzaic until it is brought into conflict with the ideal"[19] (Appendix, p. 127). Moreover, not even a belly or a phallus can be "Panzaic" in itself.

> A phallus, presented clinically, may be just a spout to urinate
> through; or, presented pornographically, it may be an object
> to thrill to. It is only Panzaic when it functions in such a
> way as to cut through what Ortega has described as the
> "crystalline orb of the ideal" -- the way the pig's pizzle in
> Hardy's *Jude the Obscure*, for example, cuts directly
> through the crystalline orb of Jude's daydreams to show the
> phallic reality that underlies them -- the reality that is to make
> a shamble of his ideals. (Appendix, p. 127).

Occurrences of "Panzaic" principles appear in the following ways:

1) When they reveal the effects of instinctual behavior on rational thought.
2) When they permeate whole scenes in order to expose the

relationship between the actions of a character and his
intentions.
3) When they operate in dialogue in order to explain the positions
of the idealist and the realist.
4) When they function as direct attacks on our ideals.

In Fielding's *Tom Jones* (1749), as Tom wanders into the fields to renew his "Meditations on his dear Sophia," he meets Molly Seagrim, and they "retire" into the "thickest Part of the Grove." Around Molly, Tom was not the "perfect Master of that wonderful Power of Reason, which so well enabled grave and wise Men to subdue their unruly Passions" (Book V, x).[20] His physical response to Molly, Burns says, "gives the lie to his apostrophe to Sophia" (Appenidx, p. 106). The Panzaic reveals the power of instinctual behavior to undermine rational thought. In Book Five, chapter five, Philosopher Square and his ideals of "true Honour" and "true Virtue" melt from the heat of his sexual desire for Molly and from his embarrassment at being revealed in the closet, "in a Posture . . . as ridiculous as can possible be conceived . . . He had a Night-cap belonging to Molly on his Head, and his two large Eyes, the Moment the Rug fell, stared directly at Jones; so that when the Idea of Philosophy was added to the Figure now discovered, it would have been very difficult for any Spectator to have refrained from immoderate Laughter" (p. 173). Here we see the Panzaic permeating a whole scene in order to reveal what we know of Philosopher Square and what his desires now reveal about him. That juxtaposition of his body with his philosophy is comic because his philosophical pretensions have been undermined by the reality of his crouching frame. And when we hear the following dialogue between Partridge and Tom in Book Eight, chapter nine, the Panzaic functions to explain the position of the idealist and the realist as they clash in vision and resolution. We see Tom and Partridge assume the roles of Don Quixote and Sancho Panza after leaving the inn at Gloucester.

> Jones made a full Stop, and turning about, cries, "Who knows, Partridge, but the loveliest Creature in the Universe may have her Eyes now fixed on that very Moon which I behold at this Instant?" "Very likely, Sir," answered Partridge, "and if my Eyes were fixed on a good Surloin of roast Beef, the Devil might take the Moon and her Horns into the Bargain." (p. 333).

In *Henry IV, Part I*, we hear the Panzaic attack one of our most cherished ideals -- military honor. Falstaff's Panzaic function, Burns says, "is to connect the poetry of our abstract ideals with the prose of our bodily senses, or more specifically, to reveal the concrete meaning of such ideals as 'honor' as that meaning is inscribed on the bodies of the living and the dead. Falstaff's cry, 'I like not such grinning honour as Sir Walter hath. Give me life,' is sufficient in itself to . . . show Hal and Prince John and Douglas and Hotspur and the king himself acting and speaking like Don Quixote's romance heroes" (Appenidx, p. 115). Henri Bergson's comments in *Le Rire* (1911) on the role of the human body in the psychology of comedy are applicable here. He claims that a human body prevented from responding to its environment in pragmatic ways is humorous, especially when the attitudes, gestures, or general movements of that body remind us of an awkward machine. But when we regard the body, Bergson continues, as a kind of obstruction to the rise of the soul to ethereal happiness, or if we put the body along side of the soul, then we have a very comic situation. If, in other words, the soul is tempted by the needs of the body, or if the ideals of the soul fall quickly aside for the body, comedy results. We experience the comic *most* strongly, he says, when we are shown the soul "tantalised" by physical needs:

> . . . on the one hand, the moral personality with its intelligently varied energy, and, on the other, the stupidly monotonous body, perpetually obstructing everything with its machine-like obstinacy. The more paltry and uniformly

repeated these claims of the body, the more striking will be the result. But that is only a matter of degree, and the general law of these phenomena may be formulated as follows: *Any incident is comic that calls our attention to the physical in a person, when it is the moral side that is concerned.* Why do we laugh at a public speaker who sneezes just at the most pathetic moment of his speech? Where lies the comic element in this sentence, taken from a funeral speech and quoted by a German philosopher: "He was virtuous and plump"? It lies in the fact that our attention is suddenly recalled from the soul to the body . . . *A person embarrassed by his body* is the image suggested to us.[21]

The body is the "constant detail in a man's changing environment" Pepper says in his chapter on contextualistic criticism from *The Basis of Criticism in the Arts.* And I have quoted Bergson because I believe he reinforces Wayne Burns' theory in *The Panzaic Principle* that a Sancho or a Falstaff can undermine, with their bodies, the idealism of a Don or a Prince. Underminings can be vivid moments, especially when the impatient body exposes the solemn mind. At the exposure of Philosopher Square in Molly's hotel bedroom, the fallen blanket concretizes the fallen ideals of the philosopher at the hands of his sexual desire for Molly -- it exposes him crouched in a square closet, naked under his nightshirt, revealed to Tom's comic eye. Bergson's discussion of these kinds of relationships between body and soul, between instincts and intellectual seriousness, reinforces Burns' discovery of such a relationship in almost all great novels and exemplifies Pepper's definition of the contextualist's interest in the conflict between instinct and social interest.

Now the operation of the Panzaic has been explained in philosophical terms by José Ortega Y Gasset's *Meditaciones Del Quijote* (1914). Using the 1957 translation "First Meditation: A Short Treatise on the Novel," a section from *Meditations on Quixote,*[22] Burns explains that Ortega "has been percipient enough and courageous enough to acknowledge, even as he deplores, the full effect of Sancho Panzism which he equates with materiality and/or realism" (Appendix, p. 120). Reality, in fiction, has a *generic function;* that is, it enters art by making an "active and combative element" out of its own "inertia and desolation" in life (*MQ*, p. 144). Therefore, "it does not actually matter what objects the realist chooses to describe. Any one at all will do, since they all have an imaginary halo around them, and the point is to show the pure materiality under it. We see in this materiality its final claim, its critical power before which, providing it is declared sufficient, man's pretentions to the ideal, to all that he loves and imagines, yields; the insufficiency, in a word, of culture, of all that is noble, clear, lofty" (*MQ*, p. 144). Surrounding culture, in other words, "copulates the barbarous, brutal, mute, meaningless reality of things" (*yace la bárbara, brutal, muda, insignificante realidad de las cosas*).[23] "It is sad," Ortega continues, "that such a thing is shown to us, but what can we do about it? It is real, it is there: terrible in its self-sufficiency. Its force and singular meaning take root in its presence. Culture is memory and promises, an irreversible past, a dreamed future, but reality is a simple and dreadful 'being there'! It is a presence, a deposit, an inertia. It is materiality" (*Quijote*, p. 156 my trans.). Crucial for Burns is that Ortega's analysis of the relationship between the real and the ideal, between materiality and culture, supports D.H. Lawrence's contentions that in the novel there is a "black tom-cat" that pounces on the "white dove of the Word" (a reality that pounces on our philosophy or mythical dream worlds of wish fulfillment), or a "banana-skin" to trip on (to show us our bodies as real and vulnerable), or a "water-closet on the premises" (to tell us of our bodily functions that undermine the "poetry" of life or culture). What both Lawrence and Ortega see as the conflict between the real and the ideal, and what Céline gives us in his description of Robinson's death, is what Burns has called the "Panzaic principle"; and this is what contextualist criticism implies, perhaps unknowingly, when it looks for conflict in a novel.

Furthermore, Ortega has claimed that the critical power of materiality is in almost every novel, and he argues that it becomes basic to the novel as a literary genre, especially when in the novel it destroys "myth." He draws an analogy between the perception of a mirage and the perception used to write mythologies. He tells the reader to visualize the dry earth of La Mancha, and to see that the real and bitter source for the water we think we see in a mirage is actually "the desperate dryness" of the land. Either we can see the water which the sun "paints" as actual, or we can see it ironically, obliquely, as the mirage it really is. If we hold this image in view, we can then understand Ortega's claim that novels of adventure, tales, and epics are all perceptions of imaginary worlds, while the realistic novel is this second, ironic, and oblique way of perception. Yet the realistic novel still needs something of the mirage to help us experience *realidad*. For not only does *Don Quixote* absorb the tradition of myth in order to expose it as a dream world, so do most novels function in this way (*MQ*, p. 139). If we see reality obliquely, if we see it ironically, we can then consider reality "as the destruction of the myth, as criticism of the myth" (*MQ*, p. 139). Subsequently, (and here is one of his most important points, the one which Burns has discovered operating in nineteenth and twentieth-century novels) "reality which is of an inert and insignificant nature, quiet and mute, revolts, and is changed into an active power of aggression against the crystalline orb of the ideal" (*la realidad, que es de naturaleza inerte e insignificante, quieta y muda, adquiere un movimiento, se convierte en un poder activo de agresión al orbe cristalino de lo ideal*) (*Quijote*, p. 151, my trans.). The spell of the ideal is broken, Ortega continues, it "falls into fine, iridescent dust which gradually loses its colours until it becomes an earthy brown." Of course the ideal does not fall without a scream. As Theodor Adorno says in *Negative Dialectics* (1973), the "system in which the sovereign mind imagined itself transfigured . . . is the belly turned mind, and rage is the mark of each and every idealism (New York: Seabury Press, 1973), pp. 22-23. "We are," Ortega y Gasset continues, "present at this scene in every novel. There is need of a book showing in detail that every novel bears the *Don Quixote* within it like an inner filigree in the same way that every epic poem contains the *Iliad* within it like the fruit its core."[24] Wayne Burns' *The Panzaic Principle* is such a book.

Let's observe how Burns pulls out of a scene from Charlotte Brontë's *Jane Eyre* the conflict between the ideal and the real. Only in writing *Jane Eyre*, Burns tell us, did Brontë actually use her deepest and most rebellious feelings to unconsciously surcharge her language with subtle attempts to break free from her religious and cultural ideals. Under the melodramatic surface of the novel there is the conflict between realism (Brontë's sexual desires) and idealism (Brontë's Methodist morality and phraseology), as illustrated by Brontë's word choice in the following passage where St. John tries to convince Jane to marry him.

> "*Could you decide now?*" asked the missionary. The
> enquiry was put in gentle tones: *he drew me to him*
> *gently. Oh, that gentleness! how far more* potent *is it than*
> *force! I could resist St. John's wrath: I grew pliant as a*
> *reed under his kindness.*
>> Yet I knew all the time, if I yielded now,
>> I should not the less be made to repent, some
>> day, of my former rebellion . . .
> "I could decide if I were but certain," I
> answered: "were I but convinced that it is
> God's will I should marry you, I could vow
> to marry you here and now -- come afterwards
> what would!"
> "My prayers are heard!" *ejaculated* St. John.
> *He pressed his hand firmer on my head, as if*
> *he* claimed me: *he* surrounded me with his arm,
> *almost as if he loved me.*
>> (I say *almost* -- I knew the difference --
>> for I had felt what it was to be loved; but,
>> like him, I had now put love out of the question,

and thought only of duty): I contended with my
inward dimness of vision, before which clouds
yet rolled.
*I was excited more than I had ever been . . . The feeling
was not like an electric shock; but it was quite as sharp, as
strange, as startling: It acted on my senses as if their utmost
activity hitherto had been but torpor, from which they were
now summoned, and forced to awake.*
"What have you heard? What do you see?" asked
St. John. I saw nothing: but I heard a voice
somewhere cry -- "Jane! Jane! Jane!" nothing more
. . . And it was the voice of a human being -- a
known, loved, well-remembered voice -- that of
Edward Fairfax Rochester; and it spoke in pain and
woe wildly, eerily, urgently.
*"I am coming!" I cried "Wait for me! Oh, I will come!"*[25]

Note how Burns has indented the more dramatic lines of the scene, while italicizing phrases or words that unconsciously express sexual implications. Given the critical tenets of contextualist criticism, the italics, Burns adds, are suggestive and not definitive, since the effect of Brontë's words "is cumulative." This is an important point to remember, for it underlies Pepper's thesis in *The Basis of Criticism in the Arts* that a perception in contextual awareness is fully achieved only if it is *cumulative*, that is, if it is a *funded* perception -- one which happens after repeated readings with an unsystemized awareness, (i.e., an awareness that does not make literature the drawing board for our own critical plans but that allows the art, the unconscious singing of the text, to illumine our lives). Burns does admit that there may be an objection to the italicizing of "coming." Critics may say that Brontë or her readers would not have known about our contemporary implication for this word. Burns answers: "I am quite willing to admit that all my italics and indentations would have mystified Charlotte Brontë and many, but not all, of her readers and critics, some of whom, if one may judge by the hysterically moralistic tone of their criticism, fully understood or sensed the veiled sexuality in the novel. But, given the aesthetic approach I have outlined, these are biographical or historical problems, and therefore critically peripheral. *Jane Eyre* cannot be reduced to the conscious intention of Charlotte Brontë, or the conscious reactions of her readers. As a work of art it includes all the meanings that its form suggests and defines within the limits of its artistic intention -- and those limits can only be determined by the most inclusive contextualist reading."[26] More aware of the demands of her own feelings than of her own "Victorian proprieties," Brontë "poured those feelings into her seemingly inadequate conceptual techniques," into her Gothic scenes and religious language. And she did with such "verbal force that she transformed her spiritual melodrama into a passionate quest for love and human fulfillment."[27] Brontë's own feelings of sexual desire acquired revolt, as it were, became the Panzaic element in her prose, and changed into Ortega's active power of aggression against the crystalline orb of Victorian ideals.

To extend Stephen Pepper's definition, then, the contextualist aesthetic field is the emotional education that arises from experiencing the *qualities* and *textures* in a scene that undermine ideals; and by ideals I mean all those intellectualized emotions men and women have about birth, sexuality, love and death -- those they have received from school, family life, religious training, and the State.

A particularly moving and significant passage in Céline's *Journey to the End of the Night* will give us one final look at how great novels can let the power of realism rumble underneath the idealism of our culture.

. . . the father, the fellow who it was supposed was the
father, that is, had gone away, disappeared for good and all.
He'd heard such a lot of talk about marriage, this young
man, that in the end he had got bored. He must have been
quite a way off by now, if he was still running. Nobody
had been able to make out why he had deserted her like that,
particularly not the girl herself. After all, he had always
seemed to get a great deal of fun out of sleeping with her.
   So now that the bird had flown, they all . . . stood round
and gazed at the infant and wept. And there you were. She
had given herself to this man, she said "body and soul." It
was bound to happen, and according to her, that explained
everything. The baby had been born from her body
suddenly, leaving it wrinkled and old. *The spirit will put up
with phrases, but the body is different; it's not so easy to
please, it must have muscle. A body is always something
that is true; that is why it's nearly always sad and repulsive
to look at.* It's true also that I have seldom seen any
maternity remove so much youth at one stroke . . . there was
only one consolation about life in Rancy -- but it was a very
great consolation: that of being able to talk freely now to all
and sundry about her "new responsibilities." Her lover's
desertion of her had awakened a certain longing in a breast
aching to be heroic and different . . . *with the romance of a
life devastated by a first love to fall back on, she accepted
with delight the great sorrow* which had been meted out to
her . . . *She squirmed with unmarried motherhood.*
(emphasis added)[28]

The capacity of this scene to do something to us emotionally, to make us "man alive again" as
D.H. Lawrence said, is the capacity of this scene to carry us headlong into those raw feelings that
will always challenge our ideal notions about birth and love.

   In the sections that follow, I offer tentative readings of novels, readings based more on my
contextualist and Panzaic awareness than on any dogmatic application of my critical perspective.
On occasion such "awareness-reading" has helped my students to make full and individual
connections to the life in a great book.

Notes

1   Hayden White argues that Pepper's contextualism represents "an ambiguous solution to the problem of constructing a narrative model of the *processes* discerned in the historical field" (*Metahistory: The Historical Imagination in Nineteenth-Century Europe* [Baltimore and London: The Johns Hopkins University Press, 1973], p. 19). And T.E. Lewis, in referring to this point in White's argument, argues in "Notes Toward a Theory of the Referent" that "contextualism refuses that gesture of conceptual abstraction without which no science can be constituted," and, "that by so delimiting the field of meaning, contextualism inhibits a larger integration of historical data into a coherent conceptualization of the historical process itself" (*PMLA*, 94, 3 [May 1979], 475). Both men forget that contextualism places no faith in a mode of analysis that claims an arrival at the *ultimate* nature of things because the present event is an "act in context."

2   John Dewey's article "Qualitative Thought" in *The Symposium*. I, (1930), pp. 5-32, contains first expressions of contextualism as a method of literary criticism: "The underlying quality that defines the work, that circumscribes it externally and integrates it internally, controls the thinking of the artist; his logic is the logic of what I have called qualitative thinking. Without an independent qualitative apprehension, the characteristics of a work of art can be translated into explicit harmonies, symmetries, etc., only in a way which substitutes mechanical formulae for esthetic quality. The value of any such translation in esthetic criticism is measured, moreover, *by the extent to which the propositional statements return to effect a heightening and deepening of a qualitative apprehension. Otherwise, aesthetic appreciation is replaced by judgment of isolated technique"* (John Dewey, *On Experience, Nature, and Freedom* [New York: Liberal Arts Press, 1960], p. 186). Emphasis added.

3   Mircea Eliade claims that today thinkers and literary artists are involved in "resistence to history, a revolt against historical *time*, an attempt to restore this historical time, freighted as it is with human experience, to a place in time that is cosmic, cyclical, and infinite . . . . The work of two of the most significant writers of our day -- T.S. Eliot and James Joyce -- is saturated with nostalgia for the myth of eternal repetition and, in the last analysis, for the abolition of time . . . . It is not inadmissable to think of an epoch . . . . when humanity . . . . will find itself reduced to desisting from any further 'making' of history in the sense in which it began to make it from the creation of the first empires, will confine itself to repeating prescribed archetypal gestures, and will strive to forget, as meaningless and dangerous, any spontaneous gesture which might entail 'historical' consequences" (*Cosmos And History: The Myth of the Eternal Return,* trans. W.R. Trask [New York: Harper and Row Torchbooks, 1959], pp. 153-154).

4   George H. Mead, *The Philosophy of the Present* (Chicago: Open Court Publishing Co., 1932), p. 18. Pepper defines these terms in the following way: "Spread -- The quality of a given event has a *spread,* or, as it is sometimes called, a *specious present.* As I am writing, *A period will be placed at the . . . .*, my act is rather thick in its duration and spreads, as we say, forward and back. I lift my pen at "the" and am just about to put down "end." The word "end" is not yet down, but it is being reached for and its meaning is already largely taken up in what has preceded. This forward reach in the quality of the event is the feeling of futurity. There is a corresponding feeling of pastness which draws into the quality all the preceding words of the sentence. "Change -- Absolute permanence or immutability in any sense is . . . . a fiction, and its appearance is interpreted in terms of historical continuities which are not changeless." "Fusion -- William James's lemonade has become famous in this regard. Lemon, sugar, and water are the ingredients or details of the taste, but the quality of lemonade is such a persistent fusion of these that it is very difficult to analyze out its components . . . .Whatever is simple and unified in experience, therefore, is the result of fusion. It is not a mere psychological affair. It reflects the active

38

structures of textures, and we may infer that qualities and fusions are as extensive as the events of our cosmic epoch" (*World Hypotheses*, pp. 239-245).

5   B. Gardner, ed. *Up The Line To Death: The War Poets* (1914-1918) (London: Methuen and Co., Lmtd., 1978), pp. 84-85.

6   Cleanth Brooks, *The Well Wrought Urn* (New York: Harcourt, Brace, and Co., 1947), p. 195.

7   J.B. McKee, *Literary Irony and the Literary Audience* (Amsterdam: Rodopi, N.V., 1974), p. 110.

8   *Ibid*

9   Paul Fussell, *The Great War and Modern Memory* (New York and London: Oxford University Press, 1975), p. 30.

10   *Ibid*, p. 31.

11   John Dewey, *Art as Experience* (New York: Capricorn Books, 1934), p. 108.

1 2   Louis-Ferdinand Céline, *Journey to the End of the Night* (New York: New Directions, 1932), pp. 501-502.

13   Céline knew well the results of his position: readers, he said, "can all get together when it is a question of loathing me. Anything is permitted expect *doubting man* -- then the laughing is over. I've tried it out ." ("Louis-Ferdinand Céline à Elie Faure," *Cahiers de L'Herne*, 5 (1965), p. 55.

14   "Much of what passes for 'new' criticism -- particularly as practiced by some of our newer Ph.D.s" Burns says, " . . . . might be called termitic criticism, since it buries itself (termite-like) so deeply in the technical interstices of a work that it cannot see the art for the technique, the forest for the trees. As a consequence it is really as far removed from art as ideological criticism; the main difference is that it reduces a work from the inside, ideological criticism from the outside" ("The Critical Relevance of Freudianism," *Western Review* 20 [Summer, 1956]; p.303). (Reprinted in *Towards a Contextualist Aesthetic of the Novel*, ed. by J. Flynn, G. Butler, and E. Butler [Seattle, Washington: Genitron Books, Inc., 1968], pp. 43-57).

1 5   "For if literary history proves anything," Burns says, "it proves that fiction cannot be written to any order without ceasing to be art; it cannot because art is creative, because, in the words of Andre Gide, 'the most beautiful things are those that madness prompts and reasons writes.' Which means, among other things, that the novelist must be free to follow his 'madness' (or as I prefer to designate it, his 'difference') wherever it leads . . . . This is not of course to suggest that the novelist can write in a vacuum . . . . he cannot avoid working from and through his beliefs in an attempt to give form and meaning to his 'difference' . . . . To be illuminative his oneness must be his own . . . . And to achieve this kind of oneness, he is obliged, like Forster,to move through and beyond the accepted and the archetypal to a point where he sees man as the measure of all things: not man as an abstraction, but the man (the 'darkness,' the 'difference') he feels inside himself. This is why the novelist . . . . must see all myths, beliefs, and systems of thought as either means or impediments, to be rejected or revolutionized or somehow made to serve his own artistic ends." ("The Genuine and Counterfeit: A Study in Victorian and Modern Fiction," *College English* 18, 3 [December, 1956], pp. 146-47). (Reprinted in *Towards,* pp. 31-41).

16   Wayne Burns, "On Wuthering Heights," *Recovering Literature*, 1, 2 (Fall, 1972), pp. 5-25. See also: Wayne Burns, *Enfin Céline Vint* (New York: Peter Lang, 1988).

17   Appendix, p. 108.

18   Appendix, p. 108.

19   In his book *What Happens in Art* (New York: Appelton-Century Crofts, 1967), Matthew Lipman devotes a chapter to what he calls the body as a qualitative prescence in art. "Whether we consider," he says, "the immense sensory appeal of the living body, the equally powerful ascetic

revulsion from it, or any of the host of intermediate expressions we are compelled to reckon with, the response to the body is an integral and inescapble component of artistic and aesthetic experience" (p. 80). See also the journal *Paunch*, which devotes its perspective to this point of view, especially issues 46-47 (1977) and 53-54 (1980).

20 Henry Fielding, *Tom Jones*, ed. S. Baker (New York: W.W. Norton and Co., Inc., 1973), pp. 195-96. Hereafter page numbers in text.

21 Henri Bergson, *Laughter: An Essay on the Meaning of the Comic* (New York: The MacMillan Company, 1911), pp. 50-51. As A.E. Pilington states it, for Bergson art is "essentially revelation; it consists in the displacement of the practical categories, the useful symbolic representations that come between the mind and reality" *Bergson and His Influence*, (Cambridge: Cambridge University Press, 1976), p. 13.

22 José Ortega Y Gasset, *Meditations on Quixote*, trans. E. Rugg and D. Marín (New York: W.W. Norton and Co., 1961). (Hereafter abbreviated as *MQ* in text).

23 José Ortega Y Gasset, *Meditaciones Del Quijote*, 2nd ed., (Madrid: Revista de Occidente, 1966), p. 155. (My trans.). (Hereafter abbreviated as *Quijote*).

24 José Ortega Y Gasset, "The Nature of the Novel," *Hudson Review*, 10 (1957), p. 40.

25 Wayne Burns, "The Critical Relevance of Freudianism," *Western Review*, 20 (Summer, 1956), pp. 308-309.

26 Ibid., p. 310.

27 Ibid., p. 311.

28 Céline, *Journey to the End of the Night*, pp. 269-71.

# PART II

# TENTATIVE APPLICATIONS

# CHAPTER 3

Lady Chatterley's Lover : D.H. Lawrence's Answer to
the "Nightmare of History"
in James Joyce and Virginia Woolf

> I hear the ruin of all space, shattered glass and
> toppling masonry, and time one livid final flame.
> What's left us then?
>
> *Ulysses* [1]

> [Giles] said (without words), "I'm damnably
> unhappy."
> "So am I," Dodge echoed.
> "And I too," Isa thought.
> They were all caught and caged: prisoners;
> watching a spectacle.
>
> *Between the Acts* [2]

> Break the cage then, start in and try.
>
> *Pansies* [3]

James Joyce and Virginia Woolf sought solutions to what was generally regarded as the failed ideal of historical progress, and to what they saw as the failure of modern love between the sexes. To relieve the tension of living under the yoke of historical consciousness, Joyce fashioned *Ulysses* (1922) to illustrate how life could be fused into art, according to his own theory of aesthetic perception, while Woolf intended *Between the Acts* (1941) to be her final statement on how present experience could be fused to literary analogues. Both authors sought refuge from sexual turmoil, too, and their fictional technique of *monologue intérieur* explained and relieved their alienation, their nightmares about history and sex. Both wanted to portray the tragedy of modern life, and they do, superbly, by giving us the clash between their ideals and twentieth-century reality. And they tell us that life is tragic -- indeed, it can be and certainly remains so in their fiction. They wanted to portray the sterility of sexual relationships between modern men and women, and they do this superbly too, as does D.H. Lawrence in the last sections of *The Rainbow* (1915) and in *Women in Love* (1920). But my purpose in this chapter is to show how Lawrence does not abstract the nightmare of history, or sex, but instead exposes and then confronts our ideas about history and sex and, in the process, and despite his own ideals, suggests possible answers to the nightmare.

D.H. Lawrence does not see, as does Joyce, that men are condemned to be at the mercy of the willful woman; nor does he see, as does Woolf, that men and women are trapped and caged forever in some primordial, cycle of sex-hate. [4] He differs from both authors because for him the relationship between men and women is the only "great relationship," the "quick and the central clue to life, not the man, nor the woman, nor the children that result from the relationship." [5] Joyce sees modern man and woman flattened to such an extent by mass conformity that the man, exhausted, assumes the terrible and automatic role of the humorous cuckold who sleeps upside down with his female archetype -- the wilful woman -- as does Bloom with Molly. The final chapter of *Ulysses*, "Penelope," seen so frequently as affirming "Life," is actually the best illustration of Molly as Joyce's personal archetype of the Irish Woman of Will. Woolf's final version of the relationship between men and women in *Between the Acts* is no less pessimistic. It concentrates on the inflexible biological role of the male who must inevitably, according to oblivious Natural Law, fight and embrace with the female. At the end of *Between the Acts*, after Lucy puts down her book, *Outline of History*, where she had been looking at pictures of prehistoric birds, and after Giles crumples up the newspaper and turns out the light, we read:

> Alone, enmity was bared; also love. Before they slept, they must fight; after they had fought, they would embrace. From that embrace another life might be born. But first they must fight, as the dog fox fights with the vixen, in the heart of darkness, in the fields of night.
> . . . It was night before roads were made, or houses. It was the night that dwellers in caves had watched from some high place among the rocks. (*BTA*, p. 219)

True enough we might say, but the whole of Woolf's last novel tells us that love is dead, and that the characters in such a dead world -- the world of 1939 -- cannot regain their feelings for life.

Lawrence had said all along, however, that historical progress, in that flabby sense of spiritual advancement, had never been real;[6] and love, he said, conscious, Western, romantic love, is just as dead because both ideas breed a compulsory disappointment in seeing their ideals collapse at the hands of physical passion. Lawrence's most successful way of breaking new ground for the novel, of breaking away from Joyce and Woolf, was to give to the relationships between men and women feelings that were different from those found in Joyce and Woolf. For example, Wayne Burns has noted that scenes like the following, where Connie sees Mellors as he is washing behind his cabin, are not "'set pieces,'" *epiphanies*, as "they are in Joyce" (like Stephen's epiphany of the bathing girl in chapter four of *Portrait*, or like Woolf's "tableaux" in *Between the Acts*). "They are not the final *Word*, . . . they are but feelings in the developing relationship between the man and the woman."[7]

> He was naked to the hips, his velveteen breeches slipping down over his slender loins . . . In spite of herself, she had had a shock. After all, merely a man washing himself; common-place enough, Heaven knows!
>
> Yet in some curious way it was a visionary experience: it had hit her in the middle of the body . . . the sense of aloneness, of a creature purely alone, overwhelmed her . . . [It was] not the stuff of beauty, not even the body of beauty, but a lambency, the warm, white flame of a single life . . . [which] with her mind she was inclined to ridicule.[8]

Lawrence is not talking about romantic love here. And he had no interest in giving us the *archetype* of the male or female. Nor is he interested in giving us the "disembodied female principle."[9] What he wanted to express in fiction by "getting beneath personality and ego" and "going behind or through our idealized self-images" was not an abstract symbol or cosmic force, but the "essential man and the essential woman, i.e., what the man feels for the woman and woman for the man -- apart from or in spite of their mental ideas and ideals and self-images."[10] This is what makes Lawrence's novels so different from Joyce's or Woolf's.

In his essay "The Novel and the Feelings," Lawrence said that if *we* can't step out into the grisly dark of unknown feelings, then we should listen to the "low, calling cries of the characters, as they wander in the dark woods of their destiny" and not to the "didactic statements of the author."[11] By having us listen to these cries, Lawrence helps us to walk through the rent he makes in the veil of aesthetic distance. As a novelist he believed that he had to "rip the old veil of a vision across, and find what the heart really believes in, after all: and what the heart really wants, for the next future."[12] Our "old veil" of vision is the worn out pose of aesthetic distance we take to really new works of art. The wall of objectivity we need to read a work like *Ulysses* crumbles when we read a Lawrence novel, because Lawrence could not make a work of art something we should "walk round and admire." By stating that a book should be either a "bandit or a rebel or a man in a crowd,"[13] Lawrence takes the novel far beyond the aesthetics of Joyce and Woolf. "Novels," he said, "are not little theatres where the reader sits aloft and watches . . . That's what you want a book to be: because it leaves you so safe and so superior."[14] This is not to say that Lawrence was not moved to despair over war and modern sex, or that he remained aloof from theories of history. He was greatly disturbed by the course of all. Indeed, his early story "England My England" (1915), often called Lawrence's "English Elegy,"[15] and his chapter "The Nightmare," from his novel *Kangaroo* (1923), beautifully testify to his struggles with the reality of war. And as far as Lawrence's struggle with the death of rural England is concerned, *The Rainbow* (1915) deals with that by exploring the historical effects that industrialization brings to our emotional and sexual lives. What remains important for Lawrence, however, and what finally distinguishes his view of conflict from Joyce's treatment of the war in *Ulysses* as well as from Woolf's image of the war in *Between the Acts,* is this: there is a brutal price men have to pay when they find themselves dragged off to a world disaster out of their own mass-minded hysteria. Joyce universalizes war with references to myth and ancient history: "Jousts. Time shocked rebounds, shock by shock. Jousts, slush and uproar of battles, the frozen deathspew of the slain, a shout of spear spikes baited with men's bloodied guts" ( *U,* p. 32). Woolf saw it as some awful cycle -- inherent in Nature: "Lucy turned the page . . . 'Prehistoric man,' she read, 'half-human, half-ape, roused himself from his semi-crouching position and raised great stones'" (*BTA,* p. 218). Lawrence, however, individualizes it:

> The torture was steadily applied, during those years after
> Asquith fell, to break the independent soul in any man who
> would not hunt with the criminal mob.

> . . . Somers tiresomely belonged to no group . . . he had
> no conscientious objection to war. It was . . . the vast mob-
> spirit, which he could never acquiesce in. The terrible,
> terrible war, made so fearful because in every country
> practically every man lost his head, and lost his own
> centrality, his own manly isolation in his own integrity,
> which along keeps life real.[16]

These passages clearly illustrate Lawrence's concern over the effects of war on the individuality of man, which helps us to understand the reality of a world that surrounds us now. The artist, Lawrence said, should follow the war "home to the heart of the individual fighters -- not to talk in armies and nations and numbers."[17] Furthermore, as Lawrence's short study *Movements in European History* (1918) suggests, man and historical events are not "caught and caged" in time, place, or predestined causes, as they are in Joyce and Woolf, but rather are organically interrelated with each other -- they are the shape of life.[18]

Clearly, what distinguishes Lawrence's difference from Joyce and Woolf is his emerging view of tragedy. As he begins to write his masterpiece, *The Rainbow,* Lawrence changes his view of classical tragedy. No longer interested --like Stephen in Joyce's *Portrait* or La Trobe in *Between the Acts* -- in glorifying through art the struggle an intellectual must have with the "shattered glass and toppling masonry" of civilization, and no longer interested in glamorizing the tragedy of middle-class ennui and sexual frustration, Lawrence envisions a new course for both history and sex. In his poem "Tragedy," he says:

> And when I think of the great tragedy of our material-
> mechanical civilization
> crushing out the natural human life
> then sometimes I feel defeated; and then again I know
> my shabby little defeat would do neither me any good
> nor anybody else.[19]

Gerald J. Butler notes that after *Sons and Lovers* (1913), Lawrence began to show characters who lived outside convention and were fulfilled. As Lawrence's art "grew there came to be nothing metaphysical about tragedy in it; tragedy was only social -- only sociology. It was something simply to avoid, as Connie and Mellors want to avoid the 'insentient iron world' -- if they can get away with it."[20] By taking us beyond Aristotelean tragedy and by refusing to give us the traditional tragic story with its cathartic delight and release in suffering, Lawrence "no longer cares to move the collective heart of mankind."[21] Instead, he presents us with a single relationship between a man and a woman in *Lady Chatterley's Lover,* and in their struggle to find fulfillment he gives us not tragedy but possibility -- even as he attacks romantic love and the marriage of compatibility. Connie and Mellors are characters who have stopped "looking for loopholes. They acknowledge that life is a struggle and they 'move along.'"[22] With *The Man Who Died* (1927) and *Lady Chatterley's Lover* (1928) Lawrence simply knocks the wind out of tragedy as high art. The very first lines of *John Thomas and Lady Jane,* for example, announce the blow: "Ours is essentially a tragic age, so we refuse to take it tragically. The cataclysm has fallen, we've got used to the ruins, and we start to build up new little habitats, new little hopes . . . Having tragically wrung our hands, we now proceed to peel the potatoes . . ."[23] Nowhere in Joyce or Woolf do we hear such pronouncements. Connie and Mellors try to build a little shelter, despite the ruins. No longer does Lawrence dramatize the tragedy of sadism in history[24] or the drama of men and women who rebel against custom and die in the end. He has simply looked long enough at tragedy, has understood it and has tired of it, has had enough of it. Tragedy begins to look to him like a man "in love with his own defeat / Which is only a sloppy way of being in love with yourself."[25] And so, with *Lady Chatterley's Lover,* Lawrence presents to the reader a new relationship between a man and a woman after the apocalypse of war and exploitive industrialization. It is new because it provides a solution to what Woolf in *To the Lighthouse* (1927) said she saw as the main problem between men and women. She said there was this "fatal sterility of the male" which consisted of his plea for sympathy as a failure to live "in the heart of life" and which would often, if not always, kill life in a woman too.[26] Bloom makes this kind of a plea all throughout *Ulysses,* until he finally submits to the reaction Molly has to such a plea: domination.

At the end of *John Thomas and Lady Jane,* sexual experience is still found in the midst of forces that try to prevent it. Woolf, at the end of *Between the Acts,* announces with great sighs of tragedy and spite that we all must be John Thomases and Lady Janes, full of despair in a brutal world (*BTA,* pp. 190, 199-200). Joyce, at the end of *Ulysses,* turns his back on fulfilling sex between men and women, and gives the last chapter over to tragic comedy and the Sheela-na-gig, that mythical and emasculating figure in Irish folklore. But by the end of Lawrence's *John Thomas and Lady Jane,* even though Connie and Parkin have lost touch with what they had gained earlier in the novel -- that tender awareness of life, free from what Lawrence called the "frictional, seething, resistant, explosive, blind sort" of modern energy in themselves -- they have learned, still, that their awareness can, at times, carry them through their days in an "iron world." Connie and Parkin take a footpath down into the little hollow of a wood. It is Sunday, and they are surrounded by churchgoers, miners and their families, and lords and ladies.

He looked up, and saw a keeper, a big-faced, middle-aged man, striding round the brambles and dog-rose thickets. Quickly he put down her dress, and as she began to lift her face he murmured:

"Keep still! There's keeper! Dunna move!" And he held her closer.

"Now then!" said the burly keeper, in ugly challenge, and Parkin felt all her body jolt in his arms. He pressed her closer. The keeper was smiling an ugly smile.

"Let us be, man, can't you!" said Parkin, in a soft, quiet voice, looking into the light-blue, half-triumphant eyes of the other fellow. "We're harmin' nothing. Have yer niver 'ad a woman in your arms yourself!" The perfect quiet rebuke of his voice was in key with the steady, unabashed rebuke in his eyes . . .

The keeper looked at the clinging woman hiding her face, and at her legs in their silk stockings. Parkin had pulled her dress tidily down. Only himself was all undone. The fat keeper slowly looked away, and the nasty smile went off his face . . . Then he looked again, fascinated, at the woman clinging motionless to the other man.

"Ay!" he said, in a changed voice. (*JTLJ*, p. 374)

Connie does not jump up and run off, nor does Parkin feel embarrassed. And that *unabashed rebuke* in Parkin's voice and eyes changes the disciplinary attitude of the gamekeeper to such a great extent that the fat keeper leaves them alone. Parkin's rebuke defeats our attempts to see this scene as tragic because his rebuke carries no plea for sympathy as a failure to live "in the heart of life." It is the strong, powerful rebuke of life, and Connie's reaction in the presence of such life is to be suddenly and involuntarily encouraged:

"Kiss me!" she whispered. "Kiss me, -- I know the old squire here --"

He kissed her many times, she was so queer and sightless . . . Then she softly rearranged his clothing, kissing the last glimpse of white flesh below his breast, and pushing down the cotton shirt . . . And she rose, and they went slowly back to the path where long ago Bryon must have limped in his unhappy inability to feel sure in his love. (*JTLJ*, p. 375)

*Queer and sightless* behavior is what Lawrence calls sexuality. And when it takes place between a man and a woman, they feel confident in their whole desires for one another, unlike the unhappy Byron or Bloom. This is what Connie and Mellors know at the end of *Lady Chatterley's Lover*, and they have discussed what "liars poets and everybody were! They made one think one wanted sentiment. When what one supremely wanted was this piercing, consuming, rather awful sensuality. To find a man who dared do it, without shame or sin or final misgiving!" (*LCL*, p. 232). Mellors learned that his feeling "all mixed up with a lot of rage" is a certain courage of his own tenderness for a woman. He learned that as he went into Connie, the "thing he had to do" was "to come into tender touch without losing his pride or his dignity or his integrity as a man" (*LCL*, p. 261). How different this all is from Woolf's conclusion about sex in her last novel, or from Joyce's ideas on sex in *Ulysses*. In all three versions of *Lady Chatterley's Lover*, "Mellors" is never presented as tragically heroic in his attempts to get what he wants out of life. In the third version, when, at the end of the novel, he describes his liking for farming, we find out that until he can purchase one of his own he will work on the Butler and Smitham Colliery

Company farm, which provides hay and oats for pit-ponies. "I like farming all right," he says. "It's not inspiring, but then I don't ask to be inspired. I'm used to horses, and cows, though they are very female, have a soothing effect on me. When I sit with my head in her side, milking, I feel very solaced" (*LCL*, p. 280). This is hardly the conventional position of the Western Hero, and hardly the popular notion of the Tragic Hero -- with head pressed against the side of a cow. Lawrence was not interested in giving us old roles of tragic melodrama, or the old roles of romance, or in giving to his characters roles which would allow them to be universalized by the reader or critic. His point was to show that if we want to see beyond our conventional beliefs, we must have the courage to drop them.

The difference, then, between Lawrence and Joyce and Woolf is provocative. Modern love is defined by Lawrence as the man getting the "better of a woman, in the sexual intercourse; the self-seeking, automatic civilized man trying to extend his ego over a woman," and the woman "putting her will over him, and thereby getting a sense of power and enlargement in herself" (*JTLJ*, p. 105). As a result, the "strange, tender flow of sex" shuts off. And so the women, eventually tired and fed up with the struggle to dominate, leave the men to "fight for the money" while they fight for the men. "This is called love. 'She is terribly in love with him,' that cant phrase means really: 'she is mad to get him under her will'" (*JTLJ*, p. 106). Virginia Woolf describes this behavior in the relationship between Giles the stockbroker, who tried the search for money and status and got tired of it, and his wife Isa:

> Inside the glass, in her eyes, she saw what she had felt overnight for the ravaged, the silent, the romantic gentleman farmer. "In love," was in her eyes. But outside, on the washstand, on the dressing-table, among the silver boxes and tooth-brushes, was the other love; love for her husband, the stockbroker -- "The father of my children," she added, slipping into the cliché conveniently provided by fiction. (*BTA*, p. 14)

Lawrence shows us Connie, too, tiring of money, status, marital domination, and sexual acquisition, yet her rebellious actions are not the solution to our modern ennui about sex and history, nor are the words of Mellors, the mouthpiece for Lawrence's own idealism; it is, instead, the relationship between them. Over the years critics have made the mistake of seeing Lawrence's solutions to our troubles in the behavior of either Connie or Mellors. Overlooking what Lawrence calls the "tremble of life" that exists apart from the egos of his characters, these critics need to read, again, Lawrence's letter to Edward Garnett, dated June 5, 1914: What is "interesting in the laugh of the woman is the same as the binding of the molecules of steel or their action in heat; it is the inhuman will, call it . . . physiology of matter, that fascinates me . . . You mustn't look in my novel for the old stable *ego* of the character. There is another *ego* , according to whose action the individual is unrecognisable" (*Collected Letters*, vol. 2, p. 282).[27] What makes up the trembling, the *senses' tender* , are the bodies of the characters, in sexual union, appearing to us as what we often know them to be in real life: strangers to our cerebral selves. Instead of contriving symbol or myth to remind us of our sexual passions,[28] as does Woolf with cows in *Between the Acts* and Joyce with Molly as "Earth-Goddess" in *Ulysses*, Lawrence shows us our sexual organs. In *The First Lady Chatterley,* we get more of Lawrence's genius at portraying human beings as "creatures" instead of egos. Parkin [Mellors] is not quite so much the preacher in this version of the novel as he is in the final version.

Drawn down into the woods to get away from Clifford's theories on the thrill of thought and the "conquest" of touch, Connie makes her way near the gamekeeper's hut and crouches in front of Parkin's chicken coop. She begins to feed the pheasant chicks, looking at their "tiny *tremble of life.*" And as she crouched among the little birds, crying, she

felt a great abandon upon her. And he, *trying to go away
from her,* was spellbound. He could not go away from that
soft, crouching female figure. In spite of himself, he went
and stood by her looking down at her.
"Y'aren't cryin' are yer!" he asked in a bewildered voice.
*She nodded blindly,* still crouched down upon herself,
her hair falling. He looked down upon her folded figure,
and almost without knowing what he did, crouched down
beside her, knees wide apart, and laid his hand softly on her
back. She continued to cry, breathing heavily. And the
touch of her soft, bowed back, breathing heavily with
abandoned weeping, filled him with such boundless desire
for her that he rose and bent over her, lifting her in his arms.
All that could ever be that was desirable, she was to him
then. And she, lifted up, for one moment saw the brilliant,
*unseeing dilation of his eyes.*[29]

There is such a glowing lambency in this scene, a delicate, unconscious, and powerful sense of desire, so different from the spite about love in *Between the Acts,* from the sadism of love in *Ulysses.* The scene is a rebuttal to our popular ideas about the ennui of modern love, with its talkiness and suffering. The yielding of these two characters to one another is not expected by them, not courted by them, and the unconscious nature of it is made all the more curiously necessary in our eyes because Lawrence does not spell out its meaning.[30] He allows the material details to speak for themselves, thus removing, I believe, about as far as they can be, our barriers of aesthetic distance. For it is here, in scenes like these, that aesthetic experience becomes human experience. The words I have italicized above communicate the tension between the impersonal and submerged material nature of our sexual desire, our "low cries," and our need to be alone. These words are missing from the final version of *Lady Chatterley's Lover,* although in that draft of the novel Mellors strokes Connie "in the blind instinctive caress" (*LCL,* p. 108). The final version of *Lady Chatterley's Lover* will go on to achieve its own famous destiny of giving us, for the first time in English literature, sexual details that speak for themselves -- although through the editorial voice of Mellors. Yet since our belief about the ennui of modern love is challenged by all three versions of this novel, our aesthetic distance is difficult to maintain. We resist what we read or call it unreal, ridiculous, not possible at all in our iron world. These kinds of reader-reactions do not happen with Woolf or Joyce. Our traditional views about unfulfilled love are upheld by their conventional novels; their traditional despair over the conventional tragedy of a loveless world is applauded. And so we declare their novels "greater," that is, easier to swallow. When we experience the scenes between Connie and Parkin or between Connie and Mellors, with their detailed sexual unions, we witness sexual feelings we either do not have and want, have had and lost, or are getting. It is the getting of them that is frightening, more frightening than the losing of them, through which we can take refuge in our conventional sadness, our popular notion of tragedy. That is why the current trend in literary criticism is to "go beyond" Lawrence, for his books, unlike most of our contemporary fiction, hold out a dangerous possibility: that sexual fulfillment can be found in a world gone mad with guilt.

After describing every neurosis Lawrence might have suffered from, critics have tried to press them into his novels in such a way as to undermine this real danger. This kind of criticism ignores the well known Lawrence warning: don't put too much emphasis on the teller at the expense of the tale.[31] Paul Eggert defines this trend in Lawrence studies this way: "We most of us live at a duller level of responsiveness, a slower intellectual pace than he -- which is no crime; the crime is in portraying Lawrence as having done so as well, portraying him as a toned-down Lawrence who is seen as extending but essentially reinforcing our own pieties about normality and society."[32] Of course there are notable exceptions to this trend. Henry Miller, in his *The World of Lawrence: A Passionate Appreciation* (Capra Press, 1980), can still say:

50

> [A] phrase which I seem to have encountered repeatedly in Lawrence's writings -- "what I am *trying* to do." It is very reminiscent of Cézanne who was always trying to *realize* something. It is a phrase which touches me deeply . . . This *trying* seems to be the creation itself. And it is this effort to go beyond oneself, to surpass, to say, and do the impossible, which makes certain men a subject of eternal debate. It mars everything they do, makes them 'failures,' as the smooth-tongued critics would say. And yet it seems to me that it is only these men who count, who really affect us and influence us. They strive to go beyond 'art' into life again.
>
> Why not let him [Lawrence] be, let him be there in the midst of his creation . . .? He whined and complained, like Job. But all the time he was *trying,* trying harder almost than any man you can think of, and if he failed to *realize* all that he was attempting, he nevertheless succeeded in trying, and that seems to me to be the most important thing about him (pp. 262-63).

And Anthony Burgess, in his homage to Lawrence, *Flame Into Being* (Arbor House, 1985), can still declare that "literature is essentially subversive, and that Lawrence is a witness . . . for that truth" (xi).

In the intense moments when human beings become creatures, *Lady Chatterley's Lover* finds its greatest importance. And even if Mellors is too preachy about sexual behavior or politics, the book still shows us the relationship wrestling to get free from his mental conceptions of it, and from our reader-response frameworks of "myth," "archetype," or "historical progress." (In one frequently overlooked scene from chapter fifteen of *Lady Chatterley's Lover,* Connie gathers up Mellors' testicles into her hands as he puffs away on some half-baked scheme to save the masses. My students laugh at this gentle satire, but cocktail-party Marxism in academia is not amused.)

Characters in Joyce and Woolf do live and battle with their old ideas on sex and history, but they stay caged in their Aristotelean concepts about such a fight. Lawrence, like Cézanne, tried to break that cage, to let out the senses' tender, the "tremble of life" in himself, and in us.[33]

Notes

[1]   James Joyce, *Ulysses* (New York: Random House, 1961), p. 24. Hereafter abbreviated in text as *U*.

[2]   Virginia Woolf, *Between the Acts* (New York: Harcourt Brace Jovanovich, 1969), p. 176. Hereafter abbreviated in text as *BTA*.

[3]   D.H. Lawrence, *The Complete Poems of D. H. Lawrence*, ed. Pinto and Roberts (New York: Viking Press, 1971), p. 485.

[4]   Bertrand Russell saw Lawrence's portrayal of sex as "a perpetual fight in which each is attempting to destroy the other" (*Portraits from Memory and Other Essays* [New York: Simon and Schuster, 1956], p. 116).

[5]   D.H. Lawrence, "Morality and the Novel," *Selected Literary Criticism*, ed. A. Beal (New York: Viking Press, 1966), p. 113.

[6]   See B. Hochman, *Another Ego: The Changing View of Self and Society in the Work of D.H. Lawrence* (Columbia: University of South Carolina Press, 1970), pp. 76-82.

[7]   Wayne Burns, "The Beginnings of a Primer to the Novels," *Towards a Contextualist Theory of the Novel* (Seattle, Washington: Genitron Books, Inc., 1968), p. 204.

[8]   D.H. Lawerence, *Lady Chatterley's Lover* (New York: New American Library, Signet Modern Classics, 1959), p. 62. Hereafter abbreviated in text as *LCL*.

[9]   W. Mitgutsch, "The Image of the Female in D.H. Lawrence's Poetry," *Salzburg Studies in English Literature*, 27 (3rd Series), 1981, p. 25.

[10]   Burns, "The Beginnings of a Primer to the Novels," p. 206.

[11]   D.H. Lawrence, *Phoenix: The Posthumous Papers of D.H. Lawrence*, ed. E.D. McDonald (New York: Viking Press, 1936), p. 760.

[12]   D.H. Lawrence, *Psychoanalysis and the Unconscious and Fantasia of the Unconscious* (New York: Viking Press, 1960), p. 57.

[13]   "To Carlo Linati" (22 January 1925), *The Collected Letters of D.H. Lawrence*, ed. H.T. Moore, vol. 2 (London: Heinemann, 1962), p. 827. Hereafter abbreviated in text as *Collected Letters*.

[14]   Ibid., p. 827.

[15]   Stephen Spender, "D.H. Lawrence, England and the War," *D.H. Lawrence: Novelist, Poet, Prophet*, ed. Stephen Spender (London: Weidenfeld and Nicolson, 1973), p. 76. See also: Paul Delany, *D.H. Lawrence's Nightmare* (New York: Basic Books, Inc., 1978).

[16]   D.H. Lawrence, *Kangaroo* (New York: Viking Press, 1960), p. 216.

[17]   "To Harriet Monroe," 17 November, 1914, *Collected Letters*, p. 295.

[18]   See James T. Boulton, "Introduction," in *Movements in European History* (London: Oxford University Press, 1971), and E.J. Hinz, "History as Education and Art: D.H. Lawrence's *Movements in European History*," *Modern British Literature*, 2 (1977), 139-52.

[19]   *The Complete Poems of D.H. Lawrence*, p. 508.

[20]   Gerald J. Butler, *"The Man Who Died* and Lawrence's Final Attitude Towards Tragedy," *Recovering Literature*, 6, 3 (Winter, 1977), p. 3.

52

Ibid., p. 7.

22 Duane Edwards, "D.H. Lawrence: Tragedy in the Modern Age," *Literary Review*, 24 (1979), p. 82.

23 D.H. Lawrence, *John Thomas and Lady Jane* (New York: Penguin Books, 1972), p· 9. Hereafter abbreviated in text as *JTLJ.*

24 See F.L. Radford, "King, Pope, Hero-Martyr: *Ulysses* and the Nightmare of Irish History," *James Joyce Quarterly* 15 (Summer, 1978), pp. 275-323.

25 Lawrence, "Tragedy," *The Complete Poems*, p. 508.

26 Virginia Woolf, *To the Lighthouse* (New York: Harcourt Brace & World, Inc., 1927), pp. 58-9.

27 Carol Dix makes the mistake with Connie in *D.H. Lawrence and Women* (Totowa, New Jersey: Rowman and Littlefield, 1980), pp. 88-92. M. Spilka makes the same mistake in "On Lawrence's Hostility to Wilful Women: The Chatterley Solution," *Lawrence and Women*, ed. Ann Smith (New York: Barnes and Noble, 1978), pp. 205-206. For my perspective, see: Wayne Burns, "D.H. Lawrence: The Beginnings of a Primer to the Novels," *Towards a Contextualist Aesthetic of the Novel* (Seattle: Genitron Books, Inc., 1968), pp. 197-215.

28 This is a "pop" view of Lawrence's technique today. See John B. Humma, "The Interpenetrating Metaphor: Nature and Myth in *Lady Chatterley's Lover*," *PMLA*, 98, 1 (January, 1983), pp. 77-86. See also Dennis Jackson, "'The Old Pagan Vision': Myth and Ritual in *Lady Chatterley's Lover*," *The D.H. Lawrence Review*, 11 (1978), pp. 260-71.

29 D.H. Lawrence, *The First Lady Chatterley* (New York: Dial Press, 1944), p. 48. Italics mine.

30 David Parker, "Lawrence and Lady Chatterley: The Teller and the Tale," *The Critical Review*, 20 (1978), pp. 31-41. Mr. Parker has explored the third and first drafts of the novel and labels the difference as one of "unconscious delicacy" and "writing unidealized" (pp. 34, 38).

31 See Keith Sagar, "Beyond D.H. Lawrence," in *D.H. Lawrence: The Man Who Lived,* ed. R.B. Partlow and H.T. Moore (Carbondale: Southern Illinois Univeristy Press, 1980), pp. 258-66. Sagar sees Ted Hughes as Lawrence's replacement. See also: Cornelia Nixon's *Lawrence's Leadership Politics and the Turn Against Women* (Berkeley: University of California Press, 1986).

32 Paul Eggert, "Lawrence Criticism: Where Next?" *The Critical Review*, 21 (1979), p. 81.

33 Eileen Barrett suggests that La Trobe's characters "are the primitive celebrants who wait for Isa's release from the 'heart of darkness,' 'the fields of night,' to celebrate her springtime reunion with her Mother/Goddess, her mythic origins, and to rewrite the plot --. 'She had screamed. She had hit him . . . . What then?' -- to prevent the rape" ("Matriarchal Myth on a Patriarchal Stage: Virginia Woolf's *Between the Acts*," *Twentieth Century Literature*, 33, 1 (Spring, 1987), p. 35. Woolf's last novel cannot, however, support this kind of idealism. Zack Bowen argues that the ending of *Ulysses* is a "comic vision of life which plays a Sancho Panza to Lawrence's Quixote," ("*Lady Chatterley's Lover* and *Ulysses*," in *D.H. Lawrence's "Lady"* eds. M. Squires and D. Jackson (Athens: University of Georgia Press, 1985), p. 134. He sees Joyce's view of sex undermining Lawrence's view of it. But how? So much of Molly's sex is in her head. Besides, Molly doesn't sleep with Mellors, Connie does.

# CHAPTER 4

## Dissident Notes on *Ulysses*

### I

Moving from Zurich with his family on October 12, 1917 to Locarno for the winter, and having undergone an iridectomy from an attack of glaucoma, James Joyce was to settle in that city to finish the first three episodes of *Ulysses*, the *Telemachiad*. He stayed in Locarno only three months, returning to Zurich early in January, 1918 -- returning closer to the European theatre of war. As World War I lurched to its conclusion, Joyce would voice a disinterest in the conflict to his friends. To the British consular authorities in Switzerland his opinions on the Great War were "offensively neutral."[1] Yet for a man who saw himself as the "tranquil gentleman who won't salute the State/or serve Nabuchodonesor or proletariat," the "meek philosopher who doesn't care a damn"[2] Joyce did care about history. He cared about it, however, in a special way: he contemplated the *concept* of it. He was cool to the realities of the front because for the first time in history, warfare, having changed itself to a war of man against matériel, removed itself in Joyce's imagination from that ancient action of man against man. It was a war unlike the literary world of the *Iliad* and the *Odyssey*, and unlike man's sentimental illusion about heroic behavior in our epic romances. It went far beyond the absurdity and chaos of men fighting as individuals (what Tolstoy gives us in *War and Peace* with his descriptions of Austerlitz and Borodino). The Great War, which initiated Joyce to the complete depersonalization of modern warfare by becoming for him one of the major symbols of the depersonalization of our age, cut deep into his Aristotelean consciousness. For just as he saw how the sudden development of new weaponry, communications, and deployments of conscripted armies to designated areas put such a final stop to the old war of long movements across open spaces, substituting for movement the stasis of trench warfare, so too did he see a similar stasis on the home front in Dublin.[3] The stalemate between desire and satisfaction in modern life, described in *Dubliners* (1916) and *Ulysses* (1922), and the stalemate of trench warfare, were equally hard to stomach. Joyce does give us, briefly, empirical details of such warfare, but they are strangely abstracted, hidden underneath rare vocabulary: "Casqued halberdiers in armour thrust forward a pentice of gutted spear points."[4] A description of fifteenth-century obsolete spears could, perhaps, be an allusion to the absurd incompetence of some of the clashes in World War I between man and machinery; however, such details are used to show us a complex theory of history.

Paradoxically, then, Joyce is concerned not with the empirical details of events (even though he lists astonishing quantities of allusions to historical names and places), but with an abstract concept of history. In "Nestor," as Stephen comes to one of his conclusions about the goals of history, we hear one of the few allusions to the details of World War I in *Ulysses*: "Jousts. Time shocked rebounds, shock by shock. Jousts, slush and uproar of battles, the frozen deathspew of the slain, a shout of spear spikes baited with men's bloodied guts" ( *U*, p. 32). The language, attempting to bridge gaps between time and history, is still oddly abstract. Presumably readers will reach an understanding about war in the author's *epiphany*: Joyce's frozen moment of action, his stasis, his "contemplative poise of the mind, whether in sorrow or in joy."[5] From that image of "shout of spear spikes" we do get fused sounds and movements of present, past, and future wars; however, fictional techniques that use materiality in this way deny reality for that larger purpose of manufacturing "epics," "myths," and "archetypes." Stephen does not, like Gabriel in "The Dead," experience an enchantment of the *heart* as he stands before empirical events. Gabriel discovers his wife's lingering desires for a dead man, feels humiliated by the "failure of his irony," and begins to see himself as a "well-meaning sentimentalist . . . idealizing

54

his own clownish lusts."[6] Stephen experiences enchantments of the *mind*, and he believes, as he says in *Portrait of the Artist as a Young Man* (1916), that in order to get a "stasis" of feeling, one must "try slowly and humbly and constantly to express, to press out again, from the gross earth or what it brings forth, from sound and shape and colour which are the prison gates of the soul, an image of the beauty we have come to understand -- that is art."[7] Happily, Lynch, and the earth itself, provide some welcome Joycean satire to Stephen's intellectual ideals here. Just as the "smell of wet branches . . . seemed to war against the course of Stephen's thought," [as did the pig's pizzle to Jude's thoughts in Thomas Hardy's *Jude The Obscure* ], so do Lynch's words. "Let us take woman," Stephen says in his attempts to define beauty. "Let us take her!" responds Lynch. When Stephen finishes defining *integritas* and *consonantia*, Lynch quips: "Bull's eye again! . . . Tell me now what is *claritas* and you win the cigar" (p. 212). Such issues, Lynch responds, have the "true scholastic stink" (p. 214). To have his epiphanies Stephen must become intellectually sensitive to reality, and ignore Lynch's quips. But the world, of course, gives the lie to his fantasies and goals.

All throughout *Ulysses* Stephen is impressed by human inabilities to face the materiality of the world. It "chilled him" earlier in *Portrait* (p. 96) and made him melancholy to the point where the material world, in *Ulysses*, became for him "nothing more than a vague fluid atmosphere seeping from his brain to impregnate space through the fluid and melancholy language of doubt; the grey monochrome of the present is the very colour of alienation." Dublin became for him a "stagnant sociohistorical setting whose 'veil' of fog and grey mist prevented his eyes and mind from making visions of a better future."[8] This collision between human goals and the material world, between Stephen's ideals and the resolute material cycles of nature, is, as we have seen, the classic confrontation between realism and idealism. It is the same conflict that Ortega Y Gasset talks about in *Meditations on Quixote*, and which Burns talks about in *The Panzaic Principle*. Joyce's stasis, his epiphanic awareness, tries to fuse the realism of war with the idealism of a solution for it. His move down to Locarno from Zurich came as the result of his doctor's advice, but there is something metaphoric about it, coming as it does at this point in his life. There is in this move his love for that warmer, more theoretical climate of speculation on history after reading Giambattista Vico's *Scienza Nuova* (1744) -- a work he admitted admiring. His move to Italy is the metaphoric movement that his mind took from the cold realism of material events to the warm idealism of speculation, from the realism of history and its brutal facts, to those ideal goals of history that Vico, Blake, Hegel, and Marx thought they had visualized. For both Stephen and Joyce insist at the beginning of "Nestor" that history "must be a movement, an actuality of the possible as possible" ( *Ulysses*, p. 25). Like Stephen, who in "Circe" taps his brow and says to Bloom that "in here it is I must kill the priest and the king" ( *U*, p. 589), so does Joyce wage a mental battle against the "nightmare" of reality. When Joyce was asked whether he believed in Vico's *Scienza Nuova*, he responded that he didn't "believe in any science," but that his imagination grew when he read Vico, as it did not when he read Freud and Jung.[9] Ellmann claims that Joyce admired Vico's famous "positive division of human history into recurring cycles, each set off by a thunderclap, of theocratic, aristocratic, and democratic ages, followed by a *ricorso*, or return"; he also says that Joyce "did not share Vico's interest in these as literal chronological divisions of 'eternal ideal history,' but as psychological ones, ingredients which kept combining and recombining in ways which seemed always to be *déjà vu*."[10] Yet, as A.M. Klein argues, these possible psychological divisions of the human mind, based on Vico's historical divisions, are not only alluded to in "Nestor," but are dispersed all throughout *Ulysses*. In fact, the entire "Nestor" chapter, Klein claims, "from the beginning to end, has been shaped and influenced by Vico's paradigms of providence; . . . there is hardly a phrase which has not been, at least in its sequence in the text, predetermined by this pattern."[11] Here are Vico's historical divisions:

1. *The age of gods*, where man created his idea of god not only out of fear of the earth, but also out of shame in the eyes of his gods, since a thunderclap caught him "under the open sky in the very act of fornication"[12]

2. *The age of heroes* which was characterized by the appearance of two classes -- intellectuals who command, strong brutes who obey.

3. *The age of man*: where those under slavery, prompted by envy of property ownership and other legal rights, revolt.

4. *The ricorso*: an age in which reflective reason falls back to beginning the cycle all over again -- from gods to heroes to men. *Ricorsi* is reflection.[13]

These divisions can, indeed, be regarded as influential to Joyce's abstract concept of history, for there is enough textual evidence to claim that these four points do provide a structure to help Joyce cope with reality, a structure to help make concrete his abstract concept of history. Stephen sees all around him in Dublin the age of *ricorso*, the "ruin of all space," the "shattered glass and toppling masonry, and time one livid final flame" (p. 24). Stephen repeats this vision only once more in *Ulysses*, near the end of "Circe," where, in the swirling vortex of violence, hallucinations, and brawls in the brothel, and, after seeing his dead mother, he lifts his "ashplant high with both hands and smashes the chandelier. Time's livid final flame leaps and, in the following darkness, ruin of all space, shattered glass and toppling masonry" ( *U*, p. 583). This is Joyce's ironic side comment on Stephen's previously serious and bitter intellectualizations in "Nestor." For Vico, "Providence" was seen in history; but for Stephen, there is only one question after his epiphany: "What's left us then?" (*U*, p. 24). Perhaps we are to accept the view that shattered glass and crashing masonry is an image not only for the nightmare of history and the nightmare of Dublin is stasis, but also for *ricorso*, an Irish age of reflection. The whole "Nestor" episode, I believe, is devoted to Stephen's search for a more satisfactory explanation to what both Vico and Joyce saw as man's "ferocity, avarice, and ambition."[14] Temporarily, Stephen settles for the Aristotelean paraphrase: "actuality of the possible as possible" (*U*, p. 25). But this phrase brings back the memory of himself reading in the library of Saint Geneviere, where he hides from the "sin of Paris, night by night," and where he sees the world calling forth that "sloth of the underworld" in himself, the stark symbol of dangerous desire "shifting her dragon scaly folds" ( *U.*, pp. 25-26). This scaly dragon is Stephen's sexuality, damned up in his body and imagination. Joyce shifts us from Stephen's abstractions on the turmoil of history to the concrete turmoil of his personal life, to the possibility of barbaric sex rising up [Vico's *ricorso*] out of Stephen's reflections, which, to my mind, confirms the inadequacies of Stephen's quest in the "real world" for "the unsubstantial image which his soul so constantly beheld" (*Portrait*, p. 65). This Aristotelean bond between realism and idealism appears not only in Joyce's decision to use the Homeric world (an ideal) as a way to expose Ireland (the real), or in his attempts to parallel Vico's perceptions of history with his discussion of history in "Nestor," but also in Stephen's observations on a fact of life: *birth*.

After his class ends, and his students go off to play ball, Stephen looks at Sargent's body, the "ugly and futile" student who stays for help with his history lessons. Sargent comes "forward slowly," like a plebian, to begin Vico's age of man.[15] Stephen sees his "lean neck and tangled hair and a stain of ink, a snail's bed," and thinks to himself: "Yet someone had loved him, borne him in her arms and in her heart. But for her the race of the world would have trampled him under foot, a squashed boneless snail. She had loved *his weak watery blood* drained from her own. *Was that then real?* The only true thing in life?" ( *U*, p. 27). This one empirical question has the power to expose the limitations of Stephen's abstract speculations about history, and perhaps even to weaken the broad idealistic generalizations Vico makes about the kind of men who usher in the "age of man." Someone loving "weak watery blood" may not be the *only* true thing in life, but it is a fact of life, a fact Stephen seems too snobbish to admit, and Sargent, simply not aware, nor could he ever be, that he might be prompted to start a revolution to begin an "age of man," is too much of a stubborn reality to be of much good for the ideal of historical progress. Stephen muses:

> *Amor matris* subjective and objective genitive. With her weak
> blood and wheysour milk she had fed him and hid from sight of
> others his swaddling bands.
> *Like him was I, these sloping shoulders, this gracelessness.*
> My childhood bends beside me. Too far for me to lay a hand there
> once or lightly. Mine is far and his secret as our eyes. *Secrets,*
> *silent, stony sit in the dark palaces of both our hearts:* secrets weary
> of their tyranny: tyrants willing to be dethroned. ( *U*, p. 28, emphasis
> added)

The fact is that Stephen is very much like Sargent, a boy who reminds him that he, too, has a body, with sloping shoulders, and one cared for and fed by a woman. The materiality of Sargent's life is too powerful for Stephen, the secrets sitting in their dark places of their hearts, secrets about the repressive realities of Dublin city life, church doctrine, and bitter politics, too awful to face. These secrets are realities in rebellion from Vico's theory of the " *storia ideale eterna.*" Every time Stephen thinks of Vico's theories about how history will progress to an understanding of itself ( *ricorsi*), every time he thinks of Aristotle's theory of the soul, there comes up in him a powerful melancholy, a reaction to the fact that none of these theories could be real. He sees what he thinks to be a sad and pathetic Sargent, but his description of the boy is *his* melancholy, *his* sentimentality about how reality will stop cultural progress every chance it gets. Ortega Y Gasset recognized such melancholy as our tension in viewing brute materiality surround the ideals in our culture. Sargent undermines Stephen's ideals on historical progress because he is a human being who cannot be easily "epiphanized." He is too anxious to play in the "jousts," in the slush and uproar, too anxious to be among the "battling bodies" ( *U*, p. 32). Sargent's contextualist qualities and textures (his dark secrets, his dullness, and appearance) are too real for Stephen, too real in the present event to be included in a philosophy of the past. Tension, then, in "Nestor," is between Stephen's wishes for what Vico called an "ideal eternal history traversed in time by the history of every nation in its rise, development, maturity, decline, and fall" (Vico, p. 62, par. 349), and the stubborn Panzaic resistance of Sargent to be included in such a scheme. Tension is also found between Joyce's wish to "transpose the myth *sub specie temporis nostri*"[16] [to get what he hoped would become in *Ulysses* a description of universal history] and the mute refusal of Sargent to be so universalized. Since realism, then, is in combat with the symbolism in this chapter (as S.L. Goldberg describes the combat in *The Classical Temper*, (New York: Barnes & Noble, Inc., 1961), the real nightmare for Stephen is to find a way to escape from brute materiality. How Joyce turned away from such materiality, however, is worthy of attention, and his attempts will explain how Molly Bloom became the solution for his nightmares, how she became, in other words, Vico's *ricorso* in Joyce's mind.

Just after World War I began, Joyce read Benedetto Croce's *Aesthetic* (1909), and knew its chapter on Vico (Ellman, p. 351). Most likely it was Croce's interpretation of the importance of Vico's theories, Ellmann suggests, that Joyce retained. Vico's philosophy of history, Croce said does not address "the concrete empirical history which unfolds itself in time: it is not history, it is a science of the ideal, a Philosophy of the Spirit . . . Vico allowed himself to suggest historical periods which do not correspond with the real periods, but are rather allegories, the mythological expressions of his philosophy of the spirit."[17] *Ulysses* is Joyce's "science of the ideal," for his "scientific" marshalling of endless realistic details in this novel adds up, in the end, to a dream, to a philosophy of the spirit. Significant Form has created context; dream has selected its reality. The power of idealisms to assuage our pain in the face of brute materiality is very seductive. By giving us Molly Bloom's monologue inside the dream of archetype, Joyce engages in seductive mythic thought, and returns us to an age Vico respected: the age of the "heroic barbarian," where thoughts and actions, Vico believed, were spontaneous and without deceit.

The conflict between realism and idealism remains a big problem for Joyce and Stephen, our historical idealists. It reminds them, among other things, that men like Sargent, in "Nestor," are not at all conscious of time or the beauty of archetypes. Vico, too, was aware of the conflict, and he tried to solve it with his principle of *ricorsi*. As Stephen pressed out of the gross event, with his "epiphany," the ideal of the oneness of the ages in "Nestor," (when he universalized Sargent) so did Vico press out of the gross event the ideal of eternal history, with his principle of *ricorsi*. Both concepts are remarkably similar. Vico's purpose in *Scienza Nuova* was to discover laws of growth and decline, and, as A.R. Caponigri points out, to "place in the hands of the nations, so to say, the power of recapturing the sources of their life and, even in the moment of decline, of initiating anew their movement toward ideality and vigorous life. This must be recognized . . . as the protoform of the concept of 'ricorsi,' and it is, clearly, thoroughly moralistic in character"[18] *Ricorsi* takes place wholly on the reflective level, supposedly capturing the spontaneous "spirit" of renewal for future history. As human reflection retreats back into events, and into itself, it supposedly advances an understanding of the present, and thereby improves the future. *Ricorsi* requires an age after the "age of man," one of oversophistication, one of decadence, an age made more inhuman "by the barbarism of reflection," but one which occurs in order to initiate a return, in this reflection, to the creative "barbarism of sense" -- Vico's age of regeneration (Vico, p. 381, par. 1106). What Vico wanted through his *ricorsi* matches what Joyce wanted through his "epiphany": an intellectual activity that fuses our senses with our intellects. As Vico's "spirit" reaches back through all "the time of the life of individual nations, and down into the depths of consciousness to bring the entire content of history before itself in a single and total act of presence," so too does Joyce reach for the same thing with his "epiphany" in the "Nestor" chapter of *Ulysses*.[19] No longer is Stephen seeing objects in reality lifted "away from everything else," as he said in *Stephen Hero* (circa 1904); [20] rather, he now believes (as does Joyce) that "life is fulfilled most completely in the reflexive act wherein it understands itself" through language (Goldberg, *Joyce*, p. 18). According to H. Cixous, this "reflexive act" is better called the "totalitarian epiphany," because it attempts to enslave empirical details to Language -- to wrap life up in "verbal clothing" (Cixous, p. 676). If our reading experiences are to be intensified at the end of the novel, with Molly's reflexive acts, then we see all along that Viconian idealism underpins *Ulysses*. For Molly is the ultimate expression of what Vico and Joyce called history -- she is the ultimate *ricorsi* : that reflexive act wherein "Life" and "Language" understand only themselves. She combines the Aristotelean, normative idealism of the combined particular (Dublin-female) with the universal (Woman-Life). She is the "totalitarian epiphany." Only in "Nestor" do we have Panzaic Sargent and the elements of realism acting in relation to Stephen, and showing us the sorrow and futility of such idealism. Reluctant to give us more of such sorrow, Joyce avoids lengthy descriptions of developed interactions between human beings in *Ulysses*. Not even Haines or Mulligan are seen in prolonged Panzaic relation to Stephen, which would expose Stephen's search for the ultimate symbol of the physical world.

Final comfort for Stephen and Bloom is supposedly provided by Molly. She is to replace Vico's Providence as the end goal of cyclic history, and be the answer to Stephen's perception of history as Irish sadism. She is to counterpoint with her humor and liveliness Bloom's apathy and resignation to melancholy. But she is also a mind present to itself, Joyce's *ricorsi* freeing itself from the tyranny of time by linking memories to the present. Yet in Joyce's idealistic denial of time there is the admission of his empirical enslavement to it, and in his celebration of memory a display of his comic sentimentality. Molly is not Vico's new "barbarism of sense," as Joyce might have wished her to be, but Vico's "barbarism of reflection," as her fictional structure forces her to be.

## II

Since the publication of *Ulysses* most readers and scholars have felt that the final solution to the sadism in Irish behavior and to the "nightmare of history" can be found in the words and feelings of Molly Bloom in "Penelope" -- especially at that point, these readers say, when the "childman weary" lies "with his unfaithful but essential (like Ireland) earth mother."[21] Giving

58

Molly Bloom the attitude of "Gea-Tellus" and emphasizing her state as "fulfilled, recumbent, big with seed" (*Ulysses,* p.737), these readers find her the symbol of fertility and "mankind's timeless answer to the nightmare of history, and the warmth of the marriage bed to the 'cold of interstellar space.'"[22] She embodies, they say, a timeless eroticism. And despite her fear of pregnancy since the death of her son, she symbolizes fertility, biological necessities, and affirmations of life. Joyce himself describes the episode as "perfectly full amoral fertilisable untrustworthy engaging shrewd limited prudent indifferent *Weib.*"[23] He wanted Molly to be representative of women; to be a comprehensive description of human female life. Other readers, however, are not so sure of Molly's positive image. They claim she is mostly the egocentric and domineering Irish woman who is not at all interested in children, who enjoys manipulating men, and that as so-called Earth-Mother she mocks fertility. Philip F. Herring summarizes most of these views and then concludes that they all miss the heart of Joyce's art. He says that Joyce rubs our noses in the humanity of his characters, and hopes that we will recognize the "verisimilitude of the portraits and consent to laugh at and thereby share in the human experience of his characters."[24] If Molly fails to fulfill her symbolic potential, he says, that does not negate her symbolic potential. What Herring sees as the "tension between the symbolic and the real" in Molly, is what for him "produces that ironic dimension which is the very heart of Joyce's comedy in *Ulysses.*"[25] Joyce does rub our noses in the humanity of his characters, and there is that tension between real and ideal in Molly that provides an ironic tension for us; yet she does not figure largely as a fully interactive female character. (The only intimate moment of conversation we get between Molly and Leopold, for example, is told in ironic and bitter third person narration at the end of "Ithaca.") Molly has been pressed out of reality and into archetype by Joyce *and* by his critics. Yet to see her as a universal archetype for female psychology or as a symbol of "Life" is very difficult. For as the ideal solution to the terrors of time and history, she limps, like Gerty, to the stage; and as the solution to the nightmare of Irish sado-masochistic history, she is hardly a match for the brute materiality of it all. She is, instead, both comic symbol for Joyce's personal view of female domination, and a kind of soft-porn movie star.[26]

At the end of the "Nestor" episode, Mr. Deasy's final remarks can be taken as allusions to the behavior of Molly in chapter eighteen. Deasy runs after Stephen to explain to him why Ireland had the honor of never persecuting the Jews. He says: "Because she never let them in" (*U.*, p. 36).[27] Ireland (Molly) will never let the Jew (Bloom) *in,* unless he bow to her conditions. The sexual implication is clear for us as readers. When Molly does let Bloom into her bed, it is only after establishing herself as the dominant figure. The joke is on Leopold-Ulysses, for Molly is no promised land, no bed of roses. When Ireland did admit Jews into her cities, she did so under the yoke of government regulations in the early 1800s. Molly lets Bloom into her bed to assume his position with a "gradual abasement" (*U.*, p.735). He is to keep his fetish for her "posterior female hemispheres," kiss her rump (*U.*, p. 734), and sleep beside her upside down -- the comic and ridiculous position of a male reduced to a fool at the foot of the Irish Woman.[28] The last sentence of "Penelope," which has been seen so frequently as affirming "Life" and giving us positive images of Molly, is actually the best example for seeing Molly as Joyce's personal archetype of the Irish Woman who possesses a titillating will. *"I got him* to propose," Molly says, *"I gave him* the bit of seedcake out of my mouth . . . *I knew I could always get round him* and I gave him all the pleasure I could *leading him on* till he asked me to say yes" (*U.*, p. 782, emphasis added). The words she has spoken here (in sentimentality over romantic love as she remembers her early courtship with Bloom) are first said, in different ways, on page 780, where, in anger over Bloom's own clichés about women, she reinforces the dilemma of their modern relationship: their stasis. She reinforces the battlelines between Bloom's independence and her own possessive will. There is hardly evidence in the following lines of the last pages of the novel to support the claim that all conflict between them is absorbed in the memory of their courtship, or in the "yes" at the end of the novel -- a word which conveys only the "mumbling of a woman falling asleep."[29] The conflict between them remains anchored in the reality of 1904 Ireland, outside of sentimental memory; and so remains the domineering on Irish Molly's part, wherein taking advantage of Bloom's various fetishes, using them to the fullest by stimulating their arrival in Bloom's psychology, she knows she can get what she wants from him: money and domination. Bloom's request for eggs in bed is hardly the announcement for a return of liveliness in Bloom, hardly the sign that Bloom has become, somehow, more virile by such a domestic request, despite, I am sure, Joyce's awareness that the word "eggs" in Spanish (*huevos*) can be used as a slang term for male testicles or for implying manliness.[30] Here is Molly's response to Bloom's request for eggs:

> Ill *throw him* up his eggs . . . I suppose hed like my nice cream too I know what Ill do Ill go about rather gay . . . Ill put on my best shift and *drawers let him have a good eyeful* out of that to *make* his micky stand for him . . . unless *I made* him stand there and put him into me Ive a mind to tell him every scrap and *make him* do it in front of me . . . its all his own fault if I am an adulteress . . . if he wants to kiss my bottom Ill drag open my drawers and *bulge it right out in his face* as large as life he can stick his tongue 7 miles up my hole as hes there my brown part *then Ill tell him I want* £1 or perhaps 30/ - Ill tell him I want to buy *underclothes.* (*U.*, p. 780, emphasis added)

The supposed ideal solution of "Penelope," the solution to the sadism of Irish history, and to the "nightmare of history" in general, is hardly provided for here, nor can romance withstand the images and actions of the willful sexual domination we see here. Joyce is reported to have said that in realism "you are down to facts on which the world is based: that sudden reality which smashes romanticism into a pulp . . . idealism is the ruin of man . . . in *Ulysses* I tried to keep close to fact."[31] Yet so many critics [perhaps even Joyce himself] have wanted Molly to be an ideal. But she does not support such a wish, she bumps around inside her own symbolic room, inside Joyce's larger scheme; she does not fit the idealistic verbal clothing the novel tries to give her. She smashes the romanticism of our solution to the "nightmare of history" to a pulp, and appears what Joyce admitted in his letters he wanted his wife Nora to be: a "strong . . . big    full proud bosom and big fat thighs" of a woman, who would "flog" him, and make him suffer with love like the whore Bella in "Nighttown."[32] This is what keeps Molly from becoming our sentimental archetype of "Earth-Goddess," or from becoming the abstract ideal of universal "Mother," -- clichés that have always denied the individuality in women. If anything, the chapter is a courageous description of Joyce's own sexual desires, or the sexual problems of a culture that surrounded him.[33]

"Penelope," then, exemplifies what Joyce believed the Irish woman to be. Darcy O'Brien makes this abundantly clear in his contention that Joyce's views on love and sexuality clearly reflect what Freud described as the common inability of modern man to unite his feelings of tenderness and sensuality toward one woman.[34] "Irishmen," O'Brien says, "continue to have it in for women, even when they have it out for them. Fear and contempt for woman as a sexual creature, that is the Irish attitude."[35] As well as pointing to the Jansenist influence on Irish Catholicism and to the great famine (1845-49), "when birth came to mean death or emigration and sexual abstinence became linked to physical survival," O'Brien also claims that there is a long literary and psychological tradition the Irish psyche is devoted to: it has looked upon woman as the "Sheela-na-gig," that pre-Christian Irish mythological figure who "seduced and emasculated her victims." For O'Brien, Joyce's portrait of Molly extends this tradition.[36] As a character, Molly may be just as one dimensional as those early stone carvings of the Sheela-na-gig, yet she does reflect the painful and complex sexual feelings, guilty desires, and masochistic leanings Joyce himself experienced with Nora, as some of his letters to his wife reveal. "The male Irish mind," O'Brien says, "fears the sexual power of woman, associates it with whorishness, and reserves love for the Virgin and her humbler surrogates on earth . . . when he set out to fashion his image of womankind in Molly Bloom, he began with the ideal of the faithful Penelope and contrasted it with what he regarded as concupiscent realities"(O'Brien, p. 147). The slyness in the realities of Bloom's masochism, Molly's wilful domination, and, as a character her ironic parallel to Homer's faithful Penelope, as well as Joyce's own psychological patterns of sexual guilt may not pull down the whole edifice of *Ulysses*, but surely they undermine the ideal in "Penelope." For the end of that chapter collapses into sentimentality and melancholy. As Lawrence's "black tom-cat" pounces on the dove of the "Word," in the novel, so does the "black tom-cat" in Molly Bloom pounce on the wish for a universal archetype of "Woman" or "Life." It is memory that Molly says yes to, not Bloom; it is the memory of Lieutenant Mulvey that stirs her melancholy outburst at the end of "Penelope," her memory of herself in "Gibraltar as a girl" (U., p. 783): memories free from the reality of masochism, sadism, and fetishism. Only with Mulvey, O'Brien claims, does Joyce come close to "describing sexuality as a positive force" (O'Brien, p. 152). Yet Mulvey is not even presented in the book -- he is a ghost. "Joyce used Molly and Mulvey's experience because of its adolescent, incomplete quality, because it reached the verge and stopped, still promising, still innocent -- at least in Joyce's mind" (O'Brien, p. 153). Here is where the sentimentality of the last chapter exists, in this incomplete dream of ideal love.[37]

The conflict between Bloom and Molly could not be absorbed in memory because it is very difficult to lose human conflict to symbolism, to fend off the particularity of it in order to universalize it. Joyce may attempt to latch human conflict to symbolism, but the reality of Molly's sexual domination of Bloom won't sink into abstract peace. Molly has become Joyce's mental ideal of the sensuous lover: the dark Moroccan Jew from Gibraltar, who shares a birthdate with the Catholic Virgin Mary, and who emerges not as a rounded character, but as a frozen mythic daydream, a private solution to Joyce's tension in the face of that conflict between reality and ideals, between artistic realism and ideational art, between sexual desire for women and tenderness for virginal purity, between what he thought women were, and what his Irish mind saw Irish women to be. Joyce suffered to enlarge the individualistic reality of female life into myth because like Stephen Dedalus, [and most of us], he is uncomfortable under reality, just as uncomfortable, in a way, as we see Gulliver to be under the desirous eye of that female Yahoo in *Gulliver's Travels*.[38]

There is one particular aspect of this uncomfortable reality that Joyce describes: "the modern theme," he told Arthur Power, "is the subterranean forces, those hidden tides which govern everything and run humanity counter to the apparent flood: those poisonous subtleties which envelop the soul, the ascending fumes of sex."[39] In his attempt to wed in the *epiphany* of "Penelope" universalized sex with his view of sexual reality, Joyce fled from the "fumes" of sex, and reinforced his earliest beliefs in ideational art, in the rubric of *arte ideativa*. As his essay "The Universal Literary Influence of the Renaissance" shows, it is the *idea* of passion or history that interests him -- the "soul" of a passion or an event.[40] There is revulsion from the flesh in "Penelope," even as the chapter insists upon the reality of it. Molly is static. D.H. Lawrence said that *Ulysses* was "stewed in the juice of deliberate, journalistic dirty-mindedness -- what old and hard-worked staleness, masquerading as the all-new!"[41] Even more to the point, the realities of history, as well as Joyce's personal view of women, are all too powerful to give "Penelope" that required status of archetype. For as we find out daily, and as Joyce I believe discovered, much to his distress, reality has "such a violent temper that it does not tolerate the ideal even when reality itself is idealized."[42]

## Notes

[1] E. Mason and R. Ellmann, eds., *The Critical Writings of James Joyce* (New York: The Viking Press, 1959), p. 246. Hereafter abbreviated as *Critical Writings.*

[2] *Ibid,* pp. 247-48.

[3] A. Rutherford, *The Literature of War* (London: The Macmillan Press, 1978), p. 66.

[4] James Joyce, *Ulysses* (New York: Random House, 1961), p. 596. (Hereafter abbreviated in text as *U.*)

[5] S.L. Goldberg, *Joyce* (New York: Barnes & Noble, Inc., 1962), p. 9. (Hereafter abbreviated as Goldberg, *Joyce*).

[6] James Joyce, *Dubliners* (New York: The Viking Press, 1961), pp. 219-20.

[7] James Joyce, *A Portrait of the Artist as a Young Man* (Penguin Books, 1968), p. 207. (Hereafter abbreviated in text as *P*).

[8] Hélène Cixous, *The Exile of James Joyce* (New York: David Lewis, 1972), p. 669. (Hereafter abbreviated in text as Cixous).

[9] Richard Ellmann, *James Joyce* (London and New York: Oxford University Press, 1959), p. 706.

[10] *Ibid.,* p. 565. (Hereafter abbreviated in the text as Ellmann).

[11] A.M. Klein, "A Shout in the Street: An Analysis of the Second Chapter of Joyce's *Ulysses,*" *New Directions in Prose and Poetry* (13, n.d.), p. 331. See also: A. Walton Litz, "Vico and Joyce," *Giambattista Vico: An International Symposium* (Baltimore: The Johns Hopkins University Press, 1969), pp. 245-55.

[12] *Ibid.,* Klein, p. 327.

[13] Giambattista Vico, *The New Science,* trans. T.G. Bergin and M.H. Fisch (Ithaca and London: Cornell University Press, 1970).

[14] *Ibid.,* p. 20 par. 132. (Hereafter abbreviated in the text as Vico).

[15] Klein, "A Shout in the Street," p. 336.

[16] Stuart Gilbert, ed., *Letters of James Joyce,* Vol. 1 (New York: The Viking Press, 1957), pp. 146-47. (Hereafter abbreviated in text as *Letters*).

[17] Benedetto Croce, *Aesthetic,* trans. D. Ainslie (New York: The Noonday Press, 1953), pp. 231-32.

[18] A.R. Caponigri, *Time and Idea: The Theory of History in Giambattista Vico* (University of Notre Dame Press, 1953), p. 133.

[19] *Ibid,* p. 141.

[20] James Joyce, *Stephen Hero* (New York: New Directions, 1944), p. 212.

[21] F.L. Radford, "King, Pope, Hero-Martyr: *Ulysses* and the Nightmare of Irish History," James Joyce Quarterly, 15 (Summer 1978), p. 318.

[22] *Ibid,* p. 318.

[23] "To Frank Budgen, 16 August 1921", Stuart Gilbert, ed., *Letters of James Joyce,* Volume I, pp. 169-70.

62

24 Philip F. Herring, "The Bedsteadfastness of Molly Bloom," *Modern Fiction Studies*, 15, 1 (Spring 1969), p. 60.

25 *Ibid*, p. 61.

26 See Leslie Fiedler, "To Whom Does Joyce Belong? Ulysses as Parody, Pop, and Porn," in *Light Rays: James Joyce and Modernism*, ed. H. Ehrlich (New York: New Horizon Press, 1984), pp. 26-37. "Ulysses . . . titillates us without the presence of real flesh . . . the pornographic dimensions of Joyce's work [critics] find . . . difficult to confess" (pp. 29-30).

27 All quotes from Ulysses are from the Random House edition of 1961. Hereafter abbreviated as *U* in text.

28 Odysseus is extremely obsequious as he approaches Penelope in Book 23 of the *Odyssey*; and she, in turn, slowly accepts her husband, calling him a "tramp."

29 Louis Gillet, *Claybook for James Joyce* (London and New York: Abelard-Schuman, 1958), p. 65.

30 Morris Beja objects to this view: ". . . what ought Bloom to do in order to prove himself 'manly' or 'masculine'? Should he slap Molly around a bit? Or, avoiding such violence, should he leave in a huff?" ("The Joyce of Sex: Sexual Relations in *Ulysses*," in The Seventh of Joyce, ed. B. Benstock [Bloomington: Indiana University Press, 1982], p. 261). D.H. Lawrence has answered these questions in *Women in Love*, "The Captain's Doll" and *Lady Chatterley's Lover*.

31 Arthur Power, *Conversation with James Joyce* (New York: Harper and Row, 1974), p. 98.

32 "To Nora Barnacle," 13 December, 1909, R. Ellmann, ed. *Letters*, II, pp. 273-74. Joyce was fully aware of his own interest in masochism. He explored it in *Exiles* with the characterization of Richard, in whom, we see Bloom's masochistic characteristics too. Just as Richard is sexually excited by the fact that Bertha may have had sexual intercourse with someone else, so does Bloom get that same excitement from his, in Freud's term, "erotogenic masochism," by groveling in front of Bella Cohen and watching through a keyhole the love-making of Boylan and Molly. (Freud, "The Economic Problem in Masochism." *Collected Papers*, London: Hogarth Press, 1948, Volume 2, pp. 257-58). E.R. Steinberg discusses Bloom's masochism in *The Stream of Consciousness and Beyond in "Ulysses"* (Pittsburgh: University of Pittsburgh Press, 1958), pp. 213-218. See also: Richard Brown, *James Joyce and Sexuality* (Cambridge University Press, 1985).

33 Critics go to great lengths to change individual sexual fetish in the novel into universal feelings for life: When "Bloom wishes Molly to lift her petticoat, orange like her chamber pot, gold like Buck's dressinggown, with its sun-rays from the sun like the nymph (with Molly as Earth-Goddess rotating around the sun) and this in the rain, one can perhaps perceive that Bloom is worshipping once again the source of human life" (Fr. R. Boyle, S.J., "Penelope," James Joyce's "Ulysses"; *Critical Essays* (Berkeley: University of California Press, 1974), pp. 426-427. See also: S. Lyman's "Revision and Intention in Joyce's 'Penelope,'" *James Joyce Quarterly*, 20, 2 (Winter, 1983), pp. 193-199; Carol Siegel, "Masochism and Fertility in *Ulysses*," *Twentieth Century Literature*, 33, 2 (Summer, 1987), pp. 179-195.

34 Darcy O'Brien, "Some Determinants of Molly Bloom," in *Approaches to Ulysses: Ten Essays*. (Pittsburgh: University of Pittsburgh Press, 1970), pp. 137-55.

35 O'Brien, "Some Determinants of Molly Bloom," pp. 137-38. See also: O'Brien's *The Conscience of James Joyce* (Princeton, New Jersey: Princeton University Press, 1968).

36 O'Brien, p. 139. See also Peter Costello, *The Heart Grown Brutal: The Irish Revolution in Literature from Parnell to the Death of Yeats, 1891-1939* (Dublin: Gill and Macmillan, Ltd., 1977): "Sexuality had become for the Irish an actual threat to their material safety, even to their very existence, as the horrors of the Famine had shown them" (p. 13). Hereafter O'Brien abbreviated in text.

37 Jane Ford claims that most of Joyce's characters are "true Quixotes" who "fail to grasp at possible joy in the present moment because they are so locked into an idealized other place,

person, or time, summed up in Molly's 'were never easy where we are.'" ("James Joyce and Those (K)nights of 'Ruful Continence,'" in *The Seventh of Joyce*, ibid., p. 244.

38 S.L. Goldberg suggests that the events of Ulysses "derive their meaning not from their relation to anything in the world in which they are enacted . . . but from the plenitude of the vision that beholds them . . . Life appears less of an activity experienced than a spectacle contemplated" (*The Classical Temper: A Study of James Joyce's "Ulysses"* [New York: Barnes and Noble, Inc., 1961], p. 206, p. 291.) For a discussion of how Joyce used for his fiction the pornographic aspects of his own life, see Richard Ellmann, *James Joyce's Hundreth Birthday* (Washington, D.C.: Library of Congress, 1982).

39 Arthur Power, Conversations with James Joyce, p. 54.

40 L. Berrone, ed., *James Joyce in Padua* (New York: Random House, 1977), pp. 49-50.

41 D.H. Lawrence, *Selected Literary Criticism*, ed. A. Beal (New York, The Viking Press, 1966), p. 148.

42 José Ortega y Gasset, *Meditations on Quixote*, trans. E. Rugg and Diego Marín (New York: W.W. Norton and Co., 1961), p. 163. Fredric Jameson points out that critics are still looking for the "happy ending" in Ulysses ("Ulysses in History," in *James Joyce and Modern Literature*, eds. McCormack and Stead [London: Routledge and Kegan Paul, 1982), p. 127. (Eg.: B.K. Scott, *Joyce and Feminism* [Bloomington: Indiana University Press, 1984], p. 203).

# PART III

# FURTHER APPLICATIONS

CHAPTER 5

*Miss Ravenel's Conversion*: The Discreet Suspension
of Melodrama for the Sake of "The Panzaic"


In America all books, novels not excepted,
suppose women to be chaste.

(Tocqueville, 1835)[1]

How imperiously, for wise ends, we are
governed by the passion of sex for sex, in
spite of the superficial pleas of selfish reason
and interest! What other quality, physical or
moral, have we that could take the place of
this beneficently despotic instinct?

(John W. De Forest, 1865)[2]


i

When John William De Forest published his American Civil War novel, *Miss Ravenel's Conversion From Secession to Loyalty*, in 1865, he did so with a full reading background of the novels of Dickens, Thackeray, George Eliot, Scott, Stendhal, and Balzac. Before serving in the war, he had spent four years abroad in England, France, Germany, and Italy, and we can see that his subsequent novels reflect some of the prevailing styles and techniques of Victorian literature. His war scenes in *Miss Ravenel's Conversion* are usually hailed as realistic, and his style is often used by critics to help with their definition of American *realism*. The novel is, in some ways, a transitional one, from the style of the American romance [Cooper's Leatherstocking Saga] to the beginnings of the realistic document [Dreiser's Cowperwood Trilogy]. De Forest did not use realistic detail in this novel to make his romance believable; in fact, with the exception of the last chapter, "A Marriage," he nearly avoided romance completely as he honestly recorded what he saw in the American North and South of the 1860's. (Lillie Ravenel is certainly one of the most realistic and fully developed female characters in nineteenth-century American literature, and not even Stephen Crane can match the brilliant realism of De Forest's war scenes [in Chapter 21]). DeForest described the relationship between Northern war efforts and the fading, landed Southern gentility by avoiding the "moonlight and magnolia" myth of the Tidewater economy, and, although he refused to "tell a good story," he did unabashedly use classic melodrama at the end of the novel for the sake of his readers. Like Zola, De Forest decided to examine men and their passions; character became for him more important than plot or action. It has been suggested, however, that those writers who use melodrama "do not have a firm sense of living in a culture."[3] Yet De Forest (using his melodrama to sell his books) is one of the first American novelists to explore the clash between American industrial interests and aristocratic interests. Most likely he advocated the reconciliation of North and South, although, as a novelist, we find him in *Ravenel* on the side of the "civilizing" North. In Chapter one, for example, Edward Colburne engages in the following conversation with Lillie Ravenel's father, the solid Northern idealist in the book:

> "It will probably be a short struggle" said Colburne,
> speaking the common belief of the North.
> "I don't know -- I don't know about that; we musn't
> be too sure of that. You must understand that they are
> barbarians, and that all barbarians are obstinate and reckless.
> They will hold out like the Florida Seminoles. They will
> resist like jackasses and heroes . . . an honor to the fortitude
> and a sarcasm on the intelligence of human nature. They will
> become an example in history of much that is great, and
> all that is foolish. (pp. 3-4)

We hear De Forest's Union sympathies in good Dr. Ravenel's speeches.

Restraint and respectability characterized most American realism in the late 1800's, long after De Forest could hardly sell his books to a prevailing market that needed love described as a sentiment. W.D. Howells warned De Forest that his books would never "catch on," as he put it; yet, admiring his work, he wrote letters of encouragement and praise to him. And so in an essay he wrote for the 9 January edition of *The Nation*, in 1868, (the title of which has since become an infamous slogan) De Forest, resting on his great respect for European realistic writers, claimed that America would never write "The Great American Novel." What are America's Irvings and Coopers to Europe's Thackerays and Balzacs? he asked. *Miss Ravenel's Conversion* is very much in the tradition of English Victorian literature, if not an American author's first attempt at writing the "Great American Novel."

ii

We are introduced to Miss Lillie Ravenel, her father, and one Edward Colburne from New Boston (New Haven, Connecticut). The Ravenels are refugees from the South, and even though Dr. Ravenel, professor of theory and practice at the Medical College of New Orleans, is rabidly anti-Confederate, Lillie remains loyal.

> She was colored by the soil in which she had germinated and
> been nurtured . . . . Accordingly the young lady listened
> to the Doctor's story of his self-imposed exile and to his
> sarcasms upon the people of her native city with certain
> pretty little starts and sniffs of disapprobation which
> reminded Colburne of the counterfeit spittings of a kitten
> playing anger . . . When he had closed his tirade and
> history she broke forth in a defense of her darling Dixie. (p.
> 10)

Miss Lillie is a plain beauty with lively blue eyes and luxuriant amber hair, and because she blushes and flutters about at meeting men,

> Each young fellow thought that she was specially
> interested in himself, that the depths of her womanly
> nature were stirred into pleasurable excitement by his advent.
> And it was frequently not altogether a mistake. Miss
> Ravenel was interested in people, in a considerable number
> of people, and often at first sight. (p. 6)

As the novel shows later, De Forest introduces us to the conflict between North and South by describing the effect Southern women have on Northern men. We have Lillie in New Boston, the bastion of Puritanism where manners and opinions are angular. Socially the city is stiff, but Lillie is not. We have Colburne, the "popular favorite" in certain circles and "considered in his set the finest and most agreeable young man in New Boston" (p. 19). There is nothing hidden or stern in his expression, and his hazel eyes are very gentle. He is humorous, a good conversationalist, free of the vices of drinking and smoking, and possesses a "truly American habit of hyperbole" (p. 19). Of course for Lillie's father, Colburne would make a fine match, especially after the young man sees his way clear to join the Union army. Colburne, grieved to learn that Lillie is a traitor to the republic, but unable to let go his preconceptions about the rightness of the Northern cause, is nevertheless impressed with Lillie.

> He actually trembled with pleasure when Lillie at parting gave him her hand in the frank Southern fashion. And after he had reached his cozy bedroom on the opposite side of the public square he had to smoke a segar to compose himself to sleep. (p. 12)

Lillie has always enjoyed the conversational games and flirtation of the parlor, especially with fine moral gentlemen that sparkle with cleanliness, good nature, and idealism, and she is quite pleased at having Colburne "hang on." She is eighteen and eye-catching, and De Forest is not at all straining to keep his descriptions of her pure. We know from her characterization that she is emotionally ready to be stirred into surrendering to a powerful male, and we can see that De Forest does not moralize or sentimentalize this stirring. At a dinner party of her father's friend, Professor Whitewood, she eyes Lieutenant Colonel Carter for the first time. He is, indeed, a powerful spectacle, and early in the novel the polarities between Colburne and Carter, respectability and passion, are given.

> A little above the middle height he was, with a full chest, broad shoulders and muscular arms, brown curling hair, and a monstrous brown mustache, forehead not very high, nose straight and chin dimpled, brown eyes at once audacious and mirthful, and a dark rich complexion which made one think of pipes of sherry wine as well as of years of sunburnt adventure. When he was presented to her he looked her full in the eyes with a bold flash of interest which causes her to color from her forehead to her shoulders . . . In manner he was a thorough man of the world without the insinuating suavity of her father, but with all his self-possession and readiness. (p. 20)

Lillie is attracted to him at once. Her father and Colburne notice her attention to him, and recognize that this colonial blue blood from Virginia, now serving in the Union army, is what De Forest calls an "alarming phenomenon." Colburne was "clever enough to recognize the stranger's gigantic social stature at a glance, and like the Isrealitish spies in the presence of the Anakim, he felt himself shrink to a grasshopper mediocrity" (p. 20).

After taking to the wine, Carter engages Lillie in conversation about the appeal of the Old South and the eventual defeat of the rebels. Everyone in the novel reacts to Carter with hints of disgust at his open enjoyment of life, except Lillie, who, much to the surprise of Colburne, is very accustomed to men such as Carter after her experiences in New Orleans society. Yet she is anxious about her father, who disapproves of bacchanalian gentility. To avoid a confrontation with him at the Whitewood dinner party, she quits talking to Carter and keeps company with John Whitewood, Jr.

> Then Miss Ravenel thought it wise to propitiate her father's searching eye by quitting the Lieutenant-Colonel

> with his pleasant worldly ways and his fascinating masculine
> maturity, and going to visit the greenhouse in company with
> that pale bit of human celery, John Whitewood . . . pure as
> the timidest of girls, he was an example of what can be done
> with youthful blood, muscle, mind and feeling by the
> studious severities of a Puritan university. (pp. 26, 19)

Carter leaves the party and Colburne shortly follows, questioning "the goodness of Providence in permitting lieutenant-colonels." (p. 27)

Lillie's father, the least lifelike character of the novel and possible mouthpiece for De Forest's opinions on temperance, the evils of slavery, and the benefits of American industry, is quite ready for both the complete destruction of the South and the removal of Carter from his daughter's life. At a picnic the doctor makes sure Carter hears his tirade against liquor, and he attempts to insult the colonel by characterizing the South as a Sodom.

> "They couldn't wait for whiskey to finish them, as it does
> other barbarous races. They must call on the political
> mountains to crush them. Their slaveholding Sodom will
> perish for the lack of five just men, or a single just idea.
> It must be razed and got out of the way, like any other
> obstacle to the progress of humanity. It must make room
> for something more consonant with the railroad, electric-
> telegraph, printing press, inductive philosophy, and practical
> Christianity." (p. 50)

De Forest is clearly aware of Northern efforts to affix Christianity upon the American social order, and he very carefully points out that had Carter not been in the Union army, he would be, for Dr. Ravenel and most of New England, the aristocratic enemy of American democracy, the oppressor of the weak, and the major obstacle for industrial interests and land speculation. Carter is a threat to Ravenel's daughter because his self-indulgences and lack of Calvinistic morality are dangerous and appealing. Patriotic hysteria, De Forest says, applies judgments of this kind to men like Carter. After all, Carter reminds Northern men and women of their own potential licentious behavior. To clarify this hysteria, De Forest gives one of the first literary descriptions of the manufacture of American mass political consciousness by the media.

> The prevailing subject, as a matter of course, was the
> rebellion. It was everybody's subject; it was the nightmare
> by night and the delirium by day of the American people; it
> was the one thing that no one ignored and no one for
> an hour forgot . . . [I]ndignation was earnest and wide-
> spread in proportion to the civilization of the century and
> the intelligence of the population. The hundreds of
> telegraph lines and thousands of printing presses in the
> United States sent the knowledge of every new treason
> and the reverberation of every throb of patriotic anger in a
> day to all Americans outside of nurseries and lunatic asylums
> (p. 58).

Colburne decides that he cannot fall in love with a Secessionist, and he calls up one of his "strongest *isms*," his patriotism, to help him avoid Lillie. After three days of "taking up the cross of exile" he "gently slides to the conclusion" that he could no longer avoid Lillie's *father*, who has proven to be a most congenial host. Besides, he is convinced that he should never "quarrel with a woman."

He colored to the tips of his repentant ears as he
thought of it and of what Miss Ravenel must think of it
. . . [H]e had lived a life of anguish as a man and a
patriot. Accordingly the old intimacy was resumed, and
the two young people seldom passed forty-eight hours
apart. But of the rebellion they said little, and of Bull Run
nothing. (p. 63)

If he is to quarrel, it will be on the battlefield. He prepares himself for the army after the battle of
Gettysburg, listening to the following verse by Edgar Allan Poe in his mind:

Thank Heaven! the crisis,
    The danger is past,
And the lingering illness
    Is over at last,
And the fever call Living
    Is conquered at last. (pp. 72-73)

Colburne solemnly gets down to business, after repressing his "fever" for Lillie, and raises a
company. All of the North has buckled down to the war, including even Colonel Carter, who
raises a regiment and even befriends Colburne. But Carter is never able to conquer his own "fever
called Living," and Colburne is still in wonder over the colonel's "slanginess and gentility, his
mingled audacity and *insouciance* of character, and all the picturesque ins and outs of his moral
architecture, so different from the severe plainness of the spiritual temples common in New
Boston" (p. 79). Colburne forgives Carter's "frank vices" since the latter has shed his blood for
the right cause and proved himself a brave and capable soldier. Even De Forest makes a small but
subtle apology for Carter's behavior.

I do venture to say that it [the American service] had also
a great many men whose moral habits were cut more or less
on the Carter pattern, who swore after the fashion of the
British army in Flanders, whose heads could carry drink . . .
and who had even other vices concerning which my discreet
pen is silent. (p. 79)

The author's discreet pen, however, is *not* silent on the growing attraction between Lillie and
Carter, and his handling of it is revealed with an unpretentious honesty not seen in American
fiction until the novels of Theodore Dreiser. Chapter eight is crucial, since there the author probes
deeply into the social and sexual polarities between Colburne and Carter. Both men are off to
war, and as Lillie says goodbye to them, De Forest very clearly describes the sexual reactions of
his heroine so that they will determine the rest of the plot. In effect, Colburne becomes the pure
lover, Carter the threatening one, and Lillie is presented as the innocent maiden, drawn physically
to Carter while entertaining, intellectually, the weak blandishments of Colburne. De Forest's
editorials would have us believe that she is duped by the colonel, but his broader artistic vision
undermines that assumption. Note how the discreet De Forest admits Lillie's "curious instinct" at
the beginning of the paragraph, but then quickly tries to "save" her from her sexual desires. Carter
s watching her with his "wide-open, unwinking eyes . . . semi-impertinent" (p. 90).

In obedience *to a curious instinct which exists in at least
some feminine natures, Miss Ravenel liked the Colonel,*
or at least felt that she could like him, just in proportion as
she feared him. A man who can make some women
tremble, can, if he chooses, make them love. Pure and

72

> modest as this girl of eighteen was, she could, and I fear,
> would have fallen desperately in love with this toughened
> worldling, had he, with his despotic temperament, resolutely
> willed it. In justice to her it must be remembered that she
> knew little or nothing about his various naughty ways. In
> her presence he never swore, nor got the worse for liquor,
> nor alluded to scenes of dissipation . . . She thought she
> stated the whole subject fairly when *she admitted that he
> might be "fast" but she had an innocently inadequate
> conception of the meaning* which the masculine sex
> attaches to that epithet. She applied it to him chiefly
> because *he had the monumental self-possession, the
> graceful audacity, the free and easy fluency, the little ways,
> the general air, of certain men in New Orleans* who had
> been pointed out to her as "fast." (p. 91)

As for Colburne, De Forest tells us that he is the only one "in love," yet he restrains himself from giving to Lillie "significant attentions." Colburne must have permission from her to *court* her *before* he will widen *his* eyes with semi-impertinence. His voice may "thrill" Miss Ravenel, and make it "difficult for her to breathe naturally" (p. 94), but there is no denying that De Forest's description of Carter's influence over Lillie is much more potent in its "monumental self-possession." Colburne will spend much of his time during the voyage to war in "meditations" on his dear Miss Ravenel. For Carter, however, it was the woman *in pretty "close personal propinquity"* that counted (p. 109). It is the same for Lillie, despite De Forest's attempts at convincing the reader of her "purity." She needs the close presence of the physical male before she is interested. For Colburne, he was "occupied with his duties to give much thought to an absent Dulcinea." (p. 109)

iii

As Union soldiers push deeper South to discover "a chance for plunder and low dissipation such as most of your simply educated and innocent country lads of New England never before imagined" (p. 123), so the author deepens the dichotomy between Colburne and Carter for a full exposure of Lillie's actual feelings. The Ravenel's have journeyed to New Orleans so that Lillie's father can engage in his humanitarian deeds and proposals for the Christianization of black slaves, and De Forest introduces us to Mrs. Larue in chapter eleven, a character who will appeal to the self-indulgence of Carter, the vulnerability of Lillie, and exemplify the "depravity" of the South. As Lillie's Creole aunt, and, at age 33, she neither belongs to the aristocracy of Louisiana nor to the patriotic camp who share Dr. Ravenel's humanitarian ideals. She is intelligent, practical, and crafty, and she says to Lillie, who has burst into tears after seeing the spoiled gayety of New Orleans:

> "*Cést effrayant*," replied Mrs. Larue. "But you are out of
> fashion to weep. We have given over that feminine
> weakness, *ma chère.* That fountain is dry. The inhumanities
> of these Yankee vandals have driven us into a despair too
> profound for tears. We do not flatter Beast Butler with a
> sob." (p. 129)

When both Colburne and Carter visit the Ravenels and meet Mrs. Larue, Colburne is shocked at her flirtation with Carter, and Carter is careful not to begin an *intrigante*. He knew "she was corrupt, and by the way he liked her none the worse for it, although he would not have married her." (p. 164) Quickly dispensing with a reunion scene between Colburne and Lillie, De Forest makes a sudden but important remark on melodrama.

Of course it would be agreeable to have a scene here between
Colburne and Miss Ravenel; some burning words to tell,
some thrilling looks to describe, such as might show how
they stood with regard to each other -- something which
would visibly advance both these young persons' heart-
histories. But they behaved in a disappointingly well-bred
manner, and entirely refrained from turning their feelings
wrong side outwards . . . *This is not the way that heroes
and heroines meet on the boards or in some romances; but
in actual human society they frequently balk our
expectations in just this manner. Melodramatically
considered real life is frequently a failure.* (p. 137)

De Forest is expressing his impatience with the expectations of his Victorian audience and turning
his back on melodrama, for a moment, in an effort to free his art. From this point on in the novel,
Lillie actually begins to play De Forest's editorial comments about her innocence off her own
desires for Carter.[4] This conflict between De Forest's unconscious perception of Lillie's sexual
impulses, and his fabrication of her innocence, provides a good look at how the sexual responses
of a heroine in American Victorian literature are handled. Wayne Burns has examined this quality
of Victorian novels in his *Charles Reade: A Study in Victorian Authorship.*

The truth is that . . . seeming hypocrisy or pruriency was
neither hypocrisy nor pruriency: it was a form of Victorian
naivete or double-think essential to . . . being a great
Victorian novelist . . . . it can be demonstrated that, with
the exception of George Eliot, nearly all the Victorian
novelists who produced genuine art were "unconscious
writers" -- mainly because, given the conditions of Victorian
authorship, there was no other way for them to let go their
imaginations.[5]

Desiring to be free to talk about Mrs. Larue and Lillie's eventual marriage to Carter, De
Forest prefaces his remarks with several significant passages in chapter twelve. "Double-think" is
operating in the following quote, but the *presence* of Carter and Larue should not be
underestimated.

Captain *Colburne* indulged in a natural expectation that the
kiss which he had laid on Miss Ravenel's hand would
draw him nearer to her and render their relations more
sentimentally sympathetic . . . he had such an exalted
opinion of the young lady's spiritual purity that he *never
thought of believing that she could be influenced by any
simply carnal impulses,* however innocent; and
furthermore he was himself in a too exalted and seraphic
state of feeling to attach much importance to *the mere
motion of the blood* and thrillings of the spinal marrow .
. . . he drifted into certain reveries of conceivable
interviews with the young lady, wherein she and he
gradually and sweetly approximated until matrimony
seemed to be the only natural conclusion. But the next
time he called at the Ravenel house, he found Mrs.
Larue there, and, what was worse, Colonel Carter. Lillie
remembered the kiss . . . I think I am able to assure the

74

reader that in her head the osculation had given birth to no
reveries . . . *she was half angry at him for troubling her
spiritual nature so potently.* (pp. 144-145)

Lillie is, and will continue to be influenced by "simply carnal impulses," and she resents Colburne
for troubling her *mind.* Colburne realizes the nature of the company he is keeping when he feels
alarmed at the "dangerous glitter" of Mrs. Larue's eyes and the freedom of her conversation. He
shrinks to an almost ethereal presence in the chapter. Meanwhile, after listening to Dr. Ravenel's
plans for the labor organization and education of blacks, Carter comes to the conclusion about
Lillie's father:

> *"What an old trump of a Don Quixote!" mused the Colonel
> as he lit his segar* in the street for the walk homeward . . .
> "He hasn't starved long enough to bring him to his milk," he
> thought. "When he gets down to his last dollar, and a
> thousand or two below it, he won't be so particular as to
> how he lines his pockets." (p. 155)

A modest yet less restrictive measure of Lillie's sexual preferences is then given:

> She positively liked the widower, and thought him the
> finest gentleman of the very few who now called on her.
> Captain Colburne was very pleasant, lively and good; but
> -- and here she ceased to reason -- she felt he was not
> magnetic. (p. 159)

In these passages, and as far as De Forest's "discreet pen" will allow, Carter emerges as Burns'
Panzaic character, except that unlike Hardy's Tess and Alec, Lillie and Carter will be sanctioned by
marriage.

In chapter thirteen, feeling he must regain censorship, De Forest resumes his double-think
for Lillie, but leaves Mrs. Larue to escape from it. Larue, who perceives Carter much as he was
and "liked him none the less for it" (p. 159), is used by De Forest to move the plot ahead and
"save" Lillie from her marriage to Carter. De Forest drops his melodrama to even greater degrees
in his descriptions of her, as she, too, emerges a Panzaic character, an even more realistic one than
Carter, since, like Dreiser's Carrie, or Thackeray's Becky Sharp, she is not punished in the end for
her proclivities.

> "Marriage will not content me, nor will single life," she
> said to him one day. "I have tried both, and I cannot
> recommend either. It is a choice between two evils, and one
> does not know to say which is the least." (p. 166)

Almost in direct proportion to the author's sudden and increased supervision of Lillie's feelings is
the relaxation of that mechanism for his characterization of Mrs. Larue. The closer we come to the
consummation of the relationship between Carter and Lillie, the less flexible his definition of
Lillie's innocence becomes.

> "Captain Colburne, you do not like women," she once said.
> "I beg your pardon -- I repel the horrible accusation."
> "Oh, I admit that you like a woman -- this one, perhaps, or
> that one. But it is the individual which interests you and
> not the sex. For woman as woman -- for woman because
> she is woman -- you care little." (p. 203)

Emerging from De Forest's double-think, the Creole, here, breaks from the author's editorializing and undermines the ideals of Colburne's conventional love. Again, with the temporary suspension of melodrama, the Panzaic exploration of a character is unconsciously sought, despite De Forest's interesting complaint at the bottom of the following paragraph.

> . . . . so the rule which guided her [Larue] in the Vanity Fair of this life was, "Wherever you see a man, set your cap at him." . . .To the Colonel she acted the part of Lady Gay Spanker; to the Doctor she was *femme raisonnable*, and, so far as she could be, *femme savante*; to Colburne she of late generally played the female Platonic philosopher. *It really annoys me to reflect how little space I must allow myself for painting the character of this remarkable woman.* (p. 207)

Carter, like Falstaff, has been the more appealing Panzaic character, but Larue, above, like Carker in Dickens' *Dombey and Son* (1848), has become the more calculating one.

The marriage of Colonel Carter and Miss Ravenel has been foreseen by the reader for some time, even while De Forest made slow preparations for it by calling their attraction for one another a "subtle and potent sense which draws the two sexes together . . . an inexorable despot" (p. 182). The groom concludes that he is "honorable in his vices" but tries not to consider himself a "fast man," while the bride has admitted that she knows he is not a good man but that "he could love fervently" (p. 185). With his admonishment that we, as readers, must "admit the power of our passions instead of their direction," De Forest, in chapter seventeen, *almost* suspends melodrama and censorship for a clear and personal admission of the power of Panzaic sexual feeling in Victorian American fiction. Of course the suspension is not complete. We are spared "the particulars" in the following quote, except for Carter's "mighty mustachios" and burning eyes. Note the reversal of opinion on Colburne.

> He could not stay away from her. As soon as he had got his brigade into such order as partially satisfied his stern professional conscience, he obtained a leave of absence for seven days and went to New Orleans. From this visit resulted *one of the most important events that will be recorded in the present history. I shall hurry over the particulars because to me the circumstance is not an agreeable one.* Having from my first acquaintance with Miss Ravenel entertained a fondness for her, *I never could fancy this match of hers with such a dubious person as Colonel Carter,* who is quite capable of making her very unhappy. *I always agreed with her father in preferring Colburne, whose character, although only half developed in consequence of youth, modesty, and Puritan education, is nevertheless one of those germs which promise much beauty and usefulness. But Miss Ravenel,* more emotional than reflective, *was fated to love Carter* rather than Colburne. To her, and probably to most women, *there was something powerfully magnetic in the ardent nature which found its physical expression in* that robust frame, that florid brunette complexion, those *mighty mustachios,* and *darkly burning eyes.*

> The consequence of this visit to New Orleans was a
> sudden marriage. The tropical blood in the Colonel's
> veins drove him to demand it, and the electric potency of
> his presence forced Miss Ravenel to concede it. (pp. 222-
> 23)

Much to De Forest's relief, Mrs. Larue helps his novel recover from what the author sees as a disaster. We find Larue and Carter on a sea voyage to Washington D.C. Their rooms happen to open upon the same passageway and they meet on the deck of the ship. De Forest has decided to bring both Panzaic characters together in an effort to use the instinctual Larue to rescue Lillie from the instinctual Carter.

> Those were perilous hours at evening, when the ship
> swept steadily through a lulling whisper of waters,
> when a trail of foamy phosphorescence, like a
> transitory Milky Way, followed in pursuit, when a
> broad bar of rippling light ran straight out to the setting
> moon, when the decks were deserted except by slumberers,
> and Mrs. Larue persisted in dallying.The temptation of
> darkness, the temptation of solitude, the fever which
> begins to turn sleepless brains at midnight, made this her
> possible hour of coquettish conquest. She varied from
> delicately phrased sentimentalities to hoydenish physical
> impertinences. He was not permitted for five minutes
> together to forget that she was a bodily as well as a spiritual
> presence. (pp. 348-49)

Carter, listening to her quote from Balzac, is speechless, but "wishes for safety." Larue, possessing "vices and virtues" that were "all instinctive, without a taint of education or effort" and "unchecked by conscience or by anything but prudence" is cool and sure in her "coquetries" (p. 350).

> *Carter saw where he was drifting to, and groaned over it
> in spirit,* and made resolutions which he broke in half an
> hour, and rowed desperately against the tide, and then
> drifted again . . . In his efforts to obtain a reconciliation
> Carter succeeded so thoroughly that the scene took place late
> at night, his arm around her waist and his lips touching her
> cheek. You must remember -- charitably or indignantly, as
> you please -- that she was his wife's relative. From this time
> forward *he pretty much stopped his futile rowing against the
> tide. He let Mrs. Larue take the helm and guide him down
> the current of his own emotions* (p. 351)

What happens, according to the hints of such discreet prose, is clear enough, but afterwards Larue says to Carter: "I never shall desire a husband, but *I have a right to claim your love.*" Carter "felt no affection, no gratitude, not even any profound pity" (p. 352). He was "absolutely ashamed of himself." Guilt of this kind, manufactured by De Forest, is completely out of character for Carter, given our knowledge of him throughout the book. Larue has now emerged as the wicked Panzaic character, while Lillie is reshaped for innocence by Carter's remorse and inevitable death in battle. The finale will be Lillie's "sensible" marriage to Colburne.

iv

In the confrontation between Carter and Larue, the author found a way to tag Carter with enough contrived self-pity to remove the reality of his simple Panzaic force; while Larue, whose emotions De Forest tells us are "so mixed that I scarcely know how to assort them" (p. 353), survives as the complicated and unmanageable Panzaic reality. Either De Forest does not have the skill to control his characterization of Larue, (which I doubt, since he gives us some of the most fully rounded female characters in American fiction) or (as I think the case), he is reluctant to pursue her significance as the destroyer of ideals on either side of the war. Whichever course critics choose to explore, they will have to admit that the meeting of Carter and Larue, underneath the conflict of the Civil War, is an important event in American literature, an event that might explain the real "reconciliation" between North and South. As De Forest sees it, instinctual surges are for the sake of respectability; however, he does point out that it was the North which defined what respectable love and politics should be.

The author's melodrama, then, has been suspended for its own survival. And even after the disappearance of naive machinations in Victorian stage plays, American newspapers, radio, television, and popular novels will show what happens to the Carters. In the end, Mrs. Larue quickly places herself in the household of a noted theologian and leading abolitionist before going on to more glittering escapades. Lillie discovers Carter's liaison with Larue and briefly mourns his death before marrying the man "whom she ought always to have loved" (p. 479). The doctor's ideals are upheld as he announces what has become an American political cliché: "The right always conquers because it always becomes the strongest" (p. 461).

The North, indeed, has won, and the last chapter of this novel is glued on with that Victorian paste of triumphal affirmation about Lillie's innocence and Colburne's rightness as a "soldier-citizen." Lillie has abolished the slavery of her instincts to the Carters, but the presence of the Colonel is never forgotten by the reader; and Mrs. Larue's cunning success *and* survival continues to undermine the concluding and purifying paragraphs of many American novels to come.

## Notes

[1] Alexis de Tocqueville, *Democracy in America, Volume II,* (New York: Vintage Books, 1945), p. 215.

[2] John William De Forest, *Miss Ravenel's Conversion From Secession to Loyalty,* (Holt, Rinehart and Winston, Inc., New York, 1955.) All quotations are from this edition, and italics are mine.

[3] Richard Chase, *The American Novel and Its Tradition,* (New York: Doubleday Anchor Books, 1957), p. 41.

[4] Edmund Wilson has said that the lack of melodrama and the unflattering appraisal of Mrs. Larue caused the novel to fail with the prevailing female reading public. He claims De Forest "couldn't make money with romance, yet he couldn't give heat to the relations between men and women." (*Patriotic Gore: Studies in the Literature of the American Civil War,* [New York: Oxford University Press, 1962], p. 671). But we do have "heat" in the relations between Lillie and Carter. Mr. Wilson, I think, underestimates the power of DeForest's discreet pen in chapters eight and fourteen.

[5] Wayne Burns, *Charles Reade: A Study in Victorian Authorship,* (New York: Bookman Associates, 1961), pp. 18-19.

CHAPTER 6

Louis-Ferdinand Céline Novels:
The Indiscreet Glance at the Real from
*Journey to the End of the Night* to *Rigadoon* *

"Ah, Ferdinand . . . as long as you live you will always
search for the secret of the universe in the loins of women!"

(*L'Eglise*).

. . . the female mystery doesn't reside between the thighs,
it's on another wave-length, a much more subtle one

(*Castle to Castle*).

"The psychoanalytic concept of narcissism," says Russell Jacoby in his study *Social Amnesia* (1975), "captures the reality of the bourgeois individual; it expresses the private regression of the ego into the id under the sway of public domination . . . it comprehends the dialectical isolation of the bourgeois individual -- dialectical in that the isolation that damns the individual to scrape along in a private world derives from a public and social one. The energy that is directed toward oneself, rather than toward others, is rooted in society, not organically in the individual . . . . The mechanism of this shift is not the least the society that puts a premium on the hardening of each individual -- the naked will to self-preservation."[1] This *naked will* to self-preservation, this *hardening* of oneself is an apt description of most protagonists in our modern novels.[2] These terms are an especially good description of Céline's main character in his first two novels: the young Ferdinand.

Still creating their storm of interest and influence after fifty years, Céline's *Journey to the End of the Night* (1932) and *Death on the Installment Plan* (1936) are novels that use narrators who express hardened feelings over their crushed ego-ideals and over their careful love choices. Major American scholarship on Céline has not explored the sexual behavior of Céline's characters as closely as it needs to do. Of course there have been important discussions of Céline's views on sex. McCarthy gives us a rather negative assessment of the author's views in his biography *Céline* (1975),[3] as does J. H. Matthews in his book, *The Inner Dream: Céline as Novelist* (1978).[4] In comparing Céline's views on sex to Baudelaire's views in *Journaux intimes*, McCarthy claims that *Journey* shows women as "predatory" (p. 69), that Céline suggests "women need to destroy men because there is a link between female sexuality and cruelty" (p. 69), and that, in the final analysis -- because of the behavior of Musyne and Lola -- "sex turns out to be disgusting" (p. 71) for Ferdinand, reflecting Céline's personal view that the male loses himself in orgasm with a woman because he is "weary" to have done "with himself" (p. 70). J.H. Matthews offers an equally negative view of sex in *Death on the Installment Plan.* He points to several episodes in the novel which support his point that sex "brings no consolation of any kind, no sense of release. It is a heightened form of terror . . . . Ferdinand's sexual contacts revitalize the cliche that represents sex

*This is a revised version of an essay that appears in *Critical Essays On Louis-Ferdinand Céline*, ed. W. K. Buckley (Boston: G.K. Hall & Co., 1989).

as a form of death and likens the ecstasy of orgasm to dying" (p. 77). Gorloge, who early in the novel invites the young Ferdinand to engage her in oral sex, and her theft of a jewel from the young boy's pocket; Gwendoline, the sex partner Ferdinand meets after crossing the Channel, and whom Matthews calls the *vagina dentata*; Nora's desperate actions with Ferdinand at Meanwell College; the astonishing scene between Antoine and Gorloge: all these scenes are examples of what Matthews calls Céline's linking of violence and eroticism. Matthews further maintains that even masturbation is "marked by terrorism" in this novel (p. 79), especially when the boys at the English boarding school cruelly beat and masturbate the retarded Jongkind for getting penalties during a soccer match. Therefore since at "no time in his life has Ferdinand felt capable of trusting women enough to love any of them," masturbation becomes the "significant feature" of his early life (pp. 79-80). "It is a direct expression of his profound need to change his destiny in a world ruled by violence and predatory sexuality, where [Ferdinand] is alternately victim and pariah" (p. 80). One could argue, for example, that Gorloge's seduction of the little Ferdinand is an example of emotional exploitation born out of the economic brutalities that exist between the classes in Paris, or that Antoine's attempt to copulate with Gorloge while Ferdinand and Robert look on and laugh, is an illustration of common but secret sexual hilarities. Yet Ferdinand's laughter, and our mix of laughter and surprise, frees us from pompous judgment, suspends our surprise in humor -- much as Chaucer does in his tales on sex. Furthermore, I believe that Ferdinand's experience with Nora, as I will show, is the exception to what Matthews and McCarthy call the predatory nature of sex in Céline's novels. In fact, his feelings over Nora are very exceptional indeed, for they begin Ferdinand's emotional education, his learning to see women as affirmations of beauty and life.

In *Céline and His Vision* (1967), Erika Ostrovsky sees Céline as debunking sex for a very special reason: "Céline tends to blacken most descriptions" of sexual gratification, but in a "spirit of mockery," because the author "finds this business of 'I lo-o-ve you' vulgar, heavy-handed, and cheaply sentimental."[5] As a result, she says, Céline intends to show us that eroticism is also "quite frequently linked to violence" (p. 53): witness Hilda, the sixteen-year-old, who waits for troop trains in *Castle to Castle*, Frau Frucht, addicted to sexual perversion in *Castle to Castle*, Ferdinand's escape from a brawl with women on board the *Bragueton* in *Journey*, or Céline's comment in *North* that the more cities burn the more crazy for sex women become.[6] Ostrovsky is quick to point out, however, that Céline can be quite positive about sex, can even see sex as regenerative. She points to the author's descriptions of Lola, Molly, Madelon, and Sophie in *Journey*, Nora in *Death on the Installment Plan* and Virginia in *Pont de Londres* -- all characters reflecting, perhaps, Céline's comment in a letter to Eveline Pollet: "I love the physical perfections of women almost to the point of madness. It's a truth I reveal to you. It governs all the others."[7] Moreover, Ostrovsky comments on Céline's astonishingly positive description of Sophie in *Journey* that "if anywhere in Céline's work there is a glimpse of hope and beauty, of sun and joy, it is in the sight of such women . . . only the physical perfection of a woman, an animal, a gesture, can offer affirmation or a momentary respite from horror" (p. 125).

Wayne Burns and Gerald Butler go even further in their positive estimations of Céline's treatment of sex. In his essay "*Journey to the End of the Night* A Primer to the Novel," (from the recently published anthology of essays edited by James Flynn entitled *Understanding Céline* [Seattle, Washington: Genitron Press, 1984]), Burns says that "Through loving the woman's body -- Sophie's, Tania's, Molly's, even Madelon's -- [Ferdinand] comes to love the woman herself. Much as Céline would have disliked having Ferdinand compared with Mellors (Céline once described *Lady Chatterley's Lover* as 'a gamekeeper's miserable prick for six hundred and fifty pages') Ferdinand's attitude towards women is essentially Lawrentian in that he comes to the woman herself through her body" (p. 86), and in *Enfin Céline Vint* (New York: Peter Lang, 1988, p. 50), Burns reminds us of Céline's long "lyrical description" of Sophie in *Journey*.[8] In his essay "The Feeling for Women in Céline and His American Counterparts," (also from *Understanding Céline*), Gerald Butler not only maintains that Céline's view of women is one of adoration when compared to the way women are seen in Miller and Kerouac, but also "that it is *not* true," as Julia Kristeva claims (in her chapter on Céline entitled "Females Who Can Wreck the

Infinite," from her book *Powers of Horror: An Essay on Abjection*)[9] that Céline's fiction "shows all women as of only two kinds: desexualized and delightful on the one hand and sexual and terrifying on the other, so that beauty is what wards off the sexual" (p. 142). "Sophie," Butler says, "is both sexual and, in her sexuality, a miracle of delight for Ferdinand" (p. 142). Her "presence and Ferdinand's reaction to it is enough to give the lie to the 'heroism' of Robinson that is the epitome of that bitterness and 'sense of superiority' and 'heaviness' that the world . . . teaches" (p. 156). And in his essay "The Meaning of the Presence of Lili in Céline's Final Trilogy,"[10] he says that Lili is "put forth in the novels as a guiding light for humanity," that even "her animal qualities, in the positive sense that Céline gives to 'animal'" (and here Butler means Lili is on the same "wave-length" as animals -- she tunes in only those who are helpless) "do not detract from her comparison to a heroine from Dickens, for Lili's 'heart' does not exclude the 'animal' but seems to be profoundly connected with it. If that is so, then all the sexuality of human beings that Céline does not at all present in these novels in a favorable light is not an expression of animality in the sense that Lili is like an animal. Rather, the implication, the message for human beings is that they should have real animality above all by having hearts, as Lili does" (p. 183-84).

These are the important discussions of Céline's view of sexual feeling. My intention here is not to discuss Dr. Destouches' views on sex and love, interesting and shadowy as this topic is turning out to be. (See, for example, Céline's own definition of love and sex in Marc Hanrez's *Céline* [Paris: Gallimard, 1961].)[11] Rather, my intention is two-fold: first, to describe how the young Ferdinand came to feel that women are regenerative, worthy of trust, and beautiful (how he learned about what Ostrovsky, Burns, and Butler are calling the *positive* aspects of sexual experience); and second, how the older Ferdinand came to realize that the sheer naked force of his will and the hardening of his heart would not help him be less narcissistic, would not help him gain sexual satisfaction. My goal is to open a more detailed investigation into those scenes of Céline's novels that describe modern sexual behavior, to look more closely at the sexual needs, desires, and secrets of Céline's characters.

In *Death on the Installment Plan*, young Ferdinand, already hardened to real connection from his brutal experiences in Paris as the son of a mother and father who want him to be a success, retains an erotic fantasy for Nora, the wife of an English school master. He has been sent by his parents to Meanwell College, in England, in order to learn English so that when he returns to Paris he will start his business career off on the right foot. Badgered by an embittered and humiliated father, watching his mother work herself to death in their lace and furniture shop, and seduced by their female customers, Ferdinand is a tight-lipped adolescent, unable to connect with anyone, and full of childhood memories that are violent and sad. He is a classic self-preservative personality who preserves gratification in fantasy. He compliments his fantasies for Nora this way: "I can still see her . . . I can bring back her image whenever I please. At the shoulders her silk blouse forms lines, curves, miracles of flesh, agonizing vision, soft and sweet and crushing . . . . The kid that came around to lap me up had his money's worth on Sunday night . . . But I wasn't satisfied, it was her I wanted . . . . Beauty comes back at you in the night . . . it attacks you, it carries you away . . . it's unbearable."[12] Ferdinand's ego-libido creates Nora as his "object-choice." In one scene, while thinking of Nora, he attacks sentimentality in love. *At the same time*, however, his attack on sentiment exhibits a deep desire for real connection, and this is what gives this novel a complexity rarely found even in our best modern British and American fiction.

> [M]y imagination kept winding me up . . . I devoured
> Nora in all her beauty . . . I'd have taken all her blood, every
> drop . . . Still it suited me better to ravage the bed, to chew
> up the sheets . . . than to let Nora or any other skirt take me
> for a ride . . . To hell with all that stinking mush! . . . Yak!
> yak! I love you. I adore you! Sure, sure! . . . Why worry,
> it's a party. Bottoms up! It's so lovely! It's so innocent!
> I'd wised up when I was a kid! Sentiment, hell! Balls! . . .

I clutched my oil can . . . You won't catch me dying like a
sucker . . . with a poem on my lips (pp. 239-40).

When Nora does, at last, come to Ferdinand's room, out of her own mad loneliness and
lack of connection to her husband, and abruptly flattens him out with her caresses, giving him, as
Céline says, "an avalanche of tenderness," young Ferdinand does surprisingly well in responding.
In bed with her he is beginning to reject, I believe, his narcissism -- if only for a moment:

> I try to soothe her pain, to make her control herself . . . I
> caulk wherever I can . . . I knock myself out . . . I try my
> best . . . I try the subtlest tricks . . . But she's too much for
> me . . . She gives me some wicked holds . . . The whole bed
> is shaking . . . She flails around like crazy . . . I fight like a
> lion . . . My hands are swollen from clutching her ass! I
> want to anchor her, to make her stop moving. There. That's
> it. She's stopped talking. Christ almighty! I plunge, I slip
> in like a breeze! I'm petrified with love . . . I'm one with her
> beauty . . . I'm in ecstasy . . . I wriggle . . . On her face I go
> looking for the exact spot next to her nose . . . the one that
> tortures me, the magic of her smile" (p. 266).

In feeling "love," and in "looking for the exact spot" which tortures him, Ferdinand
replaces his fantasy of Nora with her reality. Unfortunately Nora "breaks loose" from Ferdinand,
and runs from the school to make her way to a bridge, where she will jump into a river to her
death, a "nightgown fluttering in the wind" (p. 267). This whole scene is charged with all the
helpless desperation of human behavior. "I knew it," says Ferdinand, "she's off her rocker! . . .
Dammit to hell . . . Could I catch her? . . . But it's none of my business . . . There's nothing I can
do . . . The whole thing is beyond me . . . I listen . . . I look out through the hall door . . . to see if
I can see her on the waterfront . . . She must be down by now . . . There she is again . . . still
screaming . . . "Ferdinand! Ferdinand!" . . . her screams cut through the sky . . ." (p. 267). It is
Céline's intention, as Wayne Burns has pointed out in *Understanding Céline*, "to make the reader
hear cries he has never heard before; to make him realize that there is no end to these cries (in either
time or circumstance), for they are cries which cannot be remedied by religion or philosophy or
morality -- much less by the paltry palliatives of social reform or even social revolution."[13]

Ferdinand does go after her, but feels helpless and endangered as he stands on the bridge
with the retarded boy both he and Nora had been taking care of at the school. We hear more of her
pleas as she "flits" like a "butterfly" from one street lamp to the next. Sirens and whistles blow,
rescue squads arrive, but nothing has helped. She is a "little white square in the waves . . . caught
in the eddies . . . passing the breakwater!" (p. 268). It is Céline's intention, as he later has
Ferdinand say in *Journey to the End of the Night*, "to go deeper and hear other cries that I had not
heard yet or which I had not been able to understand before, because there seems always to be
some cries beyond those which one has heard."[14] This need to hear the "cries" of humanity is not
the impulse of a narcissist, for he is not, as Freud says in "On Narcissism: An Introduction"
(1914), "plainly seeking" himself "as a love-object."[15] Nor is Ferdinand seeking a Nora as males
would seek women to "save," those who would fulfill the male's desire to believe that "without
him she would lose all hold on respectability."[16] Even though Nora's behavior could trigger the
narcissistic impulse in Ferdinand to rescue her, "justified by her untrustworthy temperament
sexually and by the danger to her social position" (as Freud put it), it does not do so, neither in
fantasy nor in reality.[17] For there has been no "skill in argument" to win Nora, to save her from
Meanwell College, no real education on Ferdinand's part. In fact, his *self-preservative* impulse
remains defiant and hostile after her death, for he fears he will take the rap for it. Freud has it that
"the attitude of defiance in the 'saving' phantasy far outweighs the tender feeling in it, the latter
being usually directed towards the mother . . . in the rescue phantasy, that is, he identifies himself

completely with the father. All the instincts, the loving, the grateful, the sensual, the defiant, the self-assertive and independent -- all are gratified in the wish to be *the father of himself*. . . . When in a dream a man rescues a woman from the water, it means that he makes her a mother . . . his own mother."[18] Yet Nora is not rescued. The drowning is no *phantasy.* And Ferdinand, after hearing Nora's cries and feeling he was sure to get caught and blamed, runs back to the school to wake Nora's old husband out of his own torpor. The scene we see then is painful: the old man, drunk on the floor, and Ferdinand, observing, and finally giving up, leaving to pack his bags for Paris "at the crack of dawn" (p. 269).

Despite the suicide, both Nora and Ferdinand had freed themselves, momentarily, from their environments, fixed as they were to their economic realities: Ferdinand to his petit-bourgeois Paris background and Nora to her bankrupt English middle class. Without moralizing or sentimentalizing their encounter, Céline shows us Nora and Ferdinand achieving a moment of difficult tenderness. "It seems very evident," Freud says in "On Narcissism," that "one person's narcissism has a great attraction for those others who have renounced part of their own narcissism and are seeking after object-love."[19] As an adult, Nora has rejected part of her narcissism, and a kind of vulnerable, nervous, but tender compassion remains. She is no Madame Gorloge, who *orders* Ferdinand to take his clothes off and make love to her. "She grabs me by the ears . . . She pulls me down to mother nature . . . She bends me with all her might . . . 'Bite me, sweet little puppy . . . Bite into it!'" (p. 180). Ferdinand *plays* "the ardent lover," and charges into her, as he had seen Antoine do when he and Robert were spying on them, "but much more gently" (p. 181). "She squashed me against her tits! She was having a hell of a good time . . . It was stifling . . . She wanted me to work harder . . . to be more brutal . . . 'you're ripping me apart, you big thug! Oh rip me' . . ." (p. 181). Ferdinand did not have to play the "ardent lover" with Nora; nor could their lovemaking be called "ripping." She was not, as he characterized Gorloge, a "vampire" (p. 181). She was a "mirage of charm" (p. 241). Neither was Nora a Gwendoline, Ferdinand's "Greasy Jone" (p. 212), the English fish and chips girl he meets on the docks before finding Meanwell College. "She kept repeating her name. She tapped on her chest . . . Gwendoline! Gwendoline! . . . I heard her all right, I massaged her tits, but I didn't get the words . . . to hell with tenderness . . . sentiment! That stuff is like a family . . . She took advantage of the dark corners to smother me with caresses . . . We could have done our business, we'd certainly have had a good time . . . But once we'd had our sleep out, then what?" (pp. 212, 214). "Anyway I was too tired . . . And besides, it was impossible . . . It stirred up my gall . . . it cramped my cock to think of it . . . of all the treachery of things . . . as soon as you let anybody wrap you up . . . "That's all I had on my mind in the little side streets while my cutie was unbuttoning me . . . She had the grip of a working girl, rough as a grater, and not at all bashful. Everybody was screwing me. O well . . ." (p. 215).

Rather, when Ferdinand sees Nora for the first time, he is astonished at his reaction to the *gentleness* in her face: "the special charm she had, that lit up on her face when she was speaking . . . It intimidated me . . . I saw stars, I couldn't move" (p. 224). Ferdinand's narcissism is under attack by such powerful gentleness, tenderness, and charm because it is responding to it, needing it, and weakened by it in its self-preservative inner life. For all through the Meanwell College scene, Nora will be tending to the needs of a helpless retarded boy. And even though Ferdinand's young narcissism is interested in the idealized Nora -- the Nora of his dreams, the picture of her which helps him adjust to his bitterness -- he still responds, physically to *her*. This is especially remarkable when you consider Ferdinand's characterization of himself earlier in the novel: "you'll never know what obsessive hatred really smells like . . . the hatred that goes through your guts, all the way to your heart . . . Real hatred comes from deep down, from a defenseless childhood crushed with work. That's the hatred that kills you" (p. 144). Even more remarkable, is the fact that Ferdinand gets a bit of compassion from Nora, learns from her, as he too walks with the retarded boy Jongkind, who "whines like a dog" after Nora's death.

> I got to get the brat home . . . I give him a poke in the ass
> . . . He's worn out from running . . . I push him . . . I
> throw him . . . He can't see a thing without his glasses . . .
> He can't even see the lamp posts. He starts bumping into
> everything . . . He whines like a dog . . . I grab him and
> pick him up, I carry him up the hill . . . I toss him into his
> bed . . . I run to the old man's door . . . He blinks a little,
> his eyelids flutter . . . He don't know from nothing . . .
> 'She's drowning! She's drowning!' I yell at him. I repeat
> it even louder . . . I shout my lungs out . . . I make motions
> . . . I imitate the glug-glug . . . I point down . . . into the
> valley . . . out the window! (pp. 268-69)

Ferdinand's heart and naked self-will are now less hardened to women, and to those who are victims of biology, despite the memories of his defenseless childhood.

In *Journey to the End of the Night*, Ferdinand the adult is an eloquent spokesman of revulsion from European colonialism and modern warfare, the voice of revulsion from our traditional beliefs in brotherhood, marriage, and love. He does not believe in our modern love, which is, for him, a "poodle's chance of attaining the infinite" (p. 4). His travels in the novel from the front lines of World War I, to Paris, to New York City and Detroit, to Africa, and back to Paris, have given him an anti-idealistic view of human behavior. "The great weariness of life," he says near the end of the novel, "is maybe nothing but the vast trouble we take to remain always for twenty or forty or more years at a time reasonable beings -- so as not to be merely and profoundly oneself, that is to say, obscene, ghastly, and absurd" (p. 416). His first relationship with a woman in this novel is with Lola, an American nurse who believes in the existence of the soul and in patriotism, and it is a relationship characterized by a weariness because Ferdinand believes only in survival after coming home from the war. The understanding between them is of the body not the heart because the hardened heart cannot be trusted during war time. At first he accepts Lola for what she is, and this is even more of a step forward for his self-preservative personality, even less narcissistic than his relationship with Nora, for he no longer needs to see the female body in idealized images: "If I had told Lola what I thought of the war, she would only have taken me for a depraved freak and she'd deny me all intimate pleasures. So I took good care not to confess these things to her . . . she hadn't only a fine body, my Lola, -- let us get that quite clear at once; she was graced also with a piquant little face and grey-blue eyes, which gave her a slightly cruel look, because they were set a were bit on the upward slant, like those of a wildcat" (pp. 49-50). When Ferdinand does not admit that he is not going back to the front, Lola leaves him, furious at his lack of ideals, and returns to New York. But when Ferdinand arrives in New York, he meets Lola again.

> she inquired after my genital lapses and wanted to know if I
> hadn't somewhere on my wanderings produced some little
> child she could adopt. It was a curious notion of hers. The
> idea of adopting a child was an obsession with her . . . . what
> she wanted was to sacrifice herself entirely to some "little
> thing." I myself was out of luck. I had nothing to offer her
> but my own large person, which she found utterly repulsive.
> (pp. 216-17)

"Really, it's a pity, Ferdinand," Lola says, "that you haven't a little girl somewhere . . . your dreamy temperament would go very well in a woman, whereas it doesn't seem at all fitting in a man . . ." (p. 217). This is an interesting description of female narcissism, to which Ferdinand responds with some of his own. Lola's attitude toward Ferdinand is cool, but now she has found a way of object-love: through a child she could possess the ideal of what she thinks Ferdinand should be. The desire Lola has for Ferdinand is not based on a need to tend him, nor is the desire Ferdinand has for Lola based on a need to protect her. There is, therefore, no *anaclitic* object-choice here. Rather, Lola looks at Ferdinand as a lover who should be what she wants him to be. And Ferdinand looks at Lola as a source for adventure in America. Her body to him was an endless source of joy because of its "American contours" (p. 49); she is "a type" that appeals to him (p. 193). Only when Lola gives him money and he takes off for Detroit to work in the Ford plant, do we see a strong and more radical change in Ferdinand's desires for women. The mechanisms involved in his new object-choice -- Molly, the Detroit prostitute -- are now *more* anaclitic than narcissistic, more dependent than independent, and not so much concerned about being with an "American type." And although Ferdinand's relationship with Molly shows remarkable similarities with Freud's description of male love for the *grande amoureuse* (especially when Freud describes the childhood experiences, the mother-complex, and youthful masturbatory practices of those who have "love for a harlot"),[20] I believe that the following remarks show Ferdinand freeing himself of narcissistic self-absorption, and combining, if only for a time, his feelings of sex *and* tenderness, despite the fact that he is eventually fonder of his longing to "run away from everywhere in search of something" (p. 228).

> I soon felt for Molly, one of the young women in this place, an emotion of exceptional trust, which in timid people takes the place of love. I can remember, as if I'd seen her yesterday, her *gentleness and her long white legs*, marvelously lithe and muscular and noble (p. 227, emphasis added).

> "Don't go back to the works!" Molly urged me, making it worse. "Find some small job in an office instead . . . Translating, for example; that's really your line . . . you like books . . . ." She was very sweet giving me this advice; she wanted me to be happy . . . if only I'd met Molly . . . . Before I lost my enthusiasm over that slut of a Musyne and that horrid little bitch Lola!? (p. 228)

At the end of the Detroit chapter, we begin to understand the causes of Ferdinand's narcissism, and his possible solutions for his troubles:

> Molly had been right. I was beginning to understand what she meant. Studies change you, they make a man proud. Before, one was only hovering around life. You think you are a free man, but you get nowhere. Too much of your time's spent dreaming. You slither along on words. That's not the real thing at all. Only intentions and appearances. You need something else. With my medicine, though I wasn't very good at it, I had come into closer contact with men, beasts, and creation. Now it was a question of pushing right ahead, foursquare, into the heart of things. (p. 239)

No longer do we have a character at the mercy of narcissism -- like the young Ferdinand -- because the narcissist would never want to plunge "into the heart of things." Rather, the adult Ferdinand sees conventional love (i.e., ego-centric romantic love) as doomed to fail in a world where so many people have to scrape and crawl just to get by, in a world where Nature's lessons are hard to swallow. "To love is nothing, it's hanging together that's so hard . . . All our unhappiness is due to having to remain Tom, Dick, and Harry, cost what it may, throughout a whole series of years" (p. 335). And near the end of *Journey,* when Ferdinand visits a bistro for some cheap fun, living, as he says, a "capitalist's existence without capital" (p. 360), we hear him comment with irony and compassion on a female singing group from England, who are bawling out their little songs of love: "They were singing the defeat of life and they didn't see it. They thought it was only love, nothing but love; they hadn't been taught the rest of it, little dears . . ." (p. 361). Ferdinand finally realizes that conventional love, the kind we see today everywhere in American culture, richly narcissistic as it is, fails to help anyone -- especially him.

What *would* help he tried to describe for us at the end of the novel, after seeing the death of his friend Robinson at the hands of a romantic lover. Ferdinand says about himself that he is just "a quite real Ferdinand who lacked what might make a man greater than his own trivial life, a love for the life of others" (p. 501). This "love for the life of others" is not at all narcissistic, and it is the kind of love which the young Ferdinand began to achieve when he took Jongkind back to the school the night Nora died, and when he banged on the door to tell Nora's drunken husband that she was dying. It is the kind of love which would allow death to be

> imprisoned in love along with joy, and so comfortable would it be inside there, so warm, that Death, the bitch, would be given some sensation at last and would end up by having as much fun with love as every one else. Wouldn't that be pretty? Ah, wouldn't that be fine? I laughed about it, standing there alone on the river bank, as I thought of all the dodges and all the tricks I'd have to pull off to stuff myself like that full of all-powerful resolves . . . . A toad swollen out with ideals! (p. 505)

But Ferdinand dismisses even these ideas as hopelessly idealistic for a man like him.

What *does* help him are not resolves, but what he finds in Sophie, the Slovak nurse who works at the lunatic asylum with him. In his relationship with Sophie, I believe, we see a man nearly free of narcissism. For Sophie is a woman "who still from time to time caught me to her, her whole body strong with the strength of her concern for me and tenderness and a heart full also and overflowing lovely. I felt the directness of it myself, the *directness of her tender strength*" (p. 507, emphasis added). Male narcissism could never feel the directness of *tender strength* in a woman's body, the kind of strength Ferdinand now finds that he desires to have not only for himself, but also for women. It is this tender strength in a woman's body, this sex-tenderness and a full heart, which can ease the hardened heart and cruel naked self-will of a man.

I have been looking at scenes that show Ferdinand as an individual seeking meaning and sexual fulfillment. Yet there are other kinds of scenes in Céline's novels that do not emphasize individual sexual action, but rather mass sexual action. These scenes are astonishing in their impact, and they need further study -- for they show Céline as a keen observer of herd psychology. Questions, therefore, remain to be answered.

For example, what is the function of Céline's *délire*[21] and exaggeration in the episode from *Death on the Installment Plan*, where, in the Bois de Boulogne, Ferdinand and Mireille make love in public, and an orgy of sexual chaos moves and surges a crowd up to the Arc de Triomphe where they are routed by "twenty-five thousand" policemen (pp. 35-39)? Or what is the meaning of the scene in *Guignol's Band* where Virginia and Ferdinand are swept up in a chaos of orgy violence, and delight in the night club, where people are copulating in a jumble of arms and legs? There are similar scenes of mass delight in *North* and *Castle to Castle*. Are these "little narcissistic eccentricities," as Céline labels his writing in *Guignol's Band*? Or are they scenes which tell us to "Palpitate, damn it! That's where the fun is! . . . Wake up! Come on, hello! You robot crap! . . . Shit! . . . Transpose or it's death! I can't do any more for you. Kiss any girl you please! I there's still time!"[22] Perhaps these mass scenes expose the flimsiness of even our mos sophisticated ideas about love, or perhaps they speak of what Céline thought to be some ancient longing in sex, the "quite bestial act" of it, as he said.[23] Ferdinand (and later Céline himself in his World War II trilogy) are both swept up by such sights and crowds in every one of the novels -- as if this author, as a physician, wants us to understand that he sees impulses which repeat themselves on a huge scale, as if all of human life is joyously trapped into having such feelings out of the sheer biological surgings of the species, as well as out of our small motivations, brutalized as they are by war and stupid economies. Witness this description from *Castle to Castle*, where in a railway station, Céline's favorite locale for the mob's sexual *délire*, we see that:

> sadness, idleness, and female heat go together . . . and not just kids! . . . grown women and grandmothers! obviously the hottest ones, with fire in their twats, in those moments when the page turns, when History brings all the nuts together and opens its Epic Dance Halls! . . . you've got to have phosphorus and hunger so they'll rut and sperm and get with it without paying attention! pure happiness! no more hunger, cancer, or clap! . . . the station packed with eternity![24]

Are these scenes of mass erotic action in direct conflict with Ferdinand's lessons about tenderness? Or do they, then, in their juxtaposition with Ferdinand's raptures, for example, over Sophie, show us the value of individual, sexual tenderness in the face of "History"?

More comment is also needed on the intriguing relationship between what Ferdinand enjoys about women (their astonishing bodies, their compassion and intelligence, their ability to have orgasms, and their "wave-lengths"), and what Céline says about sex for men ("it allows a guy a few seconds delirium which permits him to communicate with her").[25] How do we square Céline's striking portraits of what women have to offer men with this statement from *Rigadoon* (1969):

> all our theater and literature revolve around coitus, deadly repetition! . . . the orgasm is boring, the giants of the pen and silver screen with all the ballyhoo and the millions spent on advertising . . . have never succeeded in putting it across . . . two three shakes of the ass, and there it is . . . the sperm does its work much too quietly, too intimately, the whole thing escapes us . . . but childbirth, that's worth looking at! . . . examining! . . . to the millimeter! fucking . . . God knows I've wasted hours! . . . for two three wiggles of the ass![26]

And lastly, careful analysis is needed on the relationship between what we see as the positive aspects of sexuality in Céline, what Burns calls "the essentially Lawrentian attitude" Ferdinand gains in coming to the woman, and Céline's personal comment that "(coitus is delirium): to rationalize that delirium with precise verbal maneouvers seems to me silly."[27] Perhaps Céline sees deeper than my critical phrase "positive aspects of sexuality" -- a "precise verbal maneouver" if ever I could invent one. Just how deeply and broadly Céline sees can be detected as early as 1916, the date he wrote a poem for his parents in his early twenties while traveling to Africa. Even at this early date we see that Céline's vision of sexuality is much like the "town crier's," who remains perched in a minaret:

> Stamboul est endormi sous la lune blafarde
> Le Bosphore miroite de mille feux argentés
> Seul dans la grande ville mahométane

Le vieux crieur des heures n'est pas encore couché --

Sa voix que l'écho répète avec ampleur
Announce à la ville qu'il est déjà dix heures
Mais par une fenêtre, de son haut minaret
Il plonge dans une chambre, son regard indiscret

Il reste un moment, muet, cloué par la surprise
Et caresse nerveux, sa grande barbe grise
Mais fidèle au devoir, il assure sa voix[28]

This indiscreet glance, which plunges into a bedroom, and yet remains mute, frozen with surprise, is a remarkable description of our reaction to the sexual scenes we see in Céline's works, the young Ferdinand's sights of sex behavior in *Death on the Installment Plan*, and the eventual mature view of sexual behavior in the later novels. In fact, Céline's technique as an author rests on the *indiscreet glance* at the *real*, the real that dances, always, under the ideal. For as an author Céline continues to sing that our odd sun rises, despite what he has seen either in or out of his *délire*, and no matter how many times "History brings all the nuts together and opens its Epic Dance Halls." At every reading of his novels, Céline continues to plunge us "into the heart of things."

## Notes

1 Russell Jacoby, *Social Amnesia* (Boston: Beacon Press, 1975), p. 44.

2 Works by Dickens, Hardy, Lawrence, Joyce, Woolf, Forster, Sartre, Döblin, Musil, Faulkner, Hemingway, Fitzgerald, Miller, Kerouac, Roth, Mailer, Kesey, Pynchon, and E.M. White all contain protagonists who are particularly narcissistic.

3 Patrick McCarthy, *Céline* (New York: Penguin Books, 1975).

4 J.H. Matthews, *The Inner Dream: Céline as Novelist* (New York: Syracuse University Press, 1978).

5 Erika Ostrovsky, *Céline and His Vision* (New York: New York University Press, 1967), p. 53.

6 Ostrovsky, p. 54; Matthews, p. 136.

7 Letter to Eveline Pollet, February 1933, *L'Herne*, No. 3, p. 96.

8 *Journey to the End of the Night* (New York: New Directions, 1934), pp. 475-76.

9 Trans., Leon S. Roudiez (New York: Columbia University Press, 1982).

10 James Flynn, ed., *Understanding Céline* (Seattle, WA: Genitron Press, 1984).

11 Sexual gratification is "a bonus which nature gives to coitus and reproduction: it allows a guy a few seconds' delirium which permits him to communicate with her" (Marc Hanrez, "Céline au magnétophone," *Le Nouveau Candide* [November 23, 1961]), p. 14. Quoted from Ostrovsky, p. 198. Love is "feeling, it's an act, my God! Quite bestial -- and, naturally, bestial it has to be! Warding it off with little flowers seems to me crass. Bad taste, precisely, is putting flowers where none are really needed . . . . You go into a delirium (coitus is a delirium): to rationalize that delirium with precise verbal maneouvers seems to me very silly" (Hanrez, *Céline*, p. 275). Quoted in Matthews, p. 75.

12 Translated by Ralph Manheim (New York: New Directions, 1966), p. 239. It should be noted here that Céline's *points de suspension* are retained in these quotes. I have used four periods when omitting one or more sentences.

13 Flynn, ed., *Understanding Céline*, p. 41.

14 Translated by John H.P. Marks (New York: New Directions, 1934), p. 265.

15 Sigmund Freud, "On Narcissism: An Introduction (1914)," J. Richman, ed., *A General Selection from the Works of Sigmund Freud* (New York: Liveright Publishing Corp., 1957), p. 112.

16 Freud, "A Special Type of Object Choice Made by Men (1910)," P. Rieff, ed., *Sexuality and the Psychology of Love* (New York: Collier Books, 1963), p. 52. My intention in bringing in Freud's discussion of narcissism is not to set up the lack of narcissism as an ideal, but to look at its workings in undermining ideal love.

17 Freud, p. 52.

18 Freud, pp. 56-57.

19 Freud, "On Narcissism," p. 113.

20 Freud, "A Special Type of Object Choice Made by Men (1910)," pp. 51 and 54-56.

21 See Allen Thiher's *Céline: The Novel as Delirium* (New Brunswick, NJ: Rutgers University Press, 1972).

22 Céline, *Guignol's Band* (New York: New Directions, 1954), pp. 4-5.

[23] See footnote eleven.

[24] Translated by Allen Thiher, footnote 21, p. 186.

[25] See footnote eleven.

[26] Céline, *Rigadoon* (New York: Delacorte Press, 1969), pp. 195-96.

[27] In *Céline's Imaginative Space* (Peter Lang, 1987), Jane Carson feels that Céline does not present women as saviors, or that Ferdinand can gain anything from them.

[28] L. des Touches, "Gnomography," *Cahiers Céline 4. Lettres et premiers écrits d'Afrique, 1916-17.* Ed., Jean-Pierre Dauphin (Paris: Gallimard, 1978), p. 79.

PART IV

CONCLUSION

# CHAPTER 7: CONCLUSION:

## The Unpredictable Classroom

> The obsession with symbolization is
> at bottom expressive of the reactionary
> idealism that now afflicts our literary
> life and that passes itself off as a strict
> concern with aesthetic form.
>
> (Philip Rahv)[1]
>
> [The novel] won't let you tell
> didactic lies.
>
> (D. H. Lawrence)[2]

### i

My intention in this volume has never been to provide a comprehensive theory of contextualist criticism or a finished description of it; in fact, such an aim may be too inflexible when confronted with the lively and unpredictable dynamics of the classroom. Borrowing phrases from Stephen C. Pepper's chapter on "Contextualism" in his *World Hypotheses* (1970), I will say, however, that the "structure of the verifying event" [what goes on in the classroom] "is an integration of contributions coming partly from the operations of the hunter" [the teacher] "and partly from continuous physical textures" [students and their fresh experiences.][3] Contextualism in the classroom works outward from the center of that clash between a novel and student, and it seeks to verify the integrity of unpredictable illumination because as a methodology it "is very definite about the present event and the premonitions it gives of neighboring events, but less and less definite about the wider structure of the world. It is willing to make more or less speculative wagers about the wider structures of the world. But if anyone pushes a contextualist hard, he retires into his given event and the direct verification he makes from it."[4] If someone is inclined to push me too hard, I will, as a hunter, retire to the given event of my reactive classroom, where is found the "comprehensiveness" of my approach. So consistent I am in doing this, so much of an intellectual gambler I am forced to be by the present event, that when I rely on the real connections students make with a book, I find myself upholding their lives as individuals against frozen ideology, against that "Significant Form" of the novel that academia now hunts for so strangely and seriously. My position should not be mistaken for the decentering of text, teacher, and reader, even though I emphasize the workings of the *present event* [decentering is a way of forcing text, teacher, and student to float independently in an alienated world where no visceral connection is possible: this is the current thought in so-called "reader-response" theory.][5] Nor should my position be mistaken for flabby relativism. Teachers know that opinions are part social, part personal, and part textual, and that "re-writings" of novels by defensive students are not likely to gain support ("How to find a good job" is not the theme of *Lady Chatterley's Lover.*) I am affirming *raw and informed connection* -- acts so clouded by theory today that when a human being dares believe he can utter such an "old-fashioned" thing as a meaningful response he is reduced by the critic to a ghost in his desk. So heavy is the abstract stone that has been rolled into the classroom and lowered over the genuine responses of our students that not even D.H. Lawrence could have envisioned how thoroughly *flat* our critical thought has become. Dominant academic culture in Europe and America proclaims as proven those premises that actually beg questions: one of our best minds says that literature is "fiction not because it somehow refuses to acknowledge 'reality'; but because it is not a priori certain that language functions according to the principles which are those, or which are *like* those, of the phenomenal world. It is therefore not *a priori* certain that literature is a reliable source of information about anything but its own language."[6] If we focus on the limitation of language then much the same could be said for any branch of knowledge. I simply don't know of any teacher who would spend class time telling his students that novels and student responses cannot happen according to a priori principles of the phenomenal world. In 1955 Philip Rahv described this kind of thinking as the attempt to "overcome the felt reality of art, to purge the novel of its gross immediacy and direct empirical expressiveness."[7] Rumbling underneath such gloomy views of life at school is *the classroom*, with its fresh dynamics and its eager and merciful willingness to throw off the "winding sheets" of abstract theory. That our classrooms will be permanently walled up into the tomb of the eternal "missed encounter"[8] is not very likely, especially since good classroom discussions are always too visceral for cagey thinking. There is too much unpredictable life in the *salle de classe*, too much surprise, too many obstinate and solid human beings undermining the idealism of literary criticism. Focusing on what he lives as he reads, the reader will, on many occasions, save the teacher from the fallacy of reducing him to a theory.[9]

ii

Empirical connections to literature are often made by my students, when they contextualize their feelings and ideas in D.H. Lawrence's novels. I offer the following tape-recorded session as an example.

Buckley: "Here is Lawrence from his *Psychoanalysis and the Unconscious and Fantasia of the Unconscious*, which might help us with our discussion of *John Thomas and Lady Jane*.

'It is time to drop the word love, and more than time to drop the ideal of love. Every frenzied individual is told to find fulfilment in love. So he tries. Whereas, there is no fulfilment in love. Half of our fulfilment comes *through* love, through strong, sensual love. But the central fulfilment, for a man, is that he possess his own soul in strength within him deep and alone. The deep, rich aloneness, reached and perfected through love. And the passing beyond any further *quest* of love.

This central fullness of self-possession is our goal, if goal there be any. But there are two great *ways* of fulfilment. The first, the way of fulfilment through complete love, complete passionate, deep love. And the second, the greater, the fulfilment through the accomplishment of religious purpose, the soul's earnest purpose. We work the love way falsely, from the upper self, and word it to death. The second way, of active unison in strong purpose, and in faith, this we only sneer at.'[10]

Jane: "Wow, that turns everything on its head, doesn't it?"

Mary: "Who is John Thomas? A symbol?"

(laughter)

[My students are quickly asking me for stage directions. While Jane wants institutional support from me for her insight, Mary, who has not read the introductory notes to the Penguin edition of the novel, is symbol-hunting. I am reluctant to respond to them because I don't know how deeply they are reacting. Usually such rapid-fire questions indicate anxiety, and a wish for the teacher to give them the goods, the correct answers to their defensive quizzes. I give a perfunctory answer.]

Buckley: "John Thomas and Lady Jane are English slang terms for the male and female genitals. The 'Publisher's Notes' give you the story behind them."

Jeff: "Well, first of all, I don't understand Connie's marriage to Clifford. There is something holding her, and she says there is, though she doesn't know what it is. What is it? Sympathy?"

Laura: "No, there's this wild way we go and then there's the way society goes; there are, like, set rules to love that society has, and then there is this *wild* way -- all this is confusing her! She wants to get away from Clifford, but feels obligated."

Jeff: "Well, doesn't Laura, I mean Lawrence, say love starts with desire? And desire is sometimes stronger than responsibility. Isn't it?"[11]

Buckley: "I would agree."

[Here Jeff suddenly assumes the role of lead questioner for the class, a role that Jane has dropped. The class waits in silence for my answer, and, although I could have waited for other students to have jumped in, as I did after Jane's question, I respond, partly because I wanted to pick up on the tension in the class over the issue of desire as something in conflict with responsibility, and partly because I felt obligated to get some kind of contextual awareness going over the relationship between the novel and Jeff's feelings.]

Mary: "But Parkin and Connie have nothing in common! How could it be for Connie between desire and responsibility? I mean, how much can you talk about chickens?"

[An open discussion on whether Connie's feelings for Clifford are based on guilt, hate, or responsibility could be launched; however, Mary's remarks, coming as they do after Jeff's description of desire being stronger than responsibility, can either be taken by me as defensive, trivial, or genuine. I don't stop to figure this out; instead I open the novel to the passage where Connie is holding a chick in her hand, read the description of Parkin's sudden and unexpected rush of desire and Connie's response to it, and then offer a personal anecdote. Perhaps Lawrence's words, at this point, will free Mary's trivialization from its aggressiveness and illumine her raw search for understanding the clash between her own desires and responsibilities. Whether Mary's "aggression" is alleviated is not the immediate point, however. What matters is that together the students and I create that strange contextual space for the novel, so that it can breathe there, and maintain its strength and integrity against projection, radical rewriting, or resistance.][12]

Jane: "See, you're just not getting it, Mary. Connie let her physical side go with Parkin, but then her mind would take over again. Clifford could get his revenge on her with his *words*, and that was his power over Connie -- or at least he tried to get power that way.

[I had been hoping that Jane would return to her opening remark about the passage I had read at the beginning of the class. She didn't, and since I am still not sure how serious she was, I decide once again not to return to it, but hope that the class will eventually forage its way back to what I considered a good remark.]

Jeff: "Was Clifford jealous of Connie's satisfaction with Parkin?"

Jane: "Obviously!"

Laura: "Yeah! It's like the people who have true life *can't* help those who are dead. You have to do it yourself, you have to go out and re-live yourself. The ones who have done that, like Parkin, can't help the ones who haven't."

98

(silence)

[Pauses in conversation can either mean that classes are struggling with what has just been said and need time to reflect, or they can mean that nobody else has anything to say -- that the group has reached what they want as a dead end. Without making any qualifying or introductory remarks, I take advantage of the silence to read another passage from the novel in order to try to do three things: 1. surcharge the atmosphere with the intensity of new feelings that I hope the text will bring; 2. anchor future discussions *to the text*, and 3. illustrate the tension between desire and responsibility which the class has not adequately confronted. Maybe, I think, the class will find a way back either today or the next to Jane's opening remark about how Lawrence "turns everything on it's head."]

"He's got a nice body. But you can't go down among those who have to be servants, or wage-earners, and who are under all the rest of the bosses. Parkin is far away down below Mr. Linley -- and Mrs. Linley; they'd both order him about, and he'd more or less have to obey. -- How could he be your husband? Supposing you heard Mrs. Linley giving him orders . . . "

"Yet," she said, "he is so wonderful! There's something a bit starry about him."

"What?" said Hilda. "What is starry?"

"His body! even his penis! You don't know, Hilda, how strange it is, like a little god. Surely, surely it is more sacred than Clifford's being a baronet, or father's being an artist, or that awful Sir Andrew being so stinkingly rich. Surely it *really* means more --"

"It may to you, at the moment. But even you'd get over it, and realize that Parkin's penis doesn't rule the world, whereas Clifford's baronetcy and Sir Andrew's money does, -- father's art, too."

"But Hilda, I don't care."

"Yes you do. Everybody does. Every woman does. A woman falls for the ruling man -- he can rule in what way he likes, as a saint or an aristocrat or an artist or a brewer with money or even a politician or a journalist -- and women will fall for him. Whereas a woman will despise herself for being the wife or a mere servant or a man who only takes orders, and never gives them; 'whether his penis is like a little god,' or whether it isn't."

"But I'm not like that."

"Yes you are! If your Parkin, or your phallic man as you call him, asserted himself and made himself a rule, practically any woman would want him. But it's the ruling spirit, or the authority, a woman yields to, in a man. If your Parkin was master of *anything* except just his dog and his penis, he might stand a chance. But as it is, you won't marry him . . ."[13]

Mike: "I have a question then: at the end, *after* Connie gets this fulfilment, in sex, the kind Hilda doesn't understand, and when Parkin decides he has to leave and go look for work at Tevershell . . . was that purposive activity? Reliving?"

[I have been brought back, unexpectedly, to the opening quote, and since I still feel the quote is important for us, I respond.]

Buckley: "I'm not sure if he has found any purposive activity, at least what he is doing or what he wants to do wouldn't be purposive for me. But he has given up on the modern 'quest for love' as Lawrence puts it. He still has, at the end of the book, a self-possession, partly found through Connie and partly found again within himself. And he has challenged Connie's upper-class feelings about power, money, and obligation -- although Parkin does say, on page 369: "I really don't know what love means," and about Connie he says that she is "home to me" but he doesn't care about houses. Connie does, eventually, offer him money for a farm so that he can be, as he put it, "his own boss."

Mary: "I don't get it. I mean, what *do* these two have then? Isn't Hilda's argument powerful."[14]

Jeff: "How could you *not* get it? If you had it the way Connie did?"

(laughter)

Mary: "No, no, I mean, don't they have to work at it to make it come out right? She's pregnant, don't they have to be more responsible?"

Laura: "You do if you believe in ideal love -- a thing that doesn't exist. Parkin is fighting for something that is almost impossible to get today, and Connie would like to help him. He doesn't go around "looking for love" and she realizes she *likes* that in him . . . I can just hear my *mother* telling me, though, what Hilda says here, "If your Parkin was master of anything except just his dog and his penis, he might stand a chance." My mother would win out over me I think -- although I know that Lawrence wants men to possess their own soul, something which Hilda and my mother don't get."

Mary: "Wait a minute. I can't get that either. Parkin is too interested in his own big self, too self-centered."

Jane: "Then why not have an intertwining of both mental and physical? Both desire and responsibility? Connie and her baby and Parkin and his farm?"

Mary: "Then Connie would have the best of both worlds! Yeah. Mental with Clifford and physical with Parkin."

[Both Mary and Jane have suddenly wandered off the point in trying to answer the need in this class for a quick solution to a dilemma Lawrence does not want resolved by way of a happy ending.]

Laura: "You are just not getting it! Lawrence saw or thought the sexual organs had a life of their own. It is through them that Connie finds peace and Parkin a hoped for purpose. Connie has no choice *but* to get out! I mean this stuff from Lawrence on page 312. "I *know* it was the penis which really put the evening stars into my inside self," well, *that's* too idealistic for me. But I do like the final version of *Lady Chatterley* where Mellors is spouting off about some plan or another to save the proletariat and while he is talking Connie starts holding his balls in her hands . . .

(laughter)

. . . and that makes us laugh at Mellors' sermons. It's not the man or his ideas or responsibility, it's his . . ."

Mary: "John Thomas?"

(more laughter)

These kinds of interactions, these give and take sessions between Laura, Jane, Mary, and Jeff, whatever we might say about their weaknesses, are helping the class connect up with Lawrence's words (despite the clear tension in body language I had noticed: Mike's fists were clenching and Jane's foot had wrapped itself tightly around the metal leg of her desk.) In the face of such reactions, I would be hard pressed as a teacher to regard the classroom as a place of missed encounters. For the scene in the final version of *Lady Chatterley* that Laura refers to, is, to me, the kind of scene that often leads to humorous exposures of our most cherished wishes. The gathering up of a man's testicles by a woman as he puffs away on some half-baked scheme to save the masses, is, as a bit of satire, that "banana-skin" Lawrence talks about in his essay "The Novel."

iii

In the contextualized classroom, then, a willingness in student and teacher to sink into the experiences provoked by a novel begins to flourish. Teachers release their personal experiences as they are moved or disturbed by what they have read. Students connect to the book in ways more real than note-taking. My aim in this book has not been to provide a theory that will help us psychoanalyze a student like Laura (who has catapulted this class into thinking about the tension between desire and responsibility),[15] nor has it been to burden her intense curiosity with opaque discussions on how she "knows" anything. Rather, my aim has been to describe a way of teaching and reading that fully embraces a lost idea: that novels, and the people who read them, wrestle with the problems of living. Neither does this book seek to promote the development of "well-balanced" individuals,[16] for that would force me into telling "didactic lies" about the nature of literature. My principle aim has been to offer a critical method that describes how novels illumine our unwanted connections with them. To let novels swagger about on their own terms -- that remains my difficult goal as a teacher.[17]

Notes

[1] Philip Rahv, "Fiction and the Criticism of Fiction", *Kenyon Review*, 18 (Winter, 1956): p. 287.

[2] D.H. Lawrence, "The Novel," *Phoenix II* (New York: The Viking Press, 1970), p. 417.

[3] Stephen C. Pepper, *World Hypotheses: A Study in Evidence* (Berkelely: University of California Press, 1970), p. 277.

[4] Ibid., p. 278.

[5] J.P. Tompkins, "An Introduction to Reader-Response Criticism," in *Reader-Response Criticism*, ed. J.P. Tompkins (Baltimore: John Hopkins University Press, 1980): "The later reader-response critics deny that criticism has . . . . an objective basis because they deny the existence of objective texts and indeed the possibility of objectivity altogether" (XXV). [For example, see S. Fish, *Is There a Text in This Class?* (Harvard University Press, 1980)].

[6] Paul de Mann, "The Resistance to Theory," *The Resistance to Theory* (Minneapolis: University of Minnesota Press, 1986), p. 11.

[7] Rahv, "Fiction and the Criticism of Fiction," pp. 285-86.

[8] Jacques Lacan, *The Four Fundamental Concepts of Psycho-Analysis*, ed. J.A. Miller (New York: Norton), p. 55.

[9] See especially L.M. Rosenblatt, "The Transactional Theory of the Literary Work: Implications for Research," in *Researching Response to Literature and the Teaching Literature*, ed. C.R. Cooper (Norwood, NJ: Ablex Publishing Co., 1985), pp. 33-53.

[10] D.H. Lawrence, *Psychoanalysis and the Unconscious and Fantasia of the Unconscious* (New York: The Viking Press, 1960), pp. 155-56.

[11] As I see it, Jeff's question supports the contextualist's view that reader's, in their emotional and intellectual connections with a novel, can infer what authors or characters are implying. Thus the novel, to use R.P. Blackmur's phrase, is brought to "full performance" in a classroom. See R. Beach, "Discourse Conventions and Research Response to Literary Dialogue," C.R. Cooper, ed., *Researching Response*, pp. 103-127.

[12] I am using the terms "projection" and "resistance" as defined by Norman Holland in his *5 Readers Reading* (New Haven: Yale University Press, 1975).

[13] D.H. Lawrence, *John Thomas and Lady Jane* (Penguin Books, 1977), p. 311.

[14] A side comment: This student, in asking her question the way she does, is, perhaps, reflecting what one researcher has called the current need to "dissociate" her deep feelings from sex, to "suppress" feelings of affection that would "normally accompany" sexual intercourse (W.G. Cobliner, "The Exclusion of Intimacy in the Sexuality of the Contemporary College-Age Population," *Adolescence*, 23, 89 (Spring, 1988), pp. 110-11.

[15] There is an awful lot of ego-worry these days about whether the teacher is a psychiatrist and the student a patient. Such positions are so befuddled about transference that novels get lost in the discussion. See: *College English*, volume 49, numbers 6 and 7 (October-November, 1987).

[16] See: Marshall W. Alcorn Jr., and Mark Bracher, "Literature, Psychoanalysis, and the Reformation of the Self," *PMLA*, 100 (1985), pp. 342-54, and my response "Reader-Response

Theory," *PMLA* (March, 1986), p. 250; or Simon O. Lesser's *Fiction and the Unconscious* (New York: Vintage Books, 1957).

17 By letting novels "swagger about" I mean letting novels, or other great works of art for the matter, retain their interrelatedness, quickness, and aliveness without interference. Cézanne's description of his technique is appropriate here: "I take from left, from right, here, there, everywhere, tones, colors, shades. I fix them, I bring them together. They make lines. They become objects, rocks, trees, without my thinking about it. They take on volume. They acquire value. If these volumes, these values, correspond on my canvas, in my feeling, to the planes and patches of color which are there before our eyes, very good! My canvas joins hands. It does not vacillate. It does not pass too high or too low. It is true; it is full. But if I feel the least distraction, the least weakness, above all if I interpret too much one day, if today I am carried away by a theory which is contrary to that of the day before, if I think while painting, if I intervene, why then everything is gone" (Erle Loran, *Cézanne's Composition* (Berkeley: University of California Press, 1963), p. 15. Max Horkheimer's description of our contemporary state in his essay "Art and Mass Culture," from his *Critical Theory* (New York: Herder and Herder, 1972), pp. 273-290, especially p. 287, is a remarkable description of our current literary theory.

APPENDIX

# THE PANZAIC PRINCIPLE

## WAYNE BURNS*

*The human mind
has broadened since Homer.
Sancho  Panza's belly has burst the
seams of Venus' girdle.*
Flaubert

*It is such a bore
that all great novelists have
a didactic purpose, otherwise a philosophy
directly opposite to their passional inspiration.
In their passional inspiration, they
are all phallic worshippers.*
D.H. Lawrence[1]

## Part I

In his now famous chapter on Romanticism and Classicism (in *Speculations*) T.E. Hulme suggests that "the best way of gliding into a definition [of Romanticism and Classicism] would be to start with a set of people who are prepared to fight about it -- for in them you will have no vagueness."[2] And for the same reason the best way to glide into a definition of the terms in which the Panzaic principle must be discussed (e.g., the "real" and the "ideal") may be to start with one of D.H. Lawrence's most belligerent and eloquent statements of the conflict between the real and the ideal -- his summing-up of Cezanne's artistic struggles and achievements (in his *Introduction to These Paintings*):

> After a fight tooth-and-nail for forty years, [Cezanne] did succeed in knowing an apple, fully; and not quite as fully, a jug or two. That was all he achieved.
> It seems little, and he died embittered. But it is the first step that counts, and Cezanne's apple is a great deal, more than Plato's Idea. Cezanne's apple rolled the stone from the mouth of the tomb, and if poor Cezanne couldn't unwind himself from his cerements and mental winding sheet, but had to lie still in the tomb, till he died, still he gave us a chance.

©Wayne Burns.  Reprinted with permission of the author and the editors of *Recovering Literature*, 5, 1 (Spring, 1976), pp. 5-51.  Selections from *Last Exit to Brooklyn* used by permission of Grove Press, a division of Wheatland Corporation.

The history of our era is the nauseating and repulsive history of the crucifixion of the procreative body for the glorification of the spirit, the mental consciousness. Plato was an arch-priest of this crucifixion. Art, that handmaid, humbly and honestly served the vile deed, through three thousand years at least . . .

We, dear reader, you and I, we were born corpses, and we are corpses. I doubt if there is even one of us who has ever known so much as an apple, a whole apple. All we know is shadows, even of apples. Shadows of everything, of the whole world, shadows even of ourselves. We are inside the tomb, and the tomb is wide and shadowy like hell, even if sky-blue by optimistic paint, so we think it is all the world. But our world is a wide tomb full of ghosts, replicas. We are spectres, we have not been able to touch even so much as an apple. Spectres we are to one another. Spectre you are to me, spectre I am to you. Shadow you are even to yourself. And by shadow I mean idea, concept, the abstracted reality, the ego. We are not solid. We don't live in the flesh. Our instincts and intuitions are dead, we live wound round with the winding-sheet of abstraction. And the touch of anything solid hurts us. For our instincts and intuitions, which are our feelers of touch and knowing through touch, they are dead, amputated. We talk and eat and copulate and laugh and evacuate wrapped in our winding-sheets, all the time wrapped in our winding-sheets.

So that Cezanne's apple hurts. It made people shout with pain. And it was not till his followers had turned him again into an abstraction that he was ever accepted. Then the critics stepped forth and abstracted his good apple into Significant Form, and henceforth Cezanne was saved. Saved for democracy. Put safely into the tomb again, and the stone rolled back. The resurrection was postponed once more.

As the resurrection will be postponed *ad infinitum* by the good bourgeois corpses in their cultured winding-sheets. They will run up a chapel to the risen body, even if it is only an apple, and kill it on the spot . . . All is dead, and dead breath preaching with phosphorescent effulgence about aesthetic ecstasy and Significant Form. If only the dead would bury their dead. But the dead are not dead for nothing. Who buries his own sort? The dead are cunning and alert to pounce on any spark of life and bury *it*, even as they have already buried Cezanne's apple and put up to it a white tombstone of Significant Form.[3]

Although Lawrence's rhetoric may be irritating, especially his practice of equating Platonism and Christianity with Death, there is surely no denying that he is essentially right about "us" and our reactions. For we do glorify "the spirit, the mental consciousness," although we call this glorification Christianity or humanism; and we do live wound round in our mental winding sheets, although we call these winding sheets "Culture" or "Civilization." Nor is there any denying that the touch of anything solid or material or sensual does hurt us. It hurts us, our criticism reveals, every bit as much as Cezanne's apple hurt his followers and critics, and with much the same effect.

Even the fictional apples in *Don Quixote*, "the world's best loved book," have made "people shout with pain." Nietzsche declared the novel to be "the bitterest reading I know. Here everything solemn and inspiring appears as nonsensical. It is good to keep this lesson in mind for special circumstances, but normally one would do better not to think of it."[4] In the same vein, Joseph Wood Krutch, in *Five Masters*, has affirmed that the novel arouses "a certain resentment" in most readers: "They wince rather than laugh when some new drubbing is inflicted upon the harmless hero."[5] And Salvador de Madariaga, in his *Don Quixote*, refers to "this most cruel book" with its "cruel realism,"[6] maintaining that "we should resent the infliction of unnecessary hardship upon him [Don Quixote]": that in at least one instance (Don Quixote's arrival before the Duke and Duchess: Part II, ch. XXX) "there is no point whatever in this humiliation of Don Quixote . . .[which] is painful to the mind."[7] And there is at least one page, according to Madariaga, "which every reader of *Don Quixote* would wish unwritten," the passage (in Part II, ch. LX) in which Don Quixote, after trying to "undo Sancho's breech-sashes," tells Sancho that he is "coming to repair thy negligence and to alleviate my torment: I am come to whip thee, Sancho, and to discharge in part that debt for which thou standst engaged. Dulcinea perishes, thou livest careless and I die with longing: strip therefore, of thy own will, for it is my will in this solitary spot, to give thee at least two thousand lashes."[8]

The sadistic implications of this passage -- the fact that Don Quixote's "longing" seems to be more for Sancho's backside than for any part of Dulcinea -- do not seem to bother Madariaga. What hurts him, it would seem, is that Don Quixote should long for and be overcome by the too solid flesh of either male or female. For he elsewhere describes the episode in which Sancho convinces Don Quixote that a peasant girl is Dulcinea as "that saddest of adventures, one of the cruellest in the book . . . bringing the most noble of knights, for the love of the purest illusion, to his knees before the most repulsive of realities: A Dulcinea coarse, uncouth, and reeking of garlic."[9]

To Madariaga this episode marks the beginning of the end for Don Quixote. "The reality which Sancho presented to him as vision was an insult to his dreams" from which he never quite recovers. "Our hero," Madariaga explains, has been corrupted by Sancho: the "wily squire," with "the instinctive realism of the servant," uses the "primitive, animal, almost bestial quality" of his "courage" and "virility" to drag "the noblest of knights" down to his own sensual and matter-of-fact level.[10] Yet even as Madariaga acknowledges the triumph of Panzaic reality in the novel, he refuses to accept it. To see his hero chained to the material world is more than he can bear. It is "cruel realism," explicable only in terms of Cervantes' "curious animosity against Don Quixote."[11] And in an effort to strike off the chains that bind his hero -- an effort not unlike Don Quixote's attack on the puppets in Master Pedro's puppet show -- Madariaga enters into the novel to rewrite it to his own abstract specifications, declaring that "Cervantes did not and could not see Don Quixote in his true greatness -- which, so far as we are concerned, is the greatness ["the symbolic value"] that he has attained today."[12]

A more perfect example of abstraction, of what Lawrence describes as critical entombment, can hardly be imagined. For in trying to suggest that "the greatness that Don Quixote has attained today" is "the symbolic value" we attach to him, Madariaga has turned him into an heroic statue of the type that literally tops monuments and tombstones. And it is altogether fitting that the reproduction of Don Quixote which appears on the front cover of the paperback edition of Madariaga's book should be of this type -- with the good Don (shield in hand and lance held upright) frozen into an attitude of nobility worthy of Amadis himself, or of an idealized male version of the Statue of Liberty in which the lamp is replaced by the lance.[13]

Yet Madariaga cannot be held solely or even primarily responsible for turning *Don Quixote* into this type of abstraction. He is but one of the latest in a long line of idealistic critics and commentators that extends from the seventeenth century to the present -- a line that includes, among others, Charles Lamb, who became so impatient of the petty details that stand in the way of the Knight's success that he voiced a protest against "the mind, to which, in its better moments, the image of the high-souled, high-intelligenced Quixote . . . has never presented itself, divested from the unhallowed accompaniment of a Sancho . . ."[14]

More recent idealists, following Lamb and anticipating Madariaga, have likewise tried to pry their hero loose from Sancho (that man "of the flesh, of appetites"[15]) and from Panzaic reality (the "intemperate cruelty" of Cervantes' realism,[16] "the sanchopanzism now called positivism"[17]). And from their own idealistic point of view these critics have been entirely right to attempt this separation. For Sancho's belly has not only burst the seams of Venus' girdle, it has given the lie to Dulcinea and in fact all of Don Quixote's ideals -- much as Lady Chatterley's guts give the lie to Clifford and his ideals in *Lady Chatterley's Lover.*

> "My dear, you speak as if you were ushering it all in! [i.e., "the life of the human body"] . . . Believe me, whatever God there is is slowly eliminatingthe guts and alimentary system from the human being, to evolve a higher, more spiritual being."
>
> "Why should I believe you, Clifford, when I feel that whatever God there is has at last wakened up in my guts, as you call them, and is rippling so happily there, like Dawn? Why should I believe you, when I feel so very much the contrary?"[18]

In life the rightness of the guts (as against the mind) will depend on one's point of view. In Lawrence's as in all other novels, however, the guts are always right; it is an axiom or principle of the novel that they are always right, that the senses of even a fool can give the lie to even the most profound abstractions of the noblest thinker.[19] And it is this principle I have designated the Panzaic principle, after Sancho Panza. Idealistic critics of the stamp of Lamb and Madariaga generally recognize this principle, much as they hate and deplore it. They know or sense that, in fiction, the guts are always right; this is why they want to keep them out, or cover them up, or somehow bowdlerize them. And if they cannot use any of these tactics, if, as in the case of *Lady Chatterley's Lover,* the sensuality is so direct that they must either experience it or reject the novel outright, they will of course reject it -- the way so many critics otherwise sympathetic to Lawrence, from F.R. Leavis to Katherine Anne Porter, have rejected it.

These critics, it must be stressed, are not rejecting the Panzaic principle, only its effects. But there are other critics -- those who may, for want of a better word, be identified as perspectivists -- who would dismiss the principle itself as truistic or inconsequential, or would subsume it under some form or another of the reality principle. "Modern realism," Ian Watt explains, "begins from the position that truth can be discovered by the individual through his senses . . . But the view that the external world is real, and that our senses give us a true report of it, obviously does not in itself throw much light on literary realism; since almost everyone, in all ages, has in one way or another been forced to some such conclusion about the external world by his own experience, literature has always been to some extent exposed to the same epistemological naivete . . ."[20] Thus Watt dismisses the view that underlies the Panzaic principle as of no great fictional consequence. And in discussing the history of realism in fiction he goes even further -- in an effort to dissociate realism from the "low," the "carnal," and the "seamy" (and therefore from the Panzaic principle):

> Much of the usefulness of the word [ *Realism*] was soon lost in the bitter controversies over the 'low' subjects and allegedly immoral tendencies of Flaubert and his successors. As a result, realism came to be used primarily as the antonym of 'idealism,' and in this sense . . . has in fact coloured much critical and historical writing about the novel. The prehistory of the form has commonly been envisaged as a matter of tracing the continuity between all earlier fiction which portrayed low life: the story of the Ephesian matron is 'realistic' because it shows that sexual appetite is stronger

than wifely sorrow; and the fabliau or the picaresque tale are
'realistic' because economic or carnal motives are given pride
of place in their presentation of human behaviour. By the
same implicit premise, the English eighteenth-century
novelists . . . are regarded as the eventual climax of this
tradition: the 'realism' of the novels of Defoe, Richardson
and Fielding is closely associated with the fact that Moll
Flanders is a thief, Pamela a hypocrite, and Tom Jones a
fornicator.[21]

This use of "realism" Watt considers mistaken and misleading. "If the novel were realistic merely because it saw life from the seamy side," he declares, "it would only be an inverted romance; but in fact it surely attempts to portray all the varieties of human experience, and not merely those suited to one particular literary perspective: the novel's realism does not reside in the kind of life it presents, but in the way it presents it."[22]

This final distinction, and in fact every single point in Watt's argument, has been contradicted by Ortega y Gasset in his "The Nature of the Novel" (*Hudson Review*, Spring, 1957). But discussion of the full implications of Watt's revised "realism" must wait. Of more immediate concern are the questions raised by his dismissal of the Panzaic principle; more specifically, the question of just what he means when he implies that the "realism" of *Tom Jones*, for example, is *not* "closely associated with the fact that . . . Tom Jones [is] a fornicator." This question Watt does not answer directly, but later, in discussing "the narrative mode of *Tom Jones*," he answers it indirectly, using a key passage in the novel as a means of analyzing Fielding's treatment of character:

By a great variety of devices, of which the chapter headings
are usually significant pointers, our attention is continually
drawn to the fact that the ultimate cohesive force of the book
resides not in the characters and their relationships, but in an
intellectual and literary structure which has a considerable
degree of autonomy.

The effects of this procedure and its relationship to
Fielding's treatment of character can be summarized in
relation to a brief scene which occurs after Tom has heard that
Allworthy is to recover from his illness. He takes a walk 'in
a most delicious grove,' and contemplates the cruelty of
fortune which separates him from his beloved Sophia:

Was I possessed of thee, one only suit of rags thy
whole estate, is there a man on earth whom I
would envy! How contemptible would the
brightest Circassian beauty dressed in all the jewels
of the Indies, appear to my eyes! But why do I
mention another woman? Could I think my eyes
capable of looking at any other with tenderness,
these hands should tear them from my head. No,
my Sophia, if cruel fortune separates us for ever,
my soul shall dote on thee alone. The chastest
constancy will I ever preserve to thy image . . .

At these words he started up and beheld -- not his
Sophia -- no, nor a Circassian maid richly and
elegantly attired for the grand Signior's seraglio. . .

but Molly Seagrim, with whom, 'after a parley' which Fielding omits, Tom retires to 'the thickest part of the grove.'

The least convincing aspect of the episode is the diction: the speech habits manifested here obviously bear little relation to those we expect of Tom Jones. But, of course, they are a stylistic necessity for Fielding's immediate purpose -- the comic deflation of the heroic and romantic pretences of the human word by the unheroic and unromantic eloquence of the human deed. Tom Jones is no more than a vehicle for the expression of Fielding's scepticism about lovers' vows; and he must be made to speak in terms that parody the high-flown rhetoric of the pastoral romance to give point to the succeeding wayside encounter which belongs to the very different world of the *pastourelle*. Nor can Fielding pause to detail the psychological processes whereby Tom is metamorphosed from Sophia's romantic lover to Moll's prompt gallant: to illustrate the commonplace that 'actions speak louder than words,' the actions must be very silent and they must follow very hard upon very loud words.[23]

The effect of this reading of the episode is of course to negate the Panzaic principle altogether. For if, as Watt maintains, "Tom Jones is no more than a vehicle for the expression of Fielding's scepticism about lovers' vows," it matters little that his response to the physical Molly gives the lie to his apostrophe to Sophia. Indeed, since Tom is "no more than a vehicle," his response cannot be called a response; it is, according to Watt, a metamorphosis; moreover, this metamorphosis is intended to illustrate, not the Panzaic principle, but the desexualized commonplace that "actions speak louder than words." And in relating this episode to the structure of the novel Watt (after once again metamorphosing Tom, this time into a "headstrong youth") carries his interpretation to its logical conclusion:

The relation of this episode to the larger structure of the novel is typical. One of Fielding's general organising themes is the proper place of sex in human life; this encounter neatly illustrates the conflicting tendencies of headstrong youth, and shows that Tom has not yet reached the continence of moral adulthood. The scene, therefore, plays its part in the general moral and intellectual scheme; and it is also significantly connected with the workings of the plot, since Tom's lapse eventually becomes a factor in his dismissal by Allworthy, and therefore leads to the ordeals which eventually make him a worthier mate for Sophia.[24]

So Watt very neatly structures the sensual and the carnal not only out of this episode but out of the entire novel. But neither the episode nor the novel is quite that neat, even when viewed from Watt's "perspective." For one thing he begins his analysis of the episode at just the point which enables him to gloss over the fact that, just prior to Molly's appearance, Tom has got himself sexually aroused by thinking lascivious thoughts about his Sophia: "His wanton fancy roamed unbounded over all her beauties, and his lively imagination painted the charming maid in various ravishing forms . . ."[25] His romantic maunderings which immediately follow are therefore piquantly as well as ironically euphemistic in themselves; and in addition they serve to bring the aroused Tom from sexual image to sexual reality, in the person of his Molly. At which point, for him, or for almost anyone except a character as pure as Don Quixote or as cold as Blifil, there can be but one resolution -- as the novel indicates. And to structuralize and moralize this scene and the entire novel (the way Watt does when he says that "Tom has not yet reached the continence of moral adulthood," or when he refers to "the ordeals which eventually make him [Tom] a worthier mate for Sophia") -- this is to turn the novel into little more than a structurally unified illustration of the conventional morality that Fielding preaches throughout the novel.

Yet Watt would presumably not be upset by this charge. He himself devotes some five pages of his chapter on *Tom Jones* to a specific discussion of the charges of immorality that have been brought against it and Fielding -- finally to decide, after weighing the pros and cons, that it is Fielding's intention as writer and as moralist "to put every phenomenon into its larger perspective. Sexual virtue and sexual vice, for example, are placed in a broad moral perspective . . . But, at the same time, his function as the voice of traditional social morality means that his attitude to sexual ethics is inevitably normative . . ."[26] And so it follows that "Tom Jones's carefree animality" does not mean what it seems to mean in the novel. Neither does it mean what Ford Madox Ford and others, in their denunciations of Fielding, have taken it to mean. Its meanings are positive and normative: "Tom's moral transgressions were a likely and perhaps even a necessary stage in the process of moral growth."[27]

In the succeeding and final section of his chapter on *Tom Jones* (devoted to Fielding's technical shortcomings) Watt explains that the "larger moral significance" he finds in the novel is not expressed in the dramatic action because Fielding's technique "was deficient at least in the sense that it was unable to convey this larger moral significance through character and action alone, and could only supply it by means of a somewhat intrusive patterning of the plot and by direct editorial commentary."[28] Seemingly it never occurs to Watt that Fielding may not be trying to write like George Eliot or Henry James; that he may not be trying to express "this larger moral significance" at all, much less "by character and action alone"; that, on the positive side, the moral significance Fielding is trying to express at the very least includes the "animality" that has caused critics and readers with less broad perspectives to shout with pain, and, with Ford Madox Ford, to denounce "fellows like Fielding, and to some extent Thackeray, who pretend that if you are a gay drunkard, lecher, squanderer of your goods and fumbler in placket holes you will eventually find a benevolent uncle, concealed father or benefactor who will shower on you bags of guineas, estates, and the hands of adorable mistresses -- these fellows are dangers to the body politic and horribly bad constructors of plots."[29]

In so far as this denunciation represents a serious reading of *Tom Jones* it is of course hopelessly oversimplified. But at least Ford's idealistic shout of pain -- his denunciation really amounts to little more than that -- shows that he has felt the animality, the appleyness, that Watt, with his revised realism and normative perspectivism, would transform into "this larger moral significance."

Moreover there is no denying Ford's charge (at least as it applies to Tom Jones) that "these fellows are dangers to the body politic." This is a perennial charge, not only against Tom Jones or Connie Chatterley or Sancho Panza but against every Panzaic character in literature, including of course Falstaff, who serves the same archetypal function in drama that Sancho does in the novel. "One might say," according to E.M.W. Tillyard, "that Falstaff was in unseen attendance on Satan in the Garden of Eden to make the first frivolous remark and the first dirty joke, after the Fall . . . As well as being the eternal child Falstaff is the fool . . . kin to Brer Rabbit and Fool Schweik . . . he is the active impostor and adventurer: not only Schweik but Volpone, not only Brer Rabbit but the *Miles Gloriosus* . . . But Falstaff embodies something still wider than the adventurer, something more abstract. If from Schweik he goes on to Volpone, he also goes on from the harmlessly comic Vice to the epitome of the Deadly Sins at war with law and order."[30] Then, after analyzing these various components in Falstaff's makeup, Tillyard goes on to present him as "the great symbolic figure of misrule or disorder [who] . . . stands for a perpetual and accepted human principle."[31] And for an explanation of this principle Tillyard turns to George Orwell, who in turn, in trying to explain the principle as it manifests itself in comic postcards, turns to Sancho Panza:

The comic post cards are the only existing . . . medium in which really "low" humour is considered to be printable. Only in post cards and on the variety stage can the stuck-out behind, dog and lamp-post, baby's nappy type of joke be freely exploited. Remembering that, one sees what function these post cards, in their humble way, are performing.

What they are doing is to give expression to the Sancho Panza view of life, the attitude to life that Miss Rebecca West once summed up as "extracting as much fun as possible from smacking behinds in basement kitchens." . . . If you look into your own mind, which are you, Don Quixote or Sancho Panza? Almost certainly you are both. There is one part of you that wishes to be a hero or a saint, but another part of you is a little fat man who sees very clearly the advantages of staying alive with a whole skin. He is your unofficial self, the voice of the belly protesting against the soul. His tastes lie towards safety, soft beds, no work, pots of beer and women with "voluptuous" figures. He it is who punctures your fine attitudes and urges you to look after Number One, to be unfaithful to your wife, to bilk your debts, and so on and so forth.

But though in varying forms he is one of the stock figures of literature, in real life, especially in the way society is ordered, his point of view never gets a fair hearing. There is a constant world-wide conspiracy to pretend that he is not there, or at least that he doesn't matter.[32]

Orwell himself is of course trying to give "the voice of the belly" a fair hearing. Yet his conception of the "voice" is from first to last so limited (compared, say, with Swift's conception, or Blake's, or Freud's) that his defense of it seems supererogatory. Once Sancho Panza has been reduced to Orwell's "little fat man" or to one of Rebecca West's bottom-smackers in basement kitchens it matters little whether or not he gets a fair hearing in either life or art, since in either case his function will inevitably be to provide "a harmless rebellion against virtue." For, according to Orwell, "high sentiments always win in the end . . . When it comes to the pinch human beings are heroic. Women face childbed and scrubbing brush, revolutionaries keep their mouths shut in the torture chamber, battleships go down with their guns still firing when their decks are awash. It is only that the other element in man, the lazy, cowardly, debt-bilking adulterer who is inside all of us, can never be suppressed altogether and needs a hearing occasionally."[33]

Orwell here echoes Lawrence's Sir Clifford. Yet Tillyard's response to Orwell's oversimplified and emasculated Sancho Panzism is that it "gets us pretty close to Falstaff"[34] -- in proof of which he outlines *our* reactions to Falstaff's defense of his own character (*Henry IV, Part One*, Act II, Scene IV): "With our virtuous selves we know he [Falstaff] is lying; with our unofficial selves we back up the lie, agreeing to call the misleader of youth plump Jack. But only for the moment. We end by banishing the misleader of youth. But it is not the end, for once the misleader of youth has been disposed of, with a 'Here we are again' plump Jack reappears: only to be banished again when he becomes "too threatening."[35] Tillyard here seems to be equating "our virtuous selves" with our conventional or official selves, and what he means by "too threatening" he makes unmistakably clear in his attempt to justify his reading on historical grounds: "The school of criticism that furnished him [Falstaff] with a tender heart and condemned the Prince for brutality in turning him away was deluded . . . the sense of security created in nineteenth century England by the predominance of the British navy induced men to rate that very security too cheaply and to exalt the instinct of rebellion [as exemplified by Falstaff] above its legitimate station."[36]

In contrast to this narrowly idealistic attempt to bury plump Jack, not under a tombstone of Significant Form, but under the full weight of a memorial to the British navy, there is the perspectivist attempt of Cleanth Brooks and Robert B. Heilman to give Falstaff as fair and full a hearing as Shakespeare's text warrants.[37] Pairing Hotspur and Falstaff they begin by citing Falstaff's invocation of the Panzaic principle in his famous speech on honor: "Well, 'tis no matter: honour pricks me on. Yea, but how if honour prick me off when I come on? how then? Can honour set to a leg? no: or an arm? no: or take away the grief of a wound? no . . ." Brooks and Heilman acknowledge that Falstaff's Sancho Panzism (which they call "common sense") is "devastating." But immediately they add that "it is also crippling -- or would be to a prince or ruler. If it does not cripple Falstaff, it is because Falstaff frankly refuses to accept the responsibilities of leadership." Nevertheless, still trying to be fair, they go on to suggest that Falstaff perhaps "chooses wisely in so refusing [the responsibilities of leadership]. By refusing he achieves a vantage point from which he can perceive the folly and pretentiousness which, to a degree, always tend to associate themselves with authority of any kind."

Yet despite their sympathy and insight they too must banish plump Jack (along with Hotspur): "If we assume the necessity for leadership and authority," they argue, "both Falstaff and Hotspur are *below* the serious concerns that fill the play. About both of them there is a childlike quality which relieves them of the responsibility of mature life . . ." Then, after further explanation and qualification, Brooks and Heilman repeat: "And yet, even so, the pair do not quite stand on the level of the adult world where there are jobs to be done and duties to be performed. They are either below it or else they transcend it; and Shakespeare is wise enough to let them -- particularly Falstaff -- do both."

Yet whenever Falstaff transcends the adult world, he does so, according to Brooks and Heilman, not as a man but as a child: "like the child, he is fundamentally a moral anarchist." Hence it follows that, however brilliant or penetrating his commentary on the adult world, it is true or relevant or acceptable only "on certain levels," "up to a point," or "to a degree"; and even these degrees are finally negated, in their view, by Falstaff's inability or unwillingness to be a responsible adult. In commenting on Falstaff's playing possum on the battlefield, for instance, Brooks and Heilman speak sympathetically of the way "Falstaff values his bowels" -- only to resort again to their constant demurrer: "Still, from the point of view of the need for responsibility and authority, Falstaff's conduct is childishly frivolous, if not much worse -- as is his conduct throughout the battle . . . Indeed, though Shakespeare allows Falstaff his due even here, he has made the case against Falstaff very plain." And to illustrate how plain, Brooks and Heilman cite the incident when, just after Falstaff has stabbed the dead Hotspur, Hal comes on the scene and remarks to his younger brother:

Come, brother John, full bravely hast thou flesh'd
Thy maiden sword.

"The commendation of Prince John," Brooks and Heilman point out, "applies ironically to 'Brother' John Falstaff -- here in full view of the audience -- whose sword is a 'maiden' sword too, which he has just 'flesh'd' safely in the dead Percy. The boy prince John has shown himself a man: Sir John Falstaff has shown himself a child."

This statement seems clear enough. Yet Brooks and Heilman seemingly cannot accept the final implications of their own reading. In the concluding pages of their commentary they banish Falstaff again, and still once again. Yet in every instance -- and it is to be noted that their own commentary is from first to last marked by repetitions of "Yet," "And yet," "even so," "after all," "still," etc. -- they endeavor to qualify their banishment, to insist "on the need of having the matter both ways" on the ground that "if the Prince must choose between two courses of action -- and, of course, he must choose -- we as readers are not forced to choose: indeed, perhaps the core of Shakespeare's ironic insight comes to this: that man must choose and yet that the choice can never be a wholly satisfactory one . . . that growing up is something which man must do and yet that even in growing up he loses, necessarily, something that is valuable."

In this and similar statements Brooks and Heilman try to hold the balance that they see in the play. Yet even as they say that "we as readers are not forced to choose" they use words (e.g., "must," "necessarily") which clearly indicate that they have chosen, that no matter how much they admire or sympathize with Falstaff's Sancho Panzism, they still see it, and him, as providing only a marginal commentary on serious affairs: "a criticism . . . which, on certain levels, is thoroughly valid. The rulers of the world had better not leave it totally out of account . . . Yet, after all, men must act; responsibilities must be assumed. To remain in Falstaff's world is to deny the reality of the whole world of adult concerns." What Brooks and Heilman are finally saying, then, is that regardless of how valid Falstaff's criticism may be it cannot be fully accepted -- because to accept it fully is "to deny the whole world of adult concerns," and to deny this world is to render oneself impotent to be a leader or even a "man" in this world. In still other words they are saying that Falstaff can exert a salutary influence on us only so long as we are prepared to banish him from our world when he becomes, in Tillyard's phrase, "too threatening" to our adult concerns and responsibilities and values.

In view of Brooks and Heilman's sympathetic and perceptive treatment of Falstaff it may seem unfair even to suggest that they finally invoke the same moral imperative as Tillyard. Yet they not only do, they must. Given their perspective -- the necessity for leadership and authority in this world -- they have no other choice: for as they so honestly and astutely point out, Falstaff's Sancho Panzism not only "strips Henry IV quite naked," it also lays bare "the folly and pretentiousness which, to a degree, always tend to associate themselves with authority of any kind." Ultimately, therefore, the choice they are confronted with is a choice between culture and anarchy; and they, like Tillyard, choose culture.

Of course Brooks and Heilman contend that their choice is also the choice of Shakespeare and the Elizabethan audience and the play itself. In their discussion of Hotspur, for example, they suggest that "if one assumes the necessity for leadership (and there is little doubt that the Elizabethan audience and Shakespeare did), then Hotspur points to an extreme which the truly courageous leader must avoid quite as clearly as he must avoid the other extreme represented by Falstaff." Here, in essence, is their reading of *Henry IV, Part One*, and it rests precariously on their initial "if," which in turn rests on "there is little doubt."

Needless to say Brooks and Heilman never quite manage to erase this little doubt or this big "if." Nor would it be critically decisive if they did. Quite possibly Shakespeare, assuming the necessity for leadership, did set out to portray "Falstaff . . . too practical; Hotspur not practical enough" as a means of showing that a good king must follow the golden mean. And quite possibly the Elizabethan audience saw the play as just such a study in kingship. But these are merely biographical and historical facts or hypotheses which point to the play Shakespeare consciously intended and the play his audience consciously understood. The play itself -- unless we are to reduce it to hypothesized biographical intentions or hypothesized audience reactions -- is, or may be, something quite different and infinitely more complex.

So much Brooks and Heilman themselves acknowledge, by implication at least, in their discussion of "the problem of unity" in the play. "It is possible," they admit, "that even for the mature reader, the play finally lacks unity -- that the balancing of attitudes which has been argued for in this analysis is something which perhaps Shakespeare should have attempted to accomplish but did not, for one reason or another, actually succeed in accomplishing." And the "one reason or another" they have primarily in mind, their earlier remarks show, is the relation of the comic underplot (and Falstaff) to the "history plot." Indeed they go so far, at one point, as to concede the possibility that Falstaff "became something richer and more imaginative than intended. As a matter of fact, one might, pushing this line of argument a step further, contend that Falstaff has actually so far outgrown the needs of the play, strictly considered, that he comes close to destroying it."

And so Brooks and Heilman take up their second or aesthetic line of defense against Falstaff (behind their first or moral line), their intention of course being to protect art ("they play, strictly considered") as well as culture. A play, they assume, must have dramatic unity to be a good play; and if Falstaff is permitted to become too big or too devastating for his assigned role, then "the play will probably remain a collection of brilliant but ill-assorted fragments -- the wonderful tavern scenes juxtaposed oddly with passages of dull and pawky history." Why the fragments need be "ill-assorted" or "juxtaposed oddly" is not clear. But no matter. Brooks and Heilman's argument is, in its own terms, irrefutable. If the play is to be a good play, "strictly considered," Falstaff must conform to its needs and contribute to its dramatic unity -- as that unity is defined by the thematic and structural lines which derive from their big "if" and "little doubt," which in turn derive from their moral assumptions, their belief in adult concerns and responsibilities and values, or, in a word, culture.

Brooks and Heilman's criticism is therefore wholly consistent with their moral and critical assumptions. If they have wrapped Falstaff in their own cultured winding sheets and subjugated him to their own version of Significant Form, they have done so as a matter of principle -- in an effort to demonstrate that "the play does achieve a significant unity," that "here Shakespeare has given us one of the wisest and fullest commentaries on human action possible to the comic mode -- a view which scants nothing, which covers up nothing, and which takes into account in making its affirmations the most searching criticism of that which is affirmed."

But to a modern reader not wholly committed to the need for authority and culture and dramatic unity, in the sense Brooks and Heilman have acknowledged themselves to be, their reading of the play at times verges on the arbitrary. For it not only covers up Falstaff, it negates his Panzaic function, which is to connect the poetry of our abstract ideals with the prose of our bodily senses, or,more specifically, to reveal the concrete meaning of such ideals as "honor" as that meaning is inscribed on the bodies of the living and the dead. Falstaff's cry, "I like not such grinning honour as Sir Walter hath. Give me life," is sufficient in itself to answer not only Hal's charges but Brooks and Heilman's as well, when, in trying to maintain that "Falstaff's conduct is childishly frivolous, if not much worse," throughout the battle, they solemnly declare that Falstaff "won't realize that the battlefield is no place for joking." Indeed the ultimate effect of the conduct which Brooks and Heilman would dismiss as "childishly frivolous" is to show Hal and Prince John and Douglas and Hotspur and the king himself acting and speaking like Don Quixote's romance heroes.

What a full recognition of Falstaff's Panzaic role can mean to the play itself and to Shakespearean criticism has been indicated by A.P. Rossiter (in his "Ambivalence: The Dialectic of the Histories," *Angel with Horns*, 1961).[38] And much of what Rossiter says in answer to those critics who would make *Henry IV, Part One* into "a princely morality" applies directly to the arguments of those critics who have tried to justify the idealism of the good Don himself on perspectivist grounds -- including, as in Dorothy Van Ghent's criticism of *Don Quixote*,[39] the argument that Quixote's "rescue" of the peasant boy (near the beginning of Book One) paradoxically fulfills the "ideal of human justice." In Van Ghent's own words:

> The boy has been tied to a tree and beaten by his master because he demanded honest wages. According to Quixote's interpretation of the situation, the boy's demand is just, the master had treated him unjustly, and a Righter of Wrongs and Liberator of the Oppressed might act here in the rational name of justice. On the other hand, the boy's interpretation of the situation is determined by the physical eventuality far more decidedly than by the justice or the injustice of the affair; he receives a much worse beating after he is "rescued" than before; hence, to him, Quixote's justice is an injustice. Clearly, the two outlooks are incommensurable, and yet, as clearly, the reader cannot eliminate . . . the ideal of human justice as an absurdity, without diminishing his vision of life to the scope of a brute's eye; nor can he eliminate the actualities of human psychology and practice as shown in the relationships of the boy and his master. The situation, then, is "paradoxical," in that one event shows two opposed aspects which are both "real" but which are antithetical to each other.

Actually, the situation is not paradoxical, nor is it intended to be paradoxical. For that matter the situation does not even turn on "justice" or "injustice": Quixote's proclamations can hardly be taken straight, and Cervantes' own comment on the episode reads as follows in Putnam's translation: "Such was the manner in which the valorous knight righted this particular wrong. Don Quixote was quite content with the way everything had turned out; it seemed to him that he had made a very fortunate and noble beginning with his deeds of chivalry, and he was very well satisfied with himself as he jogged along in the direction of his native village . . ."[40] The paradox, then, is of Van Ghent's own making: it represents a vain attempt on her part, first to translate Cervantes' direct and unambiguous application of the Panzaic principle into an abstract moral question, and then to negate, by an invocation of the paradoxical, the effect of Cervantes' Panzaic directness, which in this as in so many other instances in the novel is to show how foolish and even deadly, in practice, are the chivalric ideals (including the ideal of "justice") that Don Quixote professes.

But Van Ghent cannot acknowledge, much less accept, the Panzaic in the novel. For her the higher cannot be destroyed by the lower, the spiritual by the physical, "the ideal of human justice" by the cries of a boy being flayed alive. No matter what the boy feels, or the text says, "the reader cannot eliminate . . . the ideal of human justice as an absurdity, without diminishing his vision of life to the scope of a brute's eye." Van Ghent is here taking essentially the same moral position as Brooks and Heilman. Like them she feels that the reader's choice (which is of course also her own) is a choice between culture and anarchy, and that he must therefore choose culture. But unlike Brooks and Heilman, who frankly acknowledge their assumptions, Van Ghent tries to hide hers. Or at least that is the effect of her discussion of paradox, particularly when, as in her concluding remarks, she endeavors to clarify some of her abstractions, e.g., "The living reality which the book offers is that of the paradox embodied in action, the ineluctable mixture that is at once ideal and corporeal, spirit and flesh."

And from paradox she turns to parody -- to argue that *Don Quixote* is not, of course, "a parody of romances of knight-errantry" in the sense that it is "an attempt to laugh the old-fashioned romances of chivalry out of existence . . . Parody -- except that of the crudest kind -- does not ask for preferential judgments and condemnations. It is a technique of *presentation*: it offers a field for the joyful exercise of perception and not a platform for derision." And to illustrate the workings of this refined type of parody (in contrast to the "loose and inadequate kind") Van Ghent chooses Don Quixote's vigil at the horse trough, another incident from his first sally:

> In the loose and inadequate sense of parody . . . the vigil at the horse trough tells us that Quixote's world is not what he thinks it is, that "reality" is much rougher and more prosaic than what appears to his idealizing imagination: that the armor is not armor but pasteboard, that the trough is not an altar, that the inn is not a castle, that nothing "sacred" and no "consecration" has taken place but only a psychotic misinterpretation of the use of objects. This would be the meaning of the scene if the parodistic impulse were as simple as the impulse to debate the practical advisability ("truth" in the running sense) of a course of action. What else does the scene contain? Night, moonlight, a deserted innyard, a man pacing up and down alone. Arising conceptually from this poignant incantation of scene are the urgency of devotion, the conviction of mission, the subjective solitude of the individual mind, resonances of ancient stories in which Love and Beauty and Goodness impelled men to action, a sense of the sacredness and loneliness . . . of defeat. What else? The great jest, the wonderful release of laughter. The muleteers blunder up out of the night to water their mules at the "altar." Here, as in each of Quixote's and Sancho's adventures, yearning and pathos and jest flower together: emotion and burlesque, tradition and immediacy, felt time

and the atemporal time of images, brute fact and conceptual
delicacy, the abstract and the concrete, the disciplined and
the accidental -- all "real" in the intricate mixture of
experience, and here designed in a simultaneity and a
spiraling intertwining as one act of perception.

That these ebullitions derive from Van Ghent's own fancy will be immediately obvious to
any one willing to glance through even a paragraph of Cervantes' text. Although she speaks of
everything from "the urgency of devotion" to "the sacredness and loneliness of defeat" as "arising
conceptually" -- as if from some cosmic or unattached mind -- the conceptions themselves are
clearly her own sentimental responses to the conventional stimuli she has abstracted from the scene
in the form of "night, moonlight, a deserted innyard, a man pacing up and down alone." Indeed
the effect of her reading is first to transform the passage into a prevision of Dickensian melodrama,
then to garland it in critical verbiage so perspectivist as to be dizzying that is presumably intended
to show that everything is "real" and "offers a field for the joyful exercise of perception" which is
"here designed in a simultaneity and a spiraling intertwining as one act of perception."

Then, less joyfully, but more plainly, Van Ghent invokes "perspective" directly.
"Quixote's devotion to the chivalric ideal," she asserts, "is of that extreme which transforms
objects the most trivial and gross into the sacramental." In the scene at the horse trough, for
example, "consecration has taken place" -- if our perspective is right. "It is by perspective," she
explains, "that our vision is adjusted." Moreover "the perspectives that it [Don Quixote] affords
are constantly reversible . . . in depth." And by way of illustration she takes the scene in which
Sancho and Don Quixote enter Toboso, at night, looking for Dulcinea:

> Here the great experiment of the practical test of the soul's
> truth is made in a tranquil darkness, a darkness naturally
> symbolic of the subjective loneliness of Quixote's quest, both
> of its obscurity to outward view and of its serene starlit clarity
> within. This setting for an act of faith is given what we have
> called perspective by the homely, immediate foreground
> sounds of braying asses, grunting hogs, and mewing cats --
> that is, by contrast with objective detail grotesquely irrelevant
> to a spiritual quest. We see that spiritual event from a point
> of observation in the nonspiritual, and each heightens the
> significance of the other; or we could reverse our terms here,
> and say that the homely Tobosan night sounds echo in the
> perspective of that other night, the creative night of the
> dedicated soul. Similarly with that palace of Dulcinea's
> which seems, because of the tensions of Quixote's
> expectations, to loom so loftily over Toboso: as soon as
> Sancho speaks, the ghostly structure is riddled with by-lanes
> and blind alleys, hovels and bawdyhouses, all the
> commonplaces of a sleeping city; but immediately another
> displacement of vision occurs, and it rises before us again --
> only "two hundred paces" away. Both visual and spiritual
> perspective are phantasmagorically reversible . . . (Perhaps
> the most striking presentation of this double activity occurs
> when Quixote tells Sancho that, though no doubt the barber's
> basin is a barber's basin to Sancho, to Quixote it is
> Mambrino's helmet, and to another man it may well be
> something else. In other words, he refuses to falsify either
> the vision or the sense evidence.)

After further discussion Van Ghent finally acknowledges that "it is rather difficult for the rationalizing, moralizing intellect to think in this fashion. We feel the need of singling out some aspect as predominant and definitive of worth-while values." But "an eminent critic of Spanish literature," she explains, "will help us here. He [Americo Castro] says that the theme of Spanish literature, and that of *Don Quixote*, may be summarized as 'the difficulty of living, when it tries to integrate body, soul, and mind -- which is different from giving preference to the latter at the expense of the other two.'" But the difference Castro has in mind is not at all what this statement implies. "From the conjunction of Hebrew concepts with Neo-Platonic thought in Philo Judaeus," Castro observes, "sprang forth a belief in the logos-word as a divinely emanative and creative spirit: 'And the Word [logos] was made flesh and dwelt among us.'"[41] Then, invoking everything from Oriental history and tradition to "the role of the book . . . in Arabian literature," Castro proceeds from "the Word . . . made flesh" to the book made flesh, or in his own words, taken from his own title, he proceeds to "incarnation in *Don Quixote*," that comes through reading which he attempts to explain as the "incarnation of the incitement." "The basic theme of *Don Quixote* is life as a process creative of itself -- the onrush of incitements (the written or spoken word, love, wealth, possibilities of amusement, etc.) into the river bed of the life of each individual."[42] Or, as he elsewhere says more prosaically: "Books are . . . what each reader makes of them by living through them. Literature becomes personalized and individual living reveals its latent poetic dimension; this is the source of the undying beauty of *Don Quixote*."[43] For "to those capable of feeling such profound emotion, he [Don Quixote] is the paradigm of the most noble and desperate anguish . . . When Don Quixote declares: 'odious to me now are all profane stories of knight-errantry . . .' it means that he is really dying, for his soul ceases to emit reflections."[44]

So Castro integrates what he understands by body, soul, and mind into a sort of "livingness" or *Erlebnis*: "In *Don Quixote* (as generally in all Spanish life), the rational is not the real, but rather, only that is real which lives in contexture with the individuals 'livingness' (*Erlebnis*). Truth and falsity are fluid transcendencies eddied in the personal experience that serves them in each case as contents or warranty. Judgments of value, not logical judgments, lead to and build reality . . . The essential foundation for reading books is that the written word is felt as an animate, vital reality, and not as a mere expression of imagination or knowledge . . . In short the ultimate reality of *Don Quixote* cannot be understood if we keep it enclosed in the strict orbit of Western history."[45]

All this Van Ghent duly paraphrases or summarizes. "If we look on the adventures of Quixote and Sancho each as total action," she concludes, "we shall recover, through insight made body, more of ourselves and of other men -- which is to say more 'perspective' -- than if we attempt to rigidify *Don Quixote* into a system of preferences." And she completes this paragraph with a final quotation from Castro: "The scene of so prodigious a spectacle [ *Don Quixote* ] is the workshop in which the life of each one is forged, and is not a didactic or logical transcendency superimposed on the process of living. [It is] a question of showing that reality is always an aspect of the experience of the person who is living it."[46]

A more thoroughgoing denial of Cezanne's apple, or of the voice of the belly, is difficult to imagine. For Van Ghent's "perspective" as expressed through her "insight made body" (a variation on the word made flesh and incarnation in *Don Quixote* that is, in effect, an inversion of the Panzaic principle) eliminates body in the physical sense altogether. It seeks to replace bodily shaped man with, in Castro's phrase, "book-shaped man" as represented by incarnation in *Don Quixote* -- with Quixote becoming "the paradigm of the most noble and desperate anguish" until he gives up books on knight errantry, and his soul, in consequence, ceases to emit reflections.

But such a reading will not do, or at least it will not do within "the orbit of Western history." Whatever the validity of Castro's "incarnation" as mystical philosophy, it is, as criticism premised on an ostrich-like denial of the physical body (and therefore of the Panzaic principle) that simply cannot be maintained in the light of Cervantes' text. Although Cervantes was certainly not obsessed with the fact that Celia shits, or Dulcinea shits, in the sense that Swift's critics (as distinct from Swift) have been obsessed by this fact, he is at pains to show us that Don Quixote, at what must surely be (in Castro's terms) one of his supreme moments of incarnation, shits. As the scene opens (near the end of Chapter XLVIII) Sancho approaches Don Quixote's cage to inform him that he is not under a spell, that he has been put in his cage, not by enchanters, but by the barber and curate of his own village:

> "Master," he said, going up to the cage, "I want to get a load off my conscience by telling you what goes on in connection with your enchantment. The truth of the matter is that those two with their faces covered are the curate of our village and the barber, and it is my belief that they have plotted to carry you off like this out of pure spite, because your Grace is so far ahead of them in famous deeds. If this is so, then it follows that you are not under a spell at all but have been hoodwinked and made a fool of. Just to prove this, I'd like to ask you one thing, and if you answer me as I think you will have to, then you'll be able to lay your hand on what's wrong and will see that you are not enchanted but simply out of your head."
>
> "Ask me whatever you like, Sancho my son," replied Don Quixote," and I will give you an answer that will satisfy you on every point. As to what you say about those who accompany us being the curate and the barber, our fellow townsmen whom we know very well, that is who they may appear to you to be, but you are not by an manner of means to believe that that is what they really and truly are. What you are rather to understand is that if they have, as you say, this appearance in your eyes, it must be for the reason that those who have put this spell upon me have seen fit to assume that form and likeness; for it is easy enough for enchanters to take whatever form they like, and so they must have assumed the appearance of our friends expressly for the purpose of leading you to think what you do, thus involving you in a labyrinth of fancies from which you would not succeed in extricating yourself even though you had the cord of Theseus.
>
> "They also doubtless had another purpose, that of causing me to waver in my mind, so that I should not be able to form a conjecture as to the source of this wrong that is done me. For, if on the one hand you tell me it is the barber and the curate . . . who accompany us, and on the other hand I find myself shut up in a cage, knowing full well that no·human but only a superhuman power could have put me behind these bars, what would you have me say to you or what would you have me think except that my enchantment, in view of the manner in which it has been accomplished, is like none that I have ever read about in all the histories that treat of knights-errant who have been laid under a spell? And so you may set your mind at rest as to the suspicions that you have voiced, for those two are no more what you say they are than I am a Turk. But you said that you had something to ask me; speak, then and I will answer you, though you keep on asking until tomorrow morning."
>
> "May Our Lady help me!" cried Sancho in a loud voice. "Is it possible your Grace is so thick-headed and so lacking in

brains that you cannot see that I am telling you the simple
truth when I say that malice has more to do than magic with
your being in this plight? But since that is the way matters
stand, I'd like to prove to you beyond a doubt that there is no
magic about it. And now, tell me, as you would have God
rescue you from this torment, and as you hope to find
yourself in the arms of my lady Dulcinea when you least
expect it --"

"Stop conjuring me," said Don Quixote, "and ask what
you like. I have already told you that I will answer you point
by point."

"What I ask is this," Sancho went on, "and what I would
have you tell me, without adding anything to it or leaving
anything out, but in all truthfulness, as you would expect it to
be told, and as it is told, by all those who like your Grace
follow the calling of arms, under the title of knights-errant --"

"I have said that I will tell you no lies," replied Don
Quixote. "Go ahead and finish your questions; for in truth
you weary me, Sancho, with all these solemn oaths,
adjurations, and precautions."

"I am sure," said Sancho, "That my master is kindhearted
and truthful; and so, because it has a bearing on what we are
talking about, I would ask your Grace, speaking with all due
respect, if by any chance, since you have been in that cage
and, as it seems to you, under a spell, you have felt the need
of doing a major or a minor, as the saying goes."

"I do not understand what you mean by 'doing a major or
a minor,' Sancho. Speak more plainly if you wish me to give
you a direct answer."

"Is it possible that your Grace doesn't know what 'a major
or a minor' is? Why lads in school are weaned on it. What I
mean to say is, have you felt like doing that which can't be
put off?

"Ah, I understand you, Sancho! Yes, many times; and for
that matter, right now. Get me out of this, or all will not be
as clean here as it ought to be!"[47]

Here, surely, is the answer direct to Castro and Van Ghent and Madariaga and indeed all
the idealists and perspectivists. Here, in fact, the Panzaic principle manifests itself (in direct
contradiction to Van Ghent's "insight made body") as body made insight. And this is but one of
thousands of such insights in the novel that idealists and perspectivists have so long been trying to
overlook or explain away.

But at least one perspectivist critic of *Don Quixote*, Ortega y Gasset, has been percipient
enough and courageous enough to acknowledge, even as he deplores, the full effect of Sancho
Panzism which he equates with materiality and/or realism:

> The force of the concrete in things stops the movement of our
> images. The inert and harsh object rejects whatever
> "meanings" we may give it: it is just there, confronting us,
> affirming its mute, terrible materiality in the face of all
> phantoms. This is what we call realism: to bring things to a
> distance, place them under a light, incline them in such a way
> that the stress falls upon the side which slopes down towards

121

pure materiality . . . The theme of realistic poetry is the crumbling of poetry . . . the poetic quality of reality is not reality as this or that thing but reality as a generic function. Therefore it does not actually matter what objects the realist chooses to describe. Any one at all will do, since they all have an imaginary halo around them, and the point is to show the pure materiality under it. We see in this materiality a conclusive argument, a critical power which defeats the claim to self-sufficiency of all idealizations, wishes and fancies of man. The insufficiency, in a word, of culture, of all that is noble, clear, lofty . . . Cervantes recognizes that culture is all that, but that, alas, it is a fiction. Surrounding culture -- as the puppet show of fancy was surrounded by the inn -- lies the barbarous, brutal, mute, insignificant reality of things. It is sad that it is shown to us thus, but what can we do about it! It is real, it is there: it is terribly self-sufficient. Its force and its single meaning are rooted in its presence. Culture is memories and promises, an irreversible past, a dreamed future. But reality is a simple and frightening "being there." It is a presence, a deposit, an inertia. It is materiality.[48]

Ortega's critical position, it should be clear, is diametrically opposed to Lawrence's. Yet -- and this is crucial -- his analysis of the relationship between the ideal and the real, culture and materiality, substantiates Lawrence's analysis at every turn -- to show, in context, that the apple, the phallus, the guts, possess a power which "defeats the claim to self-sufficiency of all idealizations, wishes and fancies of man. The insufficiency, in a word, of culture, of all that is noble, clear, lofty . . ."

Moreover Ortega demonstrates how this power -- the power of the Panzaic principle -- becomes basic to the novel as a literary genre: how in *Don Quixote* Cervantes raises this power to its full potential, how in every novel it destroys the myth, "the crystalline orb of the ideal":

In it [*Don Quixote*] the epic comes to an end forever along with its aspiration to support a mythical orb bordering on that of material phenomena but different from it. It is true that the reality of the adventure is saved, but such a salvation involves the sharpest irony. The reality of the adventure is reduced to the psychological, to a bodily humor perhaps. It is real as far as it is vapor from a brain, so that its reality is rather that of its opposite, the material.

In summer the sun pours down torrents of fire on La Mancha, and frequently the burning earth produces the phenomenon of the mirage. The water which we see is not real water, but there is something real in it: its source. This bitter source, which produces the water of the mirage, is the desperate dryness of the land.

We can experience a similar phenomenon in two directions: one simple and straight, seeing the water which the sun paints as actual; another ironic, oblique, seeing it as a mirage, that is to say, seeing through the coolness of the water the dryness of the earth in disguise. The novel of adventures, the tale, the epic are that ingenuous manner of experiencing imaginary and significant things. The realistic novel is this second oblique manner. It requires something of the first: it needs something of the mirage to make us see it as such. So that it is not only *Don Quixote* which was written against the books of chivalry, and as a result bears the latter within it, but the novel as a literary genre consists essentially of that absorption.

This offers an explanation of . . . how reality, the actual, can be changed into poetic substance. By itself, seen in a direct way, it would never be poetic: this is the privilege of the mythical. But we can consider it obliquely as destruction of the myth, as criticism of the myth. In this form reality, which is of an inert and insignificant nature, quiet and mute, acquires movement, is changed into an active power of aggression against the crystalline orb of the ideal. The enchantment of the latter broken, it falls into fine, iridescent dust which gradually loses its colours until it becomes an earthy brown. We are present at this scene in every novel. There is need of a book showing in detail that every novel bears the *Don Quixote* within it like an inner filigree in the same way that every epic poem contains the Iliad within it like the fruit its core.[49]

Ortega's "every novel" cannot possibly include the thousands of best-selling novels (ranging from *Uncle Tom's Cabin* to *The Man in the Grey Flannel Suit*) that exclude Panzaic reality altogether. Nor does there seem to be any destruction of the myth or of the crystalline orb of the ideal in the novels that E.M. Forster has defined as "prophetic." Yet these exceptions do not invalidate -- they merely qualify -- Ortega's analysis, which serves to bring out basic critical distinctions that idealistic and perspectivistic critics have been at pains to deny. "Every novel" may not bear the *Don Quixote* within it, but nearly all the good ones do. And there is consequently a need, not only for such a book as Ortega calls for, but for books with a more critical emphasis -- including those in which I plan to show how the Panzaic principle enters into and shapes nineteenth-century English fiction.[50] For if Emma Bovary is a Don Quixote in skirts, as Ortega maintains, then Becky Sharp is a Sancho Panza to the Quixotes and Dulcineas of the nineteenth century. From Jane Austen's Lydia Bennet and Charlotte Lucas to Hardy's Arabella and Alec d'Urberville the voice of reality (i.e., the voice of the apple and the belly and the phallus) is always "there" -- in a way and to a degree and with effects that, as I shall try to demonstrate, bear out Ortega's fears and Lawrence's hopes.

Notes

¹ Gustave Flaubert, "Love, Happiness and Art" [passages from Flaubert's letters to Louise Colet], trans. Francis Steegmuller, *Partisan Review*, 20 (1953), 97. D.H. Lawrence, "The Novel," in *The Later D.H. Lawrence*, selected with introductions by William York Tindall (New York: Knopf, 1952), pp. 190-191.

² T.E. Hulme, *Speculations* (London: Routledge and Kegan Paul, 1949), p. 114.

³ D.H. Lawrence, "Introduction to These Paintings," in *Phoenix: The Posthumous Papers of D.H. Lawrence*, ed. Edward D. McDonald (New York: Viking Press, 1936), pp. 569-570.

⁴ Quoted in *Cervantes Across the Centuries*, ed. Angel Flores and M. J. Benardete (New York: Dryden Press, 1947), p. 330.

⁵ Joseph Wood Krutch, *Five Masters: A Study in the Mutations of the Novel* (Bloomington: Indiana University Press, Midland Book, 1959), p. 76.

⁶ Salvador de Madariaga, *Don Quixote: An Introductory Essay in Psychology*, rev. ed. London: Oxford University Press, Oxford Paperback, 1961), pp. 117, 162.

⁷ Ibid., pp. 4-5.

⁸ Ibid., pp. 6-7. The translation Madariaga quotes here is apparently his own.

⁹ Ibid., p. 145.

¹⁰ Ibid., pp. 151, 159, 150, 118, 124.

¹¹ Ibid., pp. 162, 8.

¹² Ibid., p. 8.

¹³ This cover design is from an engraving by Gustave Dore.

¹⁴ Charles Lamb, "Barrenness of the Imaginative Faculty in the Productions of Modern Art," in *Last Essays of Elia*, Everyman's Library (London: J.M. Dent and Sons, 1906), p. 271. For this and other references and for my general characterization of Quixote criticism I am indebted to Arthur Efron's Ph.D. thesis, "Satire Denied: A Critical History of English and American *Don Quixote* Criticism" (University of Washington, 1964). I have not yet consulted Efron's recently published study, *Don Quixote and the Dulcineated World* (Austin: University of Texas Press, 1971).

¹⁵ Joaquin Ortega, "Rethinking Cervantes," *New Mexico Quarterly Review*, 17 (1947), p. 419.

¹⁶ Thomas Mann, "Voyage with Don Quixote," in *Essays by Thomas Mann*, trans. H.T. Lowe-Porter (New York: Vintage Books, 1958), p. 346.

¹⁷ Miguel de Unamuno, *The Life of Don Quixote and Sancho*, trans. Homer T. Earle (New York: Knopf, 1927), p. 79.

¹⁸ D.H. Lawrence, *Lady Chatterley's Lover* (New York: Grove Press, 1959), pp. 297-298.

¹⁹ Why this principle holds, even for those who would consciously deny it in life, may in part be accounted for -- if one can accept Freud and his successors -- by the fact that Western man has never succeeded in his efforts to asceticize himself. As Norman O. Brown explains in *Life Against Death* (Middletown: Wesleyan University Press, 1959), p. 31: "Parental discipline, religious denunciation of bodily pleasure and philosophic exaltation of the life of reason have all left man overtly docile, but secretly in his unconscious unconvinced . . . Man remains unconvinced

124

because in infancy he tasted the fruit of the tree of life, and knows that it is good, and never forgets
. . . in spite of two thousand years of higher education based on the notion that man is essentially a
soul for mysterious accidental reasons imprisoned in a body, man remains incurably obtuse and
still secretly thinks of himself as first and foremost a body. Our repressed desires are not just for
delight, but specifically for delight in the fulfillment of the life of our own bodies." Why the
principle invariably holds in the novel (as distinct from other literary forms) has been explained by
D.H. Lawrence in his various essays on the novel, one of his more concise statements being that in
"The Novel" (in *The Later D.H. Lawrence*, p. 191):

> You can fool pretty nearly every other medium. You can
> make a poem pietistic, and still it will be a poem. You can
> write *Hamlet* in drama: if you wrote him in a novel, he'd be
> half comic, or a trifle suspicious: a suspicious character, like
> Dostoevsky's Idiot. Somehow, you sweep the ground a bit
> too clear in the poem or the drama, and you let the human
> Word fly a bit too freely. Now in a novel there's always a
> tom-cat, a black tom-cat that pounces on the white dove of the
> Word, if the dove doesn't watch it; and there is a banana-skin
> to trip on; and you know there is a water-closet on the
> premises.

[20] Ian Watt, *The Rise of the Novel* (London: Chatto and Windus, 1957), p. 12.

[21] Ibid., pp. 10-11.

[22] Ibid., pp. 11.

[23] Ibid., p. 278.

[24] Ibid.

[25] Henry Fielding, *Tom Jones*, Bk. V, chap. X (New York: Modern Library, 1950), p.
202.

[26] Watt, p. 283.

[27] Ibid., p. 282.

[28] Ibid., p. 287.

[29] Quoted by Watt, pp. 281-282.

[30] E.M.W. Tillyard, *Shakespeare's History Plays* (New York: Macmillian, 1946), pp.
285, 286, 287.

[31] Ibid., p. 289.

[32] George Orwell, "The Art of Donald McGill," in *Dickens, Dali and Others* (New York:
Reynal and Hitchcock, 1946), pp. 135-136.

[33] Ibid., p. 137.

[34] Tillyard, p. 290.

[35] Ibid., p. 291.

[36] Ibid, p. 291.

[37] Cleanth Brooks and Robert B. Heilman, "Notes on *Henry IV, Part One*," in
*Understanding Drama* (New York: Henry Holt, 1948), pp. 376-387.

[38] See also Franz Alexander, "A Note on Falstaff," *Psychoanalytic Quarterly*, 2 (1933),
592- 606. In his concluding paragraphs Alexander brings out the social-political implications of
Falstaff's childishness:

We have [in the termites] the example of a perfect social organization in which the individuals have no private life and all their functions and energies belong to the state. Here is a community in which the state does not serve the welfare of the individual, but the individual lives for the state, which appears as a higher biological unit comparable with the human body, in which the individual cells have no private life but depend on each other and function for the benefit of the whole body.

Is this the future of the human race, which is seemingly drifting towards an increasingly mechanized social organization? The state of the termites appears to us as a horrible nightmare. From this nightmare we are relieved by Falstaff, the apotheosis of self-sufficient careless individuality. So long as we applaud him and want to see him again and again, and expect our writers to create him anew in a thousand different guises, we are safe from the destiny of the termites. Our applause demonstrates that the portion of our personality which stands for individual sovereignty is still stronger than our collectivistic urges. It is difficult to tell whether the dynamic structure of the human personality is in the process of changing in the direction of a more collective type of man, but we may comfort ourselves by the belief that if, and when, the collective forces finally gain the upper hand in us, we will not deplore the loss of individual sovereignty because we will have ceased to understand what it means.

[39] Dorothy Van Ghent, "On *Don Quixote*," in *The English Novel* (New York: Rinehart and Co., 1953), pp. 9-19. I have not identified the individual quotations from this work.

[40] *Don Quixote*, trans. Samuel Putnam, 2 vols (New York: Viking Press, 1949), pp. 1, 44.

[41] Americo Castro, "Incarnation in *Don Quixote*," in *Cervantes Across the Centuries*, p. 161.

[42] Ibid., pp. 165-166.

[43] Ibid., p. 159.

[44] Ibid., pp. 161, 176.

[45] Ibid., pp. 159-160.

[46] Quoted by Van Ghent, p. 19.

[47] *Don Quixote*, I, pp. 433-435.

[48] Jose Ortega y Gasset, "The Nature of the Novel," trans. Evelyn Rugg and Diego Marin, *Hudson Review*, 10 (1957), pp. 30-31.

[49] Ibid., pp. 27, 28, 40.

[50] The present study is the first in a series of five books on the Panzaic principle that I am preparing for publication. The second is to be entitled *Dulcinea as the Immaculate Sister*, and will include chapters on *Wuthering Heights*, *The Cloister and the Hearth*, and *Vanity Fair*. The third book will be devoted to Hardy's work, the fourth to Dickens', and the fifth to the novels of Charlotte Brontë and George Eliot.

# Part II

The roundabout methods of defining the Panzaic that have been used up to this point have been used with a definite purpose in mind; viz. to suggest what the Panzaic may be without permitting the suggested possibilities to take the form of hard and fast definitions that may prove arbitrary or premature. But roundaboutness has its limits, as well as its advantages, and those limits have been reached when the reader, becoming at least partially convinced that there may be something to this Panzaic business, presumes that the next step is to look for the Panzaic in fiction the way he looks for irony, or paradox, or symbolism, or significant form. When this happens -- as it is almost bound to, given the reader's background, culture, and English-major reading habits -- he is in immediate danger of turning the Panzaic principle into another critical gimmick, one designed to turn up, say, images of defecation instead of images of incarnation. Or, proceeding in another critical direction, the reader may be in danger of turning the Panzaic principle into still another kind of critical gimmick by treating it as if it were a literary extension of Zen or one or another of the fashionable cults of body worship now heralded in magazines ranging all the way from *Look* to *Avant-Garde.*

To avoid these and related dangers, and, on the positive side, to clarify the Panzaic still further, it is necessary to reconsider and in certain instances redefine the basic distinctions that have already been made. And for this purpose there is the criticism of Ortega y Gasset.

In declaring that reality, in itself, "is of an inert and insignificant nature, quiet and mute," Ortega is of course expressing his own idealistic bias. And the same bias is apparent in his statement that "It does not actually matter what objects the realist chooses to describe. Any one at all will do, since they all have an imaginary halo around them, and the point is to show the pure materiality under it."[1] Yet, however biased these statements may be, philosophically, they point towards a crucial aspect of the Panzaic principle that cannot be too much stressed: the fact that no thing or being in fiction can be Panzaic in itself or in himself. Not even a belly! Not even a phallus! A phallus, presented clinically, may be just a spout to urinate through; or, presented pornographically, it may be an object to thrill to. It is only Panzaic when it functions in such a way as to cut through what Ortega has described as the "crystalline orb of the ideal" -- the way the pig's pizzle in Hardy's *Jude the Obscure,* for example, cuts directly through the crystalline orb of Jude's daydreams to show the phallic reality that underlies them -- the reality that is to make a shambles of his ideals.

Whether or not something is Panzaic in a novel therefore depends not on what it is like (it may, in itself, be "inert and insignificant") but on what it does. More specifically, what it does to the abstract, the ideal, "the crystalline orb," the "imaginary halo." The "two fine ladies' handkerchiefs" that Kafka's Officer wears under the collar of his uniform (in *In the Penal Colony*) may, for instance, be more Panzaic than "the seven bronze verges . . . to which the dancing women offered flowers and furious caresses . . . [until] shouting and howling, seven women suddenly hurled themselves upon the seven bronzes . . ." in Octave Mirbeau's *Le Jardin des Supplices* (1899; translated by Alvah C. Bessie as *The Torture Garden,* Citadel Press, 1948). The handkerchiefs may be more Panzaic because, "inert and insignificant" as they may be in themselves, they nevertheless function in such a way, in context, as to bring out the discrepancy between the officer's impulses and professed ideals; whereas Mirbeau's seven verges bear little if any relationship to the ideal: they merely express his notion of female lust.

Yet if the Panzaic ultimately depends on what something does, there is no denying that what something is like may to a large extent determine what it does. In most instances handkerchiefs will not be Panzaic; verges and phalluses will. There is no getting around the fact that, in our culture, we associate phalluses with the real and the crude, handkerchiefs with the genteel and the refined. Nor is there any denying that these associations necessarily affect what phalluses and handkerchiefs can do in any fictional context.

But these are theoretical considerations that can best be clarified later on, in the discussion of individual novels. The point here is that nothing is Panzaic in itself, that nothing can be Panzaic until it is brought into conflict with the ideal and serves to cut through or destroy "the crystalline orb of the ideal."

The necessary corollary to this point, as Ortega explains, is that the ideal is every bit as essential to the working of the Panzaic principle as the real. In Ortega's words:

> [The realistic novel] needs something of the mirage to make us see it as such. So that it is not only *Don Quixote* which was written against the books of chivalry, and as a result bears the latter within it, but the novel as a literary genre consists of that absorption.

Or, stated more directly, there can be no destruction of the myth unless there is a myth or ideal to be destroyed -- as well as some form of the Panzaic reality to destroy it; no destruction of Don Quixote unless there is a Don Quixote to be destroyed -- as well as a Panzaic character to destroy him.

According to this formulation, then, a Panzaic character would be one who is like Sancho Panza in both character and function, which of course raises the primary question of what Sancho Panza is like; and this question -- if it can be answered at all satisfactorily -- raises the further and perhaps even more difficult question of what the likenesses are like. Is Sam Weller, for example, like Sancho Panza because Dickens has, to some extent, modelled him after Sancho Panza, and has clearly indicated that he intends him to play Sancho Panza to Micawber's Don Quixote? My own answer would be "No," on the ground that Sam Weller is not really like Sancho, the seeming similarities in character and function are merely outward and superficial, that Sam, regardless of how Dickens consciously intended him, corresponds to a distinct Victorian type that is in most respects antithetical to Sancho Panza, a pseudo-Panzaic type sometimes defined as "The Resourceful Hero" that invariably ends up defending the mythical orb of the ideal.[2] Whereupon another critic might reply that I have misunderstood Sancho (and perhaps Sam Weller too); that the similarities I have dismissed as superficial are really fundamental; that my whole conception of the Panzaic is based on a misunderstanding of Sancho and his role in *Don Quixote*; that in point of fact I have fashioned out of my Lawrentian reading a Sancho who resembles Lawrence's Mellors far more that he does the Sancho of Cervantes' text.

To such charges I might reply that my reading of *Don Quixote* is not at all extreme or idiosyncratic; that, on the contrary, it is in all essentials much like Ortega's reading, is much like a number of the accepted readings that Arthur Efron discusses in his "Satire Denied: A Critical History of English and American *Don Quixote* Criticism."[3] And from these beginnings I might then go on to a full scale defense of my own reading, and more especially my interpretation of Sancho and his role in the novel. Indeed, if my concept of the Panzaic were dependent on my interpretation of Sancho, I would be obliged to undertake some such defense. But it is not. I am not trying to define or establish points of literary indebtedness; rather I am trying to identify a type of character common to innumerable novels, a type that I have labelled Panzaic because, in my opinion, Sancho Panza is the first and perhaps the most successful embodiment of the type. But if I am wrong about Sancho it does not follow that I am wrong about the type, which exists apart from Sancho and my application of his name. Indeed the type could just as well be identified through one or another of its 20th-century exemplifications, e.g., through Schweik in *The Good Soldier Schweik*, or Zorba in *Zorba the Greek*, or the mother in Vittorini's *Conversation in Sicily*, or Kitten in Robert Gover's *One Hundred Dollar Misunderstanding*.

Each of these characters beautifully embodies the type. The mother in Vittorini's novel, described by the narrator, who is her son, as a "Blessed Old Sow," is in her own way every bit as earthy, every bit as simple-minded, as Sancho; and it is she, in the context of the novel, who shows the nullity of the social and political ideals that her son and others would have people live by. Zorba too, for all his physical and sexual prowess, is naive if not simple-minded in his responses, and it is primarily through his responses that the novel, and more especially the movie (which is, in my opinion, far superior to the novel), exposes the inadequacy of the Quixotic hero's liberal ideals.  Schweik, unlike Zorba and Vittorini's mother, who are for their years quite striking, and even handsome, is a man after Sancho's own belly -- a man who resembles Sancho in everything from his physical features to his simple-mindedness.  And while there may be some question as to whether Schweik is actually simple-minded, or is, like Hamlet, feigning madness, the question is not, in the present context, a crucial one.  What really matters is that Schweik's simple-minded attitudes and responses, whether real or assumed, serve to devastate the pretensions and posturings of the Don Quixotes who are, in the name of God and country, trying either to kill him or get him killed.

Kitten, the fourteen-year-old Negro prostitute in Robert Gover's *One Hundred Dollar Misunderstanding*, provides still another beautiful example of a Panzaic character -- even though the novel she appears in is rather slight.  What Kitten, "lil ol blackass Pickaninny me," does to the college boy, J.C., is not just hilariously funny; it provides a contrast between her responses and his that shows how unfeeling and cruel and stupid a well-intentioned and liberal young American can be.  And this contrast could have been even more telling if Gover had created in his college boy a Don Quixote of more sensitivity and sophistication and intelligence.  As it is, Kitten has it all her own way so easily, so much of the time, that she never gets a chance to exercise her Panzaic powers to the full.  She who might have devastated the highest and most precious mythical orbs of our culture ends up by devastating only a college boy version of white, middle-class, Protestant Americanism.  But this is of course a criticism of the novel, not of Kitten.

What makes her and the other characters Panzaic, then, is not their outward or even their inward characteristics; it is their function -- which is, as I have explained, to show that the senses of even a fool can give the lie to the noblest ideals of even the most profound thinker.  But this, of course, does not mean that the Panzaic character must be a fool (although many of the greatest have been); neither does it mean that the Panzaic character must be a sensualist (although, with a few notable exceptions, the greatest have been); nor does it mean that the Panzaic character, by virtue of his giving the lie to the hero or heroine, then usurps the position of the hero or heroine and becomes a hero or heroine on his own.

The Panzaic is not synonymous with the sexual, or the Dionysian, or the Rabelaisian, or the Lawrentian, or, for that matter, any of the current forms of Zen or Hippie philosophizing.  The Panzaic principle is *not* an attempt to elevate or idealize the Panzaic or Panzaic characters at the expense of the idealistic or the heroic.  By their very nature Panzaic characters cannot be so elevated -- and still remain Panzaic.  Inevitably they become heroic.  And when this happens they can no longer function like Sancho Panza or like Schweik.  They cease being undercutters of the ideal and become embodiments of the ideal, i.e., they cease being Sancho Panzas and become spiritual Sancho Panzas or sensual Don Quixotes or, more positively, Tristans or Don Juans.

One of the first and more notable examples of this kind is Mellors in *Lady Chatterley's Lover*.  Even in the earliest version of this novel (reprinted by New Directions under the title of *The First Lady Chatterley*) Lawrence's gamekeeper, Parkin, is as much the embodiment of Lawrence's ideals as he is the undercutter of the conventional ideals of Lord Chatterley.  And in the third and final version we know as *Lady Chatterley's Lover*, Lawrence makes Parkin even more heroic, giving him a new name, Mellors, and endowing him, as the occasion demands, with the speech, manners, and even the dress of a gentleman.  Consequently, Mellors is not a Panzaic character: he is a hero -- in a sense that none of Lawrence's other great novels have heroes.  He is the man that Birkin, the hero of *Women in Love*, is only trying to be; that the heroes of *Kangaroo, Aaron's Rod,* and *The Rainbow* are trying to be.  He is, in short, Lawrence's idealized self-image -- a sensual Don Quixote with no Sancho Panza to challenge his sensual pretensions.  He has all the right feelings, all the right ideas, and knows all the right answers.  And, like Lawrence, he is constantly exercising his rightness and his knowingness, giving Connie, the other characters, and us, the readers, the final word on everything from sex to bolshevism, to painting.

With such a hero, the novel should be as bad as Lawrence's detractors have declared it to be.  Why it is not, why it is, on the contrary, a masterful novel of a very special kind, I have tried to explain in a separate essay, *"Lady Chatterley's Lover: A Pilgrim's Progress* for Our Time." [4] And I shall not rehearse my arguments here, except to point out that if Mellors is not Panzaic,

Connie is (in relation to everyone but Mellors himself); that if Mellors' guts do not give the lie to Clifford and his "insentient iron world," Connie's guts do. But in any case Lawrence was not trying to write another *Rainbow* or *Women in Love*. He knew perfectly well that in presenting Mellors as his savior-hero he was, to a large extent, substituting assertion and illustration for the "subtle inter-relatedness" of his earlier novels. But he did not care. His message, he felt, was a holy one -- a matter of life against death -- and he wanted to express it as directly, as clearly, as forcefully, and as propagandistically as the Bible expresses Christianity. In other words he was trying to write as a prophet, and if the novel succeeds, as I think it does, it succeeds as prophecy, as a new *Pilgrim's Progress* for our time, with the phallus as the bridge to the new heavenly city, Lawrence's new crystalline orb of the ideal.

The uniqueness of the novel is therefore ultimately attributable to Lawrence's prophetic power, his power of writing as if he were the last sane man in a world gone mad, his power of convincing the reader that whatever Mellors may be like, the phallic message he brings is a holy one. And this power, as E.M. Forster has explained (in his chapter on "Prophecy" in *Aspects of the Novel*), is a power that sets Lawrence's novels apart from those of his contemporaries, since it is a power that Lawrence shares with only three earlier novelists, and that only he, of all our 20th-century novelists, possesses. In any case, whether one can accept Lawrence as prophetic novelist or not, there is no denying that he is just about the only modern novelist who has been able to write directly as a phallic worshipper (apart from or in spite of the Panzaic principle) without having his work degenerate into case history, therapy, or pornography. Certainly none of the novelists who have followed him, from Aldous Huxley to Ken Kesey, have been able to write anything comparable to *Lady Chatterley*. Invariably the sexed-up savior-heroes in their novels become pep figures overcoming spurious difficulties, even when, as in the case of *Point Counter Point* and *One Flew over the Cuckoo's Nest*, the savior-heroes are modelled after Lawrence and Jesus Christ.

The efforts of these novelists, are, in fact, much like those of the movie-makers who have been trying so desperately to exploit their new sexual freedom. Trying, that is, with their heads, for their hearts, or more accurately, their phalluses, just do not seem to be in their work. They want to believe that the sexual connection that they would celebrate is really significant. They try to convince themselves. But apparently they cannot. And seemingly they cannot convince us, the viewers, even though we too want to believe. The most they can do is to present more and more body, more and more writhing, in the hope that somehow it will mean something. But of course it does not. It is just so much sensual and sentimental Quixoticism, with out new Don Quixotes laying our new Dulcineas in the French, Italian, Scandinavian, English and American hay.

*A Man and a Woman*, one of the most popular and one of the worst examples of this type, can be briefly described as *Peyton Place* for the jet set, since it turns on the question of whether or not the heroine can forget her former husband and learn to "come" with her new boyfriend. And we are invited to share her fears and frustrations and triumphs -- just as the news media, after raising much the same question in connection with Jackie Kennedy's marriage to Onassis, would have liked us to share her supposed fears and frustrations and triumphs. But such appeals to pruriency, no matter how much flesh is bared, are in no sense Panzaic.[5]

And the movie version of D.H. Lawrence's *The Fox* grossly oversimplifies Lawrence's novella in order to achieve the same type of sensational appeal. Will Banford win March? Or will Henry? Does March like homosexual love-making best? or heterosexual? or maybe she really prefers the fox? It is indeed a titillating triangle (or quadrangle, if we include the fox), especially as the movie-makers exploit its possibilities, finally to resolve the conflict by means of a long drawn out second murder (Henry's killing the fox is, in the movie, the first murder) that presumably assuages March's doubts. In short, the movie is an unintended parody of the novella in everything from its sexiness to its symbol mongering. For the novella is not about sex or murder at all, it is about the man-woman relationship between March and Henry, as Henry becomes a man and brings March a good part of the way towards womanhood and marriage. But not all the way; at the end of the novella March still cannot become "a seaweed," still cannot "go to sleep" in Henry --

although the text does suggest that she may, in time, become a woman, and that they may, in time, have a marriage, in Lawrence's sense of marriage.

The movie-makers, as well as the audiences who have thrilled to the sex and murder the movie-makers have presented in Lawrence's name,[6] thus serve to illustrate once again the truth of Lawrence's own observations in his much-quoted letter to Aldous Huxley, apropos of Huxley's efforts in *Point Counter Point* to espouse Lawrence's philosophy:

> Intellectual appreciation does not amount to so much, it's what you thrill to . . . if you can only palpitate to murder, suicide, and rape, in their various degrees -- and you state plainly that it is so -- *caro*, however are we going to live through the days? Preparing still another murder, suicide, and rape? But it becomes of a phantasmal boredom and produces ultimately inertia, inertia, inertia and final atrophy of the feelings. Till, I suppose, comes a final super-war, and murder, suicide, rape sweeps away the vast bulk of mankind.

The distinction Lawrence draws here cannot be too much stressed. Murder, suicide, and rape neither express nor appeal to our feelings or animal impulses: in their native habitats animals do not murder or rape each other, nor do they commit suicide. What murder, suicide, and rape appeal to is our sense of frustration and our consequent urges to beat and kill and destroy. And the effect of these appeals, constantly repeated, may be, as Lawrence suggests, to produce inertia and final atrophy of the feelings.

How close we have come to the final atrophy and the final super-war that Lawrence speaks of it is difficult if not impossible to say -- although there can be little doubt about the direction in which we are moving. The murder, suicide, and rape that Lawrence found so terrifying in *Point Counter Point* , for example, will not bear comparison, either in quality or quantity, with the murder, suicide, and rape in *Last Exit to Brooklyn*. In this novel the section entitled "Tralala" opens with this statement: "Tralala was 15 the first time she was laid." And the section concludes, after some twenty pages of her exploits, in this way:

> Tralala still bounced her tits on the palms of her hands turning to everyone as she was dragged out the door by the arm by 2 or 3 and she yelled to Jack to comeon and she/d fuckim blind not like like that fuckin douchebag he was with and someone yelled we/re coming and she was dragged down the steps tripping over someones feet and scraping her ankles on the stone steps and yelling but the mob not slowing their pace dragged her by an arm and Jack and Fred still hung on the bar roaring and Ruthy took off her apron getting ready to leave before something happened to louse up their deal and the 10 or 15 drunks dragged Tralala to a wrecked car in the lot on the corner of 57th street and yanked her clothes off and pushed her inside and a few guys fought to see who would be first and finally a sort of line was formed everyone yelling and laughing and someone yelled to the guys on the end to go get some beer and they left and came back with cans of beer which were passed around the daisychain and the guys from the Greeks cameover and some of the other kids from the neighborhood stood around watching and waiting and Tralala yelled and shoved her tits into the faces as they occurred before her and beers were passed around and the empties dropped or thrown and guys

left the car and went back on the line and had a few beers
and waited their turn again and more guys came from Willies
and a phone call to the Armybase brought more seamen and
doggies and more beer was brought from Willies and Tralala
drank beer while being laid and someone asked if anyone
was keeping score and someone yelled who can count that
far and Tralalas back was streaked with dirt and sweat and
her ankles stung from the sweat and dirt in the scrapes from
the steps and sweat and beer dripped from the faces onto
hers but she kept yelling she had the biggest goddamn pair
of tits in the world and someone answered ya bet ya sweet
ass yado and more came 40 maybe 50 and they screwed her
and went back on line and had a beer and yelled and laughed
and someone yelled that the car stunk of cunt so Tralala and
the seat were taken out of the car and laid in the lot and she
lay there naked on the seat and their shadows hid her
pimples and scabs and she drank flipping her tits with the
other hand and somebody shoved the beer against her mouth
and they all laughed and Tralala cursed and spit out a piece
of tooth and someone shoved it again and they laughed and
yelled and the next one mounted her and her lips were split
this time and the blood trickled to her chin and someone
mopped her brown with a beer soaked handkerchief and
another can of beer was handed to her and she drank and
yelled about her tits and another tooth was chipped and the
split in her lips was widened and everyone laughed and she
laughed and she drank more and more and soon she
passedout and they slapped her a few times and she
mumbled and turned her head but they couldnt revive her so
they continued to fuck her as she lay unconscious on the seat
in the lot and soon they tired of the dead piece and the
daisychain brokeup and they went back to Willies the Greeks
and the base and the kids who were watching and waiting to
take a turn took out their disappointment on Tralala and torn
her clothes to small scraps put out a few cigarettes on her
nipples pissed on her jerkedoff on her jammed a broomstick
up her snatch then bored they left her lying amongst the
broken bottled rusty cans and rubble of the lot and Jack and
Fred and Ruthy and Annie stumbled into a cab still laughing
and they leaned toward the window as they passed the lot
and got a good look at Tralala lying naked covered with
blood urine and semen and a small blot forming on the seat
between her legs as blood seeped from her crotch.[7]

In this scene, and throughout the novel, Selby succumbs to the violence he presumably
intends to deplore. It is not just the characters who are unfeeling; the novel is. Tralala, as the
novel presents her, is merely receiving the treatment she has given others. She is vile; her killers
are vile; Jack and Fred and Ruthy and Annie are vile; everyone is vile, because everyone is sexual,
especially women, and sex is vile, or at the very least debasing.

The only character whom the novel present sympathetically as a human being is a little old
lady named Ada who is introduced near the end of the novel:

Ada opened the window. The air was still and warm. She smiled and looked at the trees; the old ones, tall, big and strong; the young ones small, springy, hopeful; sun-shine lighting the new leaves and buds. Even the budding leaves on the hedges and the young thin grass and dandelion sprouts were alive with sunshine. O, it is so lovely. And Ada praised god, the being and creator of the universe who brought forth the spring with the warmth of his sun. She leaned out the window, her favorite window. From it the factory and the empty lots and junkyards were not visible; she could see only landscaping and the playground. And everything was coming to life and it was warm with sunshine. There were dozens of shades of green and now that spring was *really* here it would get greener and life would multiply on the earth and the birds would be more plentiful and their song would wake her in the mornings. All would be beautiful.[8]

And Ada has no sex life; she has love:

Ada hummed as she washed the dishes. She scoured the sink then made her bed, first opening the windows so the bed clothes should air out, then carefully tucking in the sheets and blankets, fluffing up the pillows (Hymie always liked his pillow thick and fluffy), then hanging up her nightgown and the pajamas she laid out on Hymies side of the bed each night. (Hymie had always liked a clean pair of pajamas every night and though he had been dead these 5 years, 6 in October, October the 23rd, she still laid out a pair of pajamas every night, though now she used the same pair each night, washing them once a month, ironing them and putting them back on the bed.) Then she tidied up the apartment, sweeping the kitchen floor and adjusting the furniture, before wiping the dishes and putting them away with the other dairy dishes. The humming evolved into light singing as she put on her sweater and coat and readied herself to go downstairs. She looked around the apartment, making certain the stove was off and all the lights out, before closing the door and going out. Near the entrance to the building was a small area bordered with benches and a few young trees. Here Ada sat whenever the weather permitted. She sat on a bench on the near side as she knew it would be in the sun longer than any of the others. This was *her* bench and here she sat and watched the children, the people passing or sitting, and enjoying the warmth of the sunshine. She closed her eyes and faced the sun, lifting her face, and sat thus for many minutes feeling the heat on her forehead, her eyelids, her cheeks, feeling the suns rays . . . warming her heart, making her feel almost happy. She breathed deeply, sighing inaudibly, and lowered her head and opened her eyes, then raised her feet slightly and wiggled her toes in her shoes. Her poor feet had such a burden to carry and they suffered so in the winter, but now even they were alive and relieved. It would be many, many wonderfully warm and sunny months before her feet would have to be tortured with thick heavy socks and forced to feel the cold. Soon she could go one day to Coney Island and sit on the Boardwalk and watch the swimmers or maybe she could even walk in the surf, but she wasn't sure if she should. She might slip, or someone might knock her over. Anyway, the beach was nice even just sitting on a bench getting the sun. She watched a small child ride by on his tricycle then watched a group of children running after each other and yelling. Occasionally she would be able to distinguish the words they were yelling and she blushed and immediately pushed it from her mind (this too would be remembered next winter) then turned abruptly as she heard a baby crying, seeing the overturned carriage, hearing the voice from a window, seeing a blur as 2 children ran away; trying to locate the baby, getting up from the bench when she saw a woman coming out of the building. Those children really should be more careful. She watched the mother pick up the child and drop him in the carriage and shove a bottle in his mouth and go upstairs. I hope it wasnt hurt. The baby eventually stopped crying and Ada turned away and once more watched the child circling the benches on its tricycle. She saw a woman passing with her children and shopping cart. The woman smiled, nodded and said Hello. Ada returned her greeting but didnt smile. She was a nice lady but her husband was no good. He always looked at Ada funny like he was going to hurt her. Not like her Hymie. Her Hymie was always friendly. Such a good man. They would have been married 43 years this summer, July 29th, if he was still alive. Hymie used to help her all the time. And he too loved the beach. But so seldom could they go. Only on Mondays when they closed the store and then sometimes it wouldnt be so nice. But many times they would go and she would make sandwiches and a thermos of a cold drink and Hymie always got for her a beach chair and umbrella. He always insisted. I want you should be comfortable and enjoy yourself. Thats what he said. She would always say no, dont bother. Who needs it? and they would laugh. But always Hymie insisted she should have the umbrella in case she might want to sit in the shade, but she never did and they would sit on the beach chairs getting the sun and once, maybe twice, during the day they would go down to the surf and splash around. He was so good her Hymie. And sometimes when her Ira got older he would tell them to go to the beach and they would mind the store and they would go an extra day to the beach. Her Ira was the best boy any Mother could have. (Everynight before going to bed she kissed their pictures.) Still only a boy already when they killed him. Just a boy. Not even married. Not even married when the Army took him. And he was such a good boy. When he was still just a little one he would come home from school and tell her to take a nap, hed help papa in the store and Hymie would smile so big and rub little Iras head and say yes, take a nap, Iras a big boy now and he will help me and Ira would smile up at his father and Ada would go back to the

small rooms behind the candy store and lie down. And
sometimes, when maybe it wasnt too busy, Hymie would fix
the supper while Ira watched the store and then Ira would
come back and wake her up and say suppers ready Mommy.
See? And everything would be on the table and they would
eat and she would go out and take care of the store while
Hymie ate. And Hymie worked so hard. Opening the store
at 6 in the morning and going out and getting the papers off
the street, and sometimes it would be cold and raining, and he
would carry in the big bundles of paper all by himself (he
would never let her help him with that) and cut the cords and
arrange them on the stand and she would lie in bed,
pretending to be asleep, and all the years they were married
Hymie got out of bed so quietly so she should sleeplonger
and every morning she would wake up but she never let him
know she was awake so he wouldnt worry about her. Then
he would come back at 8 oclock and she would pretend to
wake up when he touched her, and she would get up and fix
the breakfast. For 20 years they had the store and they were
so happy -- the child ran his tricycle into a tree and toppled
off, but got right up and started riding again -- maybe they
didnt always have so much, but they were happy and she
could still smell the soda fountain; the sweet smell of ice
cream, syrups, mixed fruits, hot fudge, marshmallow,
whipped cream and fudgicles, popsicles and ices and the
candy and chewing gum on the counter and the candy shelves
on the opposite side of the store, the sliding glass doors
smeared by the smudgy hands of thousands of children. She
used to lean on the counter and watch them look at the
candies pointing with their fingers pressed against the glass.
Many times each day this would happen and Ada would
wonder why they had to lean against the glass with their
hands and why it took them so long to make up their minds
what candy they wanted. And then when Ira came, late in her
life, it didnt annoy her as much. They were young like her
Ira. But when they get older they werent so nice and said bad
things to you. But Ira was always such a good boy. And
they had to kill him. And they didnt even see his body. Just
a telegram and many years later a sealed coffin. My poor Ira.
So young. Not even a father and now dead . . . . Dead 15
years and not even children to remember you. I dont know
why they did this to me. Even dead before Hymie, his
father. And even Hymie left me. Such a good man. Worked
so hard his back bent -- someone passed and Ada smiled, but
they just walked past not noticing Ada and Ada almost yelled
at them, but stopped as she noticed that now women were
coming down and people were going to the store and children
were running and laughing and the sun was getting brighter
and warmer and a few men straddled a bench with a checker
board between them and maybe someone would sit down
next to her and they would talk.[9]

But no one does sit next to her, or talk with her. And because she is so lost and lonely Ada
at times comes close to despair. But she can still pray ("praying to the Father as did the trees with

136

their bared limbs raised to heaven . . . hearing only the voice of God"). And she can still "sit on a bench and feel the sun, watch the birds, the children playing." And she still has her memories of Hymie and Ira and the good life they had together.

Nor is there any irony intended here. For all his sophistication Selby actually does present Ada and her seemingly sexless life with Hymie and Ira as, if not *the good life*, at least the best life that is possible in Brooklyn. Of course, Selby might, if he chose, justify the sentimentality of his presentation by pointing out that it is not really his, but Ada's, and that Ada is by this time a somewhat crazed old lady conjuring up a past that is idyllic only because she remembers it that way. But for Selby to attempt such a justification would be to hide behind a technicality. Ada is his creation; she is the only character in the novel who recognizes the "hate" in the people around her; and she is certainly the only character who hears "the voice of God," and hears it, seemingly, in much the same way that Selby does in his biblical epigraphs to the various sections of the novel.

Ada, then, is the Don Quixote, the upholder of the ideal, in the novel -- even though Selby, as novelist, is apparently either too ashamed or too self-conscious to acknowledge her openly. And her visions of her past life with Hymie and Ira, reminiscent of Dickens at his Victorian worst, are therefore the novel's ideal alternatives to the murder, suicide, and rape of Brooklyn -- even though Selby, as moralist, can neither acknowledge these ideals nor bring them into open collision with the world the other characters are living in. The most he can do is to sentimentalize Ada and her visions still further by having the other characters (usually the anonymous "Womens Chorus" of sadistic females) ignore, or mistreat, or vilify her in their commentaries:

> The housewives were on a bench. They looked at Ada and laughed. Everything comes out in this weather. Even Ada. I guess shes airing out her clothes. Laughter. Same shitty coat. She wears it all winter. Why dont she take it off? She got nothin on underneath. Whattaya mean? I bet shes wearing scabs. Laughter. Shes a filthy slob. I bet even the fumigator is afraid to go up to her house. I bet her crotch smells like limburger cheese. Laughter. (One picked her nose, exploring each nostril first with the pinky, locating the choice deposits, then with the forefinger broke loose the nights accumulations, scraping with the thumb and plucking forth, with thumb and forefinger, a choice meaty snot, long and green, spotted with yellows, waving it about, then rolling it in a ball, caressing it between her fingers, trying to flip it off but it clung tenaciously, adhesively to the finger until it was finally rubbed off on the bench.) . . . Looka Ada smilin. I think shes nuts the way she smiles all the time like that. She is. Shes got people talking to/er in her head. Somebody oughtta call up Kings County and turn her in. Laughter. Yeah, it aint safe with nuts running around. All she needs is a good fuckin. Maybe I should send Henry ova, hed do a good job. Laughter. I bet shes got money put away somewhere. You know those kind. Yeah. Her husband was in business for himself and cant tell me shes gotta go on Relief. Look atter sittin alone and smilin. If I had her money you wouldnt catch me sittin here. (A scab is picked off a leg, examined from various angles then flicked away.)[10]

There can be no doubt as to how these lines are intended. Selby is trying to turn the Panzaic principle inside out, upside down, in an effort to suggest that the ideal is right, the senses wrong. But these women are not speaking from their senses: they no longer have any senses to speak from. They might just as well be named "envy," "lust," "greed," etc., like characters in a medieval play. And the more elaborately drawn characters, like Tralala, are every bit as stereotyped. Presented more fully and sympathetically, they might be elemental Don Quixotes being destroyed by their own ideals and the psychopathic world that is Brooklyn -- the way so many of the characters in Celine's great novel *Death on the Installment Plan* are crippled or destroyed, not so much by the forces of reality, although they take their toll, but by their own Quixotic devotion to their own ideals.

But Celine is one of the great masters of the Panzaic whereas the closest Selby comes to it is in his treatment of Harry, the protagonist of the long section of the novel entitled "Strike." Harry is, in the beginning, a dim-witted, sadistic slob, who shares the outlook and attitudes of "the guys from the Greeks." Nevertheless he somehow meets a fairy, Alberta, who takes him home and, in one night, literally sucks and fucks him into a state of emotional well-being in which, for the first time in his life, he actually feels happy:

> When she finished the preparations she rolled back onto her back, Harry rolling over on her, and moved rhythmically with Harry, her legs and arms wrapped around him, rolling, squirming, groaning.
>
> Harry lunged at first, then, looking at Alberta, slowed to an exciting movement; and as he moved he was conscious of his movements, of his excitement and enjoyment and not wanting it to end; and though he clenched his teeth from lust and pinched her back and bit her neck there was a comparative relaxing, the tautness and spasms being caused by pleasure and desire to be where he was and to do what he was doing. Harry could hear her and his moans blending, could feel her under him, could feel her flesh in his mouth; there were many tangible things and yet there was still a confusion, but it stemmed from inexperience, from the sudden overpowering sensations of pleasure, a pleasure he had never known, a pleasure that he, with its excitement and tenderness, had never experienced -- he wanted to grab and squeeze the flesh he felt in his hands, he wanted to bite it, yet he didn't want to destroy it; he wanted it to be there, he wanted to come back to it. Harry continued to move with the same satisfying rhythm; continued to blend his moans with her through the whirlygig of confusion; bewildered but not distracted or disturbed by these new emotions giving birth to each other in his mind, but just concentrating on the pleasure and allowing it to guide him as Alberta had. When he stopped moving he lay still for a moment hearing their heavy breathing then kissed her, caressed her arms then rolled slowing and gently onto the bed, stretched out and soon slept. Harry was happy.
>
> Harry didnt open his eyes immediately when he awoke, but lay thinking then opened them suddenly, very wide, and turned and looked at Alberta. Harry sat up. The entire evening jammed itself into Harrys mind and his eyes clouded from his terrible anxiety and confusion. For the briefest moment he hid behind alcohol and overlapping images hung in front of him, then passed. He dropped back on the bed and fell asleep once more. When he awoke again later he no

longer wanted to run. The frightening clarity felt for the
moment when he first awoke assimilated itself with the usual
confusion of Harrys mind and now he was able to look at
Alberta and remember the night, in a general penumbrous
way, and not be afraid to be there -- though still fearing the
consequences of having someone find out -- but the fears and
confusion were overshadowed by his feeling of happiness.

Actually it was this feeling of happiness that bothered
Harry more than anything else at the immediate moment he
sat in the bed and looked at Alberta and remembered, with
pleasure, the night before. He knew he felt good, yet he
couldn't define his feeling. He couldnt say, Im happy. He
had nothing with which to compare his feeling. He felt good
when he was telling wilson off; he felt good when he was
with the guys having a drink; at those times he told himself he
was happy, but his feeling now went so much beyond that
that it was incomprehensible. He didn't realize that he had
never been happy, this happy, before.[11]

While this scene may not be wholly convincing -- for one thing it is too "literary" -- it is, in its
intention at least, Panzaic, inasmuch as it shows Harry's senses giving the lie to his manly ideals.

Yet Selby cannot permit even this one Panzaic revelation to stand. The flesh is wicked,
whether it be homosexual or heterosexual, and poor Harry, when he cannot find a fairy who will
love him for himself, and not for his money, tries to seduce (or rape) a ten-year-old boy --
whereupon he is murdered by his old buddies, "the guys from the Greeks":

They started slowly up 57th street, Harrys hand still on the
back of Joeys neck. When they had walked a few feet Harry
stopped. They stood still a second then Harry started
walking into the empty lot. Hey, where yagoin. Over there.
Comeon, I wanna show yasomethin. What yawant ta show
me? Comeon. They crossed the lot and went behind the
large advertising sign. Whats here? Harry leaned against the
billboard for a moment then lowered himself to his knees.
Joey watched him, his hands in his jacket pockets. Harry
reached up and opened Joeys fly and pulled out his cock.
Hey, whatta yadoin, trying to back away. Harry clutched
Joey by the legs and put Joeys small warm cock in his
mouth, his head being tossed from side to side by Joeys
attempts to free himself, but he clung to Joeys legs, keeping
his cock in his mouth and muttering please . . . please. Joey
pounded him on the head and tried to kick him with his knee.
LETME GO! LETME GO YA FUCKIN FREAK! Harry felt
the fists on his head, the cold ground under his knees; felt the
legs squirming and his hands starting to cramp from holding
them so tight; and felt the warm prick in his mouth and the
spittle dribbling down his chin; and Joey continued to
scream, squirm and pound his head until he finally broke
loose and ran from the lot, still screaming to the Greeks.
When Joey broke loose Harry fell on his face, his eyes
swelling and tears starting to ooze out and roll down his
cheeks. He tried to stand but kept falling to his knees then

flat on his face, still muttering please. A minute later Joey,
Vinnie and Sal and the rest of the guys from the Greeks came
running down 2nd avenue to the lot. Harry was almost
standing, holding on to the billboard, when they reached him.
THERE HE IS. THERE HEIS. THE SONOFABITCH
TRIED TA SUCK ME OFF. Harry let go of the billboard
and started to extend his arms when Vinnie hit him on the
cheek. Ya fuckin freak. Someone else hit him on the back of
the neck and Harry fell to the ground and they kicked and
stomped him, Joey squeezing in between to kick him too, and
Harry barely moved, barely made a sound beyond a
whimpering. A couple of guys picked him up and stretched
his arms across and around one of the crossbars of the sign
and hung on his arms with all their weight and strength until
Harrys arms were straining at the shoulder sockets,
threatening to snap, and they took turns punching his
stomach and chest and face until both eyes were drowned
with blood, then a few of the guys joined the two pulling on
his arms and they all tugged until they heard a snap and then
they twisted his arms behind him almost tying them in a knot
and when they let go he continued to hang from the bar then
slowly started to slide down and to one side until one arm
jerked around the bar and flopped back and forth like a
snapped twig held only be a thin piece of bark and his
shoulder jerked up until it was almost on a level with the top
of his head and the guys watched Harry Black as he slowly
descended from the billboard, his arms flapping back and
forth until his jacket got caught on a splinter and the other arm
spun around and he hung, impaled, and they hit and kicked
him until the splinter snapped and Harry descended to the
ground.

Harry lay still, sobbing. He cried then screamed a long
loud AAAAAAAAAAAAAAAAAAAAAAAAAAAAA that was
muffled as his face fell back into the dirt of the lot.

He tried to raise his head but could not. He could only
turn it slightly so he rested on a cheek. He was able to open
his eyes slightly, but was blinded by the blood. He yelled
again. He heard the sound loud inside his head, GOD O
GOD he yelled but no sound came from his mouth. He heard
his voice loud in his head but only a slight gurgle came from
his lips.

GOD          GOD

YOU SUCK COCK

The moon neither noticed nor ignored Harry as he lay at the
foot of the billboard, but continued on its unalterable journey.
The guys washed up in the Greeks, drying their hands with
toilet paper and tossing the wet wads at each other, laughing.
It was the first real kick since blowing up the trucks. The

> first good rumble since they dumped that doggy. They
> sprawled at the counter and the tables and order coffee and.[12]

Despite the symbolic trimmings -- the crucifixion, the moon, God, YOU SUCK COCK -- this finale neither follows nor gives meaning to what has gone before. It is just one more example of the rape and murder the novel palpitates to, rationalized morally to enforce the reiterated theme of the novel: the wages of sex are death.

The theme itself is, of course, as old as Christianity. What is different and modern in Selby's treatment is his thoroughgoing use of the flesh to deny the flesh. Quantitatively the novel probably contains more sex and violence more explicitly expressed than any serious novel of comparable length that has yet been published. But the difference is not merely or even primarily quantitative. It is qualitative. Except for Harry's response to Alberta (in the passage quoted above) there is not a single instance in the entire novel of one character responding sexually to another -- the way Connie Chatterley, for example, responds to Mellors when she sees him washing up behind the shed. The fucking, heterosexual and homosexual, is invariably a coldhearted attempt to get something or prove something. (Hardy's copulating earthworms in *Jude the Obscure* are warm in comparison.) It is not until the fucking begins to verge on rape and murder, as it does in almost every instance, that Selby's prose really begins to palpitate -- and, if one may judge by the comments of reviewers, really begins to give his readers something to palpitate to.

The following are excerpts from the reviews cited in the opening pages of the novel:

> His style has the clean economy of a battering ram . . . This is art, not scatology.
>
> -- *Chicago Sun-Times*

> As dramatic and immediate as the click of a switchblade knife.
>
> -- *Los Angeles Times*

> This is an important book . . . Police or sociological reports could not be so graphic.
>
> -- *Kansas City Star*

> Drops like a sledge hammer. Emotionally beaten, one leaves it a different person.
>
> -- Webster Schott -- *The Nation*

> His style is the most arrestingly original since *Naked Lunch* and *One Hundred Dollar Misunderstanding*. Also, like Burroughs, Selby is one of the really strong moralists.
>
> -- Terry Southern[13]

Except for Southern's remarks, which I shall mention later, there can be no doubt as to what these reviewers have thrilled to; nor is it surprising that three of the five have expressed their appreciation through symbols much like those which Harry Black conjures up in his sadistic fantasies in the novel. Indeed Webster Schott not only seems to enjoy being emotionally beaten; he actually seems to imply that such a beating with "a sledge hammer" constitutes the ultimate literary experience -- although in fairness to Schott, it must be acknowledged that he goes on to imply that the beating must enforce a high moral purpose, which he, along with Terry Southern, apparently finds in the novel's use of images of the flesh to castigate the flesh. But even if Schott's criticism is defensible, in moralistic Christian terms, it does not follow, as he would have us believe, that Selby's treatment of the spirit-flesh conflict is at all like the treatment accorded this conflict in the work of Dostoevski and other great 19th-century novelists. For one thing, as I have already pointed out, Selby presents the ideals of his one clear-cut Quixotic character (Ada) as sentimental memories that, by their very nature, cannot come into conflict with Ada's or any other character's senses. As for the more elemental and marginal Quixotes in the novel, from Tralala to Harry, they have neither feelings nor ideals that are distinguishable from the stock responses of the characters around them. In the last analysis, therefore, the novel has no ideals to be undercut, and neither a Sancho Panza nor any other form of the Panzaic to undercut them.

A number of other present-day novelists (to be noted presently) have also managed to eliminate the Panzaic. But for the most part the serious novelists of today appear to be as epistemologically naive, as Panzaic, as in the past. Some indeed have continued to use the Panzaic in almost exactly the same way that their 19th-century predecessors did -- the most notable though by no means the most successful example being Pasternak's use of Kamarovsky, a conventional 19th-century villain, as the prime Panzaic character in *Dr. Zhivago*. Still another and more successful example would be the black college president in Ellison's *Invisible Man*, a Dickensian villain very nearly as big as any of Dickens', and one who functions Panzaically in much the way that Dickens' villains do.

But most contemporary novelists have been as reluctant as Selby to embody their own positive ideals in a Quixote character (the way, for example, Pasternak embodies his positive ideals in Zhivago). They have, instead, embodied the positive ideals of our society in Quixotic characters whom they then proceed to destroy by means of the Panzaic, primarily as embodied in a character who functions as both unheroic hero and Panzaic character and has come to be identified as the anti-hero. The way, for example, the ideals of our society (as embodied in our police, our priests, and our jurists) are destroyed by Meursault in Camus' *The Stranger*. And it can be argued that the destruction of the crystalline orb of the ideal is all the more complete and devastating in *The Stranger* because Camus, by refusing to include his own positive ideals in the novel, has left himself free to be as negative, as Panzaic, as his subject warrants. Or, as Leslie Fiedler has expressed it, Camus has left himself free to say "No, In Thunder."

It is just this freedom (and the consequent "No, In Thunder") that has so upset Wayne Booth in his *Rhetoric of Fiction*, and caused him to try and insist that the novelist provide the reader with a positive moral perspective for reading his novel -- when, in point of fact, the novelist (in this instance Camus) has deliberately avoided such a moral perspective because it would prevent him from saying what he wants to say. Which is not, of course, what Booth wants him to say and therefore believes that he is rhetorically obliged to say. For rhetoric as Booth conceives of it implies the acceptance of Booth's own values, which he presents as "universal," e.g., "He [the novelist] must first plumb to universal values about which his readers can really care . . . In short, the writer should worry less about whether his *narrators* are realistic than about whether the *image he creates of himself*, his implied author, is one that his most intelligent and perceptive readers can admire."[14] And if the novelist does not present an image that Booth can admire he is, according to Booth, either irresponsible, like Camus, or vicious, like Celine in *Journey to the End of the Night*. "It [*Journey* ] is *not* an honest picture . . . These things have not been 'judged and given each its appointed place in the whole scheme.' . . . We cannot excuse him [Celine] for writing a book which, if taken seriously by the reader, must corrupt him. The better it is understood the more immoral it looks."[15]

Yet if Booth's "rhetoric" is a newer and more ponderously pontifical version of the old Philistinism of the forties and early fifties, the fact remains that freedom from commitment does have its liabilities. For one thing it permits the novelist to evade the full implications of his own Panzaic revelations -- the way Kesey does, for example, in *One Flew over the Cuckoo's Nest* by transforming his anti-hero (who is, in the first half of the novel, a Falstaffian rogue) into a responsible leader of men who finally sacrifices himself (crucifixion through shock therapy) that the men may live. Or the way Joseph Heller does towards the end of *Catch 22* by transforming his anti-hero, who is in many ways a World War II version of Schweik, into a man of moral principle. The effect of these transformations is to mute or negate the effect of the Panzaic revelations by assuring the reader that, however terrifying the revelations may be, they can be corrected and made right, that in the last analysis the seemingly Panzaic anti-hero is not a Sancho Panza at all but a Don Quixote who will sacrifice himself in an effort to see that his revelations are corrected and made right.

Novelists have always found it difficult to end their novels, however, and so long as an ending does not completely negate what has gone before -- and the ending of *Catch 22* certainly does not do that -- it should be viewed indulgently. A more serious liability of such freedom from commitment derives from the fact that this freedom can be used, not just to evade but to completely deny the Panzaic, the way Selby has denied it in *Last Exit to Brooklyn*, or the way Gunter Grass has denied it in *The Tin Drum*. In most respects these two novels are completely antithetical to each other: *Last Exit to Brooklyn* is about as loose structurally as a novel can be, consisting as it does of a group of related short stories. And in matters of style and technique it is straight-forward, direct, simple. Whereas *The Tin Drum*, on the other hand, is massive, highly wrought, highly unified, and highly symbolic as well as being tremendously clever and witty and ironical. Yet for all Grass's technical virtuosity the novel is a complete denial of the Panzaic. Once again, as in *Last Exit to Brooklyn*, it is not just the characters (including the three-year-old anti-hero) who lack feelings, the novel itself does; and once again, in the absence of feelings, it is murder, suicide, and rape that the novel palpitates to, even though its palpitations have been cushioned and camouflaged by wit and irony.

How many more novels should be included with *Last Exit to Brooklyn* and *The Tin Drum* must remain a moot question, turning as it does on matters of interpretation that can hardly be objectified in a few words or even a few lines, e.g., should Donleavy's *The Ginger Man* be included? Should Kerouac's *On the Road*? Or Capote's *In Cold Blood*? And how are these serious novels related to those that have been written to formulas which rigorously exclude the Panzaic? To the novels of Ian Fleming, for example? Or those of Mickey Spillane? Or those of Chester Himes? Moreover these questions are still further complicated by the encroachment of the movies, by the fact that serious as well as popular novelists have for years been writing with at least one eye cocked toward Hollywood or London. On a popular level the phenomenal success of *Love Story* (originally written as a movie script and then published as a novel) may even mark the advent of a new era in which the old process of turning novels into movies will be reversed and the only commercially successful novels will be those adapted from movies.

In any event *The Tin Drum* and *Last Exit to Brooklyn* and others like them (however many that includes) may well mark last exits of the serious novel. Quite possibly these novels have arrived at the complete dead end that Ortega predicted more than a half century earlier: "The ideals attacked by . . . the contemporary novel," Ortega wrote, "are hardly removed from the reality with which they are attacked. The tension is very weak: the ideal falls from a very small height."[16] For this reason Ortega believes that the novel as an art form is doomed, that the time will come when the tension will not only be "very weak" but will disappear altogether since the ideals will be indistinguishable from the reality with which they are attacked.

At the moment it still seems safe to say that this time has not yet come. But if it ever does -- if *The Tin Drum* and *Last Exit to Brooklyn* and other such novels ever do come to be recognized as the highest examples of fictional art -- then there will no longer be any Panzaic principle, or, for that matter, any novels, in the sense that Ortega defines novels. There will only be more *Tin Drums*, more *Last Exits*, along with their more popular and cinematic counterparts such as *Love Story* or the Masterpiece Theatre version of *Jude the Obscure* which recently appeared on NET.

But good novels, in the sense that Ortega defines novels, are still being written. In fact, have just read one in manuscript. And the original *Jude* is still in print, along with most of the better-known Victorian novels. And in the studies that follow -- studies intended to complemen the present work -- I hope to cut away the winding sheets in which we have wrapped these novels and show how powerfully Panzaic some of them really are.

Notes

[1] Jose Ortega y Gasset, "The Nature of the Novel," trans. Evelyn Rigg and Diego Marin, *Hudson Review,* 10 (1957), pp. 27, 28, 40.

[2] Ibid., pp. 30-31.

[3] Wayne Burns, *Charles Reade: A Study in Victorian Authorship* (New York: Bookman Associates, 1961), pp. 52-53, 55, 77, 90, 97, 143, 158, 162, 203, 214, 216-217, 269-270, 274-278, 282-283, 289, 316.

[4] University of Washington, 1964.

[5] Wayne Burns, *Towards a Contextualist Aesthetic of the Novel* (Seattle: Genitron Books, 1968), pp. 169-183.

[6] When I made these generalizations I had not seen *I Am Curious (Yellow)*, which is doubtless one of the great movies of all time. But unless I am mistaken its greatness derives in part from the fact that it is a Panzaic spoof of the very films I am referring to. Vilgot Sjoman, the director, acknowledged both his realistic and satirical intentions in the film in his testimony before the U.S. District Court:

> Q. "Would you say it was generally correct that it was your objective in making this film with respect to the sex scenes to show things as they actually happened?"
>
> A. "Yes, to break away from the ordinary way of presenting very arranged love scenes,and to approach reality and reconstruct reality, and to give the audience the feeling that this is more likely to be the real behavior than what is shown in many other films. But I must add one thing: that part of the intention is also to satirize, so there is also a lot of parody. Since you are particularly talking about the sex scenes now, there is a lot of parody and satire in the tree, in the pond, or the swamp, the balcony scene. All these are not supposed to be ordinary, realistic behavior but I am making fun of certain things."

This testimony is reprinted in *I Am Curious (Yellow)*, trans. Martin Minow and Jenny Bohman (New York: Grove Press, 1968), pp. 242-243.

[7] The movie version of *Women in Love* would now have to be added to the list.

[8] Hubert Selby, Jr., *Last Exit to Brooklyn* (New York: Grove Press, 1965), pp. 114-116.

[9] Ibid., p. 238.

[10] Ibid., pp. 253-257.

[11] Ibid., pp. 257-258.

[12] Ibid., pp. 198-200.

[13] Ibid., pp. 228-231.

[14] Ibid., unnumbered pages at the beginning of the book.

146

15 Wayne Booth, *The Rhetoric of Fiction* (Chicago and London: University of Chicago Press, 1961), p. 395.

16 Ibid., p. 383. Milton A. Mays has written a brilliant review of *The Rhetoric of Fiction* (*Critique*, V, 2 [Fall, 1962], 84-90), in which he discusses at some length Booth's use of the term "rhetoric."

17 Ortega y Gasset, p. 41.

# BIBLIOGRAPHY

148

Contextualist Criticism: A Bibliography*

Aiken, Henry David. "Review of *The Basis of Criticism in the Arts*." *The Journal of Philosophy*, 43 (August 1, 1946), 441-46.

Ames, Van Meter. "John Dewey as Aesthetician." *Journal of Aesthetics and Art Criticism*, 12 (December, 1953), 145-67.

Berall, Nathan. "A Note on Professor Pepper's Aesthetic Object." *The Journal of Philosophy*, 48 (November 22, 1951), 750-54.

Bergson, Henri. *Laughter: An Essay on the Meaning of the Comic*. London: Macmillan and Company, 1935.

Boas, George. "Communication in Dewey's Aesthetics." *The Journal of Aesthetics and Art Criticism*, 12 (December, 1953), 177-83.

Buchler, Justus, ed. *The Philosophy of Peirce and Selected Writings*. New York: Harcourt, Brace and World, 1950.

Buckley, William K. "A Selected Bibliography of Contextualist Aesthetics and Criticism." *Recovering Literature*, 8, 1 (Spring, 1980), 15-23.

*_____. "Contextualist Criticism in the Classroom." *Recovering Literature*, 8, 1 (Spring, 1980), 5-14.

_____. "George Gissing's *The Odd Women*." *Recovering Literature*, 6, 1 (Spring, 1977), 27-50.
*_____. "*Journey Through The Dark Woods* by Wayne Burns." *Arizona Quarterly*, 40, 3 (Autumn, 1984), 282-85.

_____. "Louis-Ferdinand Céline's Novels: From Narcissism to Sexual Connection," in *Critical Essays On Céline*. Boston: G.K. Hall & Co., 1988.

_____. "*Miss Ravenel's Conversion*: The Temporary Suspension of Melodrama for the Sake of the 'Panzaic'." *Recovering Literature*, 5, 3 (Winter, 1976), 53-75.

*_____. "Reader-Response Theory." *PMLA* , (March, 1986), 250.

_____. "Realism Still Knocking on Academe's Door." *Studies in the Novel* , 18, 3 (Fall, 1986), 314-19.

_____. "Michael Squires, *The Creation of Lady Chatterley's Lover*." *Studies in the Novel*, 16, 4 (Winter, 1984), 464-67.

---

* I have placed an asterisk by those items that give various summaries of contextualism.

Burns, Wayne. "A Seminar on D.H. Lawrence's *The Fox.*" *Recovering Literature*, 4, 2 (Fall, 1975), 5-47.

_____. "Critical Relevance of Freudianism," *Western Review*, 20 (Summer, 1956), 301-14.

_____. *Enfin Céline Vint* New York: Peter Lang, 1988.

_____. "Freudianism, Criticism, and Jane Eyre." *Literature and Psychology*, II, 5 (November, 1952), 4-13.

*_____. *Journey Through The Dark Woods* Seattle: Howe Street Press, 1982.

_____. "*Lady Chatterley's Lover.* A Pilgrim's Progress for Our Time." *Paunch*, 26 (April, 1966), 16-33.

_____. "Marxism, Criticism, and the Disappearing Individual." *Recovering Literature*, 12 (1984), 7-28.

*_____. "On Reading Novels: An Outline for a Contextualist Primer." *Recovering Literature*, 10 (1982), 33-41.

_____. "On Wuthering Heights." *Recovering Literature*, 1, 2 (Fall, 1972), 5-25.

_____. "The Genuine and Counterfeit: A Study in Victorian and Modern Fiction." *College English*, 18, 3 (December, 1956), 143-50.

_____. "The Novelist as Revolutionary," *Arizona Quarterly*, 7, 1 (Spring, 1951), 13-27.

_____. "The One Bright Book of Life." *West Coast Review*, 13 (April, 1979), 3-10.

_____. "The Panzaic Principle in Hardy's *Tess of the D'Urbervilles.*" *Recovering Literature*, 1, 1 (Spring, 1972), 26-41.

*_____. *The Panzaic Principle Parts I & II* Pendejo Press, ltd., Vancouver, 1965. Reprinted in *Recovering Literature*, 5, 1 (Spring, 1976), 5-51.

*_____. *Towards a Contextualist Aesthetic of the Novel.* Seattle, Washington: Genitron Books, Inc., 1968.

Butler, Gerald J. "Against Responsibility: An Answer to Arthur Efron's Critique of 'The Panzaic Principle in Hardy's *Tess of the D'Urbervilles*' by Wayne Burns." *Recovering Literature* 1, 2 (Fall, 1972), 67-75.

*_____. "Critical Afterword to the Panzaic Principle." *Recovering Literature*, 5, 1 (Spring, 1976), 52-59.

*_____. "Recovering Fiction." *Recovering Literature*, 1, 1 (Spring, 1972), 5-25.

_____. "The Panzaic Principle in Faulkner's *The Hamlet.*" *Recovering Literature*, 15 (Summer, 1987), 1-17.

_____. *This is Carbon: A Defense of D.H. Lawrence's The Rainbow Against His Admirers* Seattle, Washington: Genitron Press, 1986.

150

Croce, Benedetto. *Aesthetic: As Science of Expression and General Linguistic.* New York: Farrar, Straus and Co., 1966.

Dewey, John. *A Quest for Certainty: A Study of the Relation of Knowledge and Action.* New York: Minton, Balch and Co., 1929.

_____. *Art as Experience.* New York: Capricorn Books, 1934.

_____. *On Experience, Nature , and Freedom.* Ed. R.J. Bernstein. New York: The Liberal Arts Press, 1960.

Duncan, Elmer H. "Stephen C. Pepper: A Bibliography." *Journal of Aesthetics and Art Criticism,* 28 (Spring, 1970), 287-93.

_____. "The Philosophy of Stephen C. Pepper: An Appraisal." *Paunch,* 53-54 (1980), 63-73.

Eason, Douglas O. "Demonic Eschatology, Demonic Grammar." *Recovering Literature,* 13 (Spring, 1985), 37-52.

Edman, Irwin. *Arts and the Man: A Short Introduction to Aesthetics.* New York: W.W. Norton and Co., Inc., 1939.

_____. "Review of Aesthetic Quality: A Contextualist Theory of Beauty." *Journal of Philosophy,* 35 (August 18, 1938), 470-75.

Efron, Arthur. *Don Quixote and the Dulcineated World.* Austin, Texas: University of Texas Press, 1971.

_____. "Just What and Where is the Panzaic Principle in *Tess of the D'Urbervilles?*" *Recovering Literature,* 1, 2 (Fall, 1972), 50-66.

_____. "Pepper's Continuing Value." *Paunch,* 53-54 (1980), 5-53.

Ehrenzweig, Anton. *The Hidden Order of Art: A Study in the Psychology of Artistic Imagination.* Berkeley: University of California Press, 1967.

Flynn, James. "Bureaucratic Criticism." *Recovering Literature,* 4, 1, (Spring, 1975), 5-18.

_____. "Céline: Beyond the Gesture." *Recovering Literature,* 2, 1, (Spring, 1973), 5-35.

* _____. "Introduction" to *Understanding Céline* . Seattle, Washington: Genitron Press, 1984, 1-27.

Forster, E.M. *Aspects of the Novel.* New York: Harcourt, Brace & World, Inc., 1955.

Greene, M. Theodore. "Review of Aesthetic Quality: A Contextualist Theory of Beauty." *The Philosophical Review,* 49 (September, 1939), 544-56.

Hahn, Lewis Edwin. "A Contextualist Theory of Perception." *University of California Publications in Philosophy,* 22 (1942), 1-24, 106-121.

151

Hartshorne, C. and Weiss, P., eds. *Collected Papers of Charles Sanders Peirce.* Cambridge, Massachusetts: The Belknap Press of Harvard University, 1960.

Henze, Donald F. "Is The Work of Art a Construct? A Reply to Professor Pepper." *The Journal of Philosophy,* 52 (August 4, 1955), 433-39.

_____. "The Work of Art." *The Journal of Philosophy* 54 (July 4, 1957), 429-42.

Heyl, Bernard. "'Relativism' and 'Objectivity' in Stephen C. Pepper's Theory of Criticism." *Journal of Aesthetics and Art Criticism,* 18 (March, 1960), 378-93.

Hill, James L. "Defensive Strategies in Nineteenth and Twentieth-Century Criticism." *Journal of Aesthetics and Art Criticism,* 27 (Summer, 1969), 177-85.

Hill, John M. "Pepper's Contextualism and the Reader's Values." *Paunch,* 53-54 (1980), 122-34.

Hyman, Lawrence W. "Autonomy and Distance in a Literary Work: A New Approach to Contextualism." *Journal of Aesthetics and Art Criticism,* 31 (Summer, 1973), 467-71.

James, William. *Essays in Radical Empiricism: A Pluralistic Universe.* New York: Longmans, Green and Co., 1943.

Jarrett, James L. "More on Professor Pepper's Aesthetic Object." *The Journal of Philosophy,* 48 (November 22, 1951), 750-54.

Jenkins, Iredell. *Art and the Human Enterprise.* Cambridge, Massachusetts: Harvard University Press, 1958.

Johnson, Stephanie. "The Last Perfection: José Ortega Y Gassett and the Taming of the Novel." *Recovering Literature,* 5, 3 (Winter, 1976), 5-20.

Kaplan, Abraham. "Review of the Basis of Criticism in the Arts." *Journal of Aesthetics and Art Criticism,* 5 (September, 1946), 70-71.

Lawrence, D.H. *Selected Literary Criticism.* Ed. Anthony Beal. New York: The Viking Press, 1966.

_____. "The Novel." *Phoenix II.* New York: The Viking Press, 1970.

_____. "Introduction To These Paintings." *Phoenix: The Posthumous Papers of D.H. Lawrence.* New York: The Viking Press, 1936.

Lee, Otis. "Value and the Situation." *The Journal of Philosophy,* 41 (1944), 337-60.

Lewis, C.I. *An Analysis of Knowledge and Valuation.* La Salle, Illinois: The Open Court Publishing Co., 1946.

Lipman, Matthew. *What Happens In Art.* New York: Appleton-Century-Crofts, 1967.

Massey, Irving. *The Uncreating Word.* Bloomington: Indiana University Press, 1970.

Ortega Y Gasset, José. *Meditations on Quixote.* New York: W.W. Norton and Co., Inc. 1961.

152

Parker, DeWitt H. "Review of *The Basis of Criticism in the Arts.*" *The Philosophical Review*, 56 (January, 1947), 90-95.

*Paunch.* Number 53-54 (1980). Stephen Pepper Issue.

*Paunch.* Number 46-47 (1976). Wayne Burns Issue.

Pepper, Stephen C. "A Contextualistic Theory of Possibility." *University of California Publications In Philosophy*, 17, (1934), 177-97.

*_____. Aesthetic Quality: A Contextualistic Theory of Beauty.* New York: Charles Scribner's Sons, 1937.

_____. "A Proposal for a World Hypothesis," *The Monist*, 47 (Winter, 1963), 267-86.

_____. "Art and Experience." *The Review of Metaphysics*, 12 (September, 1958-June, 1959), 294-99.

*_____. "Autobiography of an Aesthetics" *Journal of Aesthetics and Art Criticism*, 28 (Spring, 1970), 275-86.

_____. *Concept and Quality: A World Hypothesis.* La Salle, Illinois: The Open Court Publishing Co., 1967.

_____. "Description of Aesthetic Experience." *Proceedings of the Sixth International Congress of Philosophy.* Harvard, 1926, 423-27.

_____. "Emotional Distance in Art." *Journal of Aesthetics and Art Criticism*, 4, (June, 1946), 235-39.

_____. "Further Consideration of the Aesthetic Work of Art." *Journal of Philosophy*, 49 (April 10, 1952), 274-79.

_____. "On Professor Jarrett's Questions About the Aesthetic Object," *Journal of Philosophy*, 49 (September 25, 1952), 633-41.

_____. *Principles of Art Appreciation.* New York: Harcourt, Brace and World, Inc., 1949.

*_____. *The Basis of Criticism in the Arts.* Cambridge, Massachusetts: Harvard University Press, 1945.

_____. "The Concept of Fusion in Dewey's Aesthetic Theory." *The Journal of Aesthetics and Art Criticism*, 12 (December, 1953), 169-76.

*_____. "The Development of Contextualistic Aesthetics." *Antioch Review*, 28 (Summer, 1968), 169-85.

_____. "The Esthetic Object." *The Journal of Philosophy*, 40 (September 2, 1943), 477-82.

_____. "The Individuality of a Work of Art." *University of California Publications in Philosophy*, 20 (1937), 81-98.

\*_____. *World Hypotheses: A Study in Evidence.* Berkeley: University of California Press, 1942.

Powell, A.E. *The Romantic Theory of Poetry: An Examination in the Light of Croce's Aesthetics.* London: Edward Arnold and Co., 1926.

Rahv, Philip. "Fiction and the Criticism of Fiction." *Kenyon Review* (Spring, 1956), 276-99.

*Recovering Literature: A Journal of Contextualist Criticism.* . Volume 10 (1982) contains a complete listing of articles from 1972 to 1982. Volume 2, No. 1 (Spring, 1973), is devoted to Céline.

Rosenblatt, Louise M. *The Reader, the Text, the Poem.* Carbondale: Southern-Illinois University Press, 1978.

_____. *Literature As Exploration.* New York: Noble and Noble, 1976.

Slatoff, W.J. *With Respect To Readers.* Ithaca, New York: Cornell University Press, 1970.

Steig, Michael. "*Towards a Contextualist Aesthetic of the Novel by Wayne Burns.*" *Minnesota Review,* 8 (1968), 376-78.

Stein, Leo. *The A-B-C of Aesthetics.* New York: Boni and Liveright, 1927.

Tilghman, B.R. "Aesthetic Perception and the Problem of the Aesthetic Object." *Mind,* 75 (July, 1966), 351-67.

Zaslove, J. "Counterfeit and the Use of Literature." *West Coast Review,* 3, 3 (Winter, 1969), 5-12.

_____. "Look! We Have Come Through . . . . Then And Now: An Afterward to Wayne Burns' Talk" *West Coast Review,* 13 (1979), 11-13.

# INDEX

Abrams, M.H., 15
Adorno, Theodor, 17
Aesthetic distance, 10-11
Artaud, Antonin, 16
*Aspects of the Novel*, 9
Barthes, Roland, 16
Becker, George J., 14
Bergson, Henri, 31-32
*Between the Acts*, 43
Bleich, David, 3
Brecht, Bertolt, 14
Brooks, Cleanth, 26
Burns, Wayne, on the novel, 3;
    his definition of the panzaic
    principle and contextualist
    criticism, 29-32; 73; 82;
    Appendix
Butler, Gerald J., 46; 82-83
Cary, Joyce, 2
*Castle to Castle*, 89
Céline, Louis-Ferdinand, 28-29; 35; 81ff.
Cezanne, Paul, 102:17n.; 106
Comfort, Alex, 15
Contextualist criticism, its independence,
    3; questions it asks, 3-4; brief
    definition, 9; 26; conflict, 9-10;
    its definition of realism, 15;
    contextualized classroom, 95ff.
Danger in art, 2
Davie, Donald, 11-12
*Death on the Installment Plan*, 83ff.
DeForest, John William, 67ff.
Dewey, John, 2, 13, 27
*Don Quixote,* see Appendix, 107ff.
*Down and Out in Paris and London,* 13; 27
Engels, Friedrich, 9
Feelings and Emotions, 11-14
Fielding, Henry, on literary criticism, 1
Flynn, James, 82
Formistic criticism, 9
Forster, E.M., on the novel, 2-3; 9
Freud, Sigmund, 84-85; 87
Freund, Elizabeth, 19
Function of teacher of fiction, 3
Fusion, 25
Fussell, Paul, 26-27
Gibson, Wilfred, 25
Graff, Gerald, 3; 11
*Heart of Darkness,* 2; 11
Hegel, 9
*Henry IV, Part I,* See Appendix, 112ff.

Howells, W.D., 14
Ideals, 11; 15
Irony, 26
Jacoby, Russell, 11; 81
James, William, 19
*Jane Eyre*, 33-34
*John Thomas and Lady Jane*,
    46ff.
*Journey to the End of the Night*,
    28-29; 34-35
Joyce, James, 43ff.; 53ff.
*Lady Chatterley's Lover*, 43ff.;
    108; 129ff.
*Last Exit to Brooklyn*, see
    Appendix, 131ff.
Lawrence, D.H., 2; his definition
    of the novel, 17-19; 30, 43ff.
*Le Rire*, 31-32
Levin, Harry, 15
Mechanistic criticism, 9
*Meditations on Quixote,* 32-33
Miller, Henry, 49-50
O'Brien, Darcy, 59-60
Organicist criticism, 9
Ortega Y Gasset, José, 32-33
Orwell, George, 13
Ostrovsky, Erika, 82
Panzaic principle, 29-35; Appendix
Pepper, Stephen, conflict in art, 3;
    10; historic event, 9; "funded"
    perception, 34
*Portrait of the Artist as a Young Man*,
    10
Proust, Marcel, 14
Rahv, Philip, 96
Reader's sense of life, 19
Reading experience, 19
Realism, 14
Reality, its generic function, 32
Rilke, 10; 16
Santayana, 9
The novel, 17-19
*Tom Jones,* 16; 31; see Appendix,
    109-111
*Twelfth Night,* 10
*Ulysses,* 53ff.
Vico, Giambattista, 54ff.
Watt, Ian, 16, 108-111
*Women in Love,* 10
Woolf, Virginia, 14; 43ff.
*World Hypotheses,* 95

A. P. Foulkes

# THE SEARCH FOR LITERARY MEANING. A SEMIOTIC APPROACH TO THE PROBLEM OF INTERPRETATION IN EDUCATION

ISBN 3-261-01536-5          259 pages          pb., US $ 33.40

Recommended price – alterations reserved

*Aspect:* The principal aim of the study is to comment on institutional literary interpretation against the current background of various reformist tendencies in literary studies. Descriptive and analytic techniques derived from semiotics are used in an attempt both to illuminate the function of interpretation within systems of literary education and to examine critically the theoretical assumptions which underlie many contemporary approaches to the subject.

*Contents:* The concept of interpretation in the humanities and literary studies – Semiotic approaches to meaning – Literary semantics – Fictionality – Literary persuasion and propaganda – Connotation and implication – Affective meaning and controlled reception of literary texts.

*Groups interested:* Teachers and students in literary studies, linguistics, education. sociology and philosophy.

*About the author:* A. P. Foulkes is Senior Lecturer in German at the University of Stirling, Scotland. His main interests are modern literature, history and theory of criticism, and literary education. Earlier publications include *The Reluctant Pessimist: a study of Franz Kafka, Deutsche Novellen von Tieck bis Hauptmann, Das deutsche Drama von Kleist bis Hauptmann.*

PETER LANG PUBLISHING, INC.
62 West 45th Street
USA – New York, NY 10036

Constantin Ponomareff

# THE SILENCED VISION
An Essay in Modern European Fiction

European University Papers: Series 18 (Comparative Literature). Vol. 20
ISBN 3-8204-06463-8                102 pages                pb. US $ 24.10

Recommended price – alterations reserved

This essay explores the historical impact of war and totalitarianism on the literary imagination of several major Soviet Russian and West German writers. The painful experience which has become muted in this fiction is articulated through a 'second', more subconscious and metaphorical, language. It is this subliminal poetic voice in the works of Borchert, Aitmatov, Grass, Pasternak and Nossack which provides us with a heightened sense of the spiritual condition of European man and the nature of modern and contemporary European writing.

Contents: Wolfgang Borchert, Nightmares of Primordial Sea – Chingiz Aitmatov, Reincarnations of the Virgin and Child – Günter Grass, The Burden of Conscience – Boris Pasternak, Art of Self-Concealment – Hans Erich Nossack, Audible Silence.

Interested groups: Germanists, Slawists, Psychologists.

The Author is Associate Professor for Russian Literature at Scarborough College of the University of Toronto.

PETER LANG PUBLISHING, INC.
62 West 45th Street
USA – New York, NY 10036